1ST SCHOOL REPORT, 1981

G10B	SEAN P. CONDON

FRENCH | E

THE CROSS INDICATES TEACHER'S ASSESSMENT

	Excellent	Good	Fair	Poor
Understands the Spoken Language		✓		
Understands the Written Language			✓	
Speaking the Language		✓		
Writing the Language			✓	

COMMENTS:

Sean has much ability which he channels with great gusto into the comic, the foolish and the fruitless approach. Relying on his memory and intelligence, he has coasted along, promised to turn over a new leaf and inevitably thumbed his way back to page 1.

His remarks can be irritating and his complaints will receive little sympathy when he so obviously has a whale of a time mucking about. He has promised to improve, once again — we'll see.

What they said about *Sean & David's Long Drive*

'A darn good read.'
New Woman

'A rude and reckless romp – definitely not to everyone's taste.'
Wanderlust

'One of the funniest road-stories in print . . . An iconoclastic, rambling tour through startling geography and the changing values of different generations: shocking, desperate, insightful, provoking. A wonderful read.'
Toronto *Globe & Mail*

'Scurrilous, not to mention scatological . . . The one indispensable guide to Australia.'
Scotsman

'A strange but strangely compelling look at the country, which the Australian Tourist Board would probably rather you didn't read.'
Guernsey Evening Post

'A cool wit who comes off like Hunter S. Thompson on prescription drugs. It's a great drive, a good read and is packed with "smart-arse one-liners".'
Australian

'A funny, offbeat road book (and genre send-up).'
Patriot – News

'Set to become a cult classic.'
Melbourne *Age*

'This is not a book for the queasy and the easily offended . . . A roaringly funny introduction to the continent.'
Notes from Underground, the Solar Light newsletter

'Funny, pithy, kitsch and surreal . . . This book will do for Australia what Chernobyl did for Kiev.'
Time Out

'I'd never hire these guys to write a guidebook.'
Tony Wheeler, *Lonely Planet*

'In fact, Condon can be quite funny.'
Times Literary Supplement

Drive Thru America

Sean Condon

LONELY PLANET PUBLICATIONS
Melbourne • Oakland • London • Paris

Drive Thru America

Published by Lonely Planet Publications
   Head Office: PO Box 617, Hawthorn, Vic 3122, Australia
   Branches: 155 Filbert St, Suite 251, Oakland, CA 94607, USA
                10a Spring Place, London NW5 3BH, UK
                71 bis rue du Cardinal Lemoine, 75005 Paris, France

Published 1998

Printed by SNP Printing Pte Ltd, Singapore

Author photograph by Simon Bracken
Map by David O'Brien
Designed by Adam McCrow
Edited by Janet Austin

National Library of Australia Cataloguing in Publication Data

Condon, Sean, 1965-
Drive thru America

ISBN 0 86442 506 6.

1. Condon, Sean, 1965- – Journeys – North America.
2. North America – Description and travel.
3. North America – Social life and customs – Humor.
I. Title. (Series: Lonely Planet journeys.)

970.0539

To Sally and David,
who endured my absence and presence
respectively.

The author and publisher would like to thank Metro Goldwyn Mayer for permission to reprint copyright material from *Manhattan* on page 44, and from *Raging Bull* on page 182.

Contents

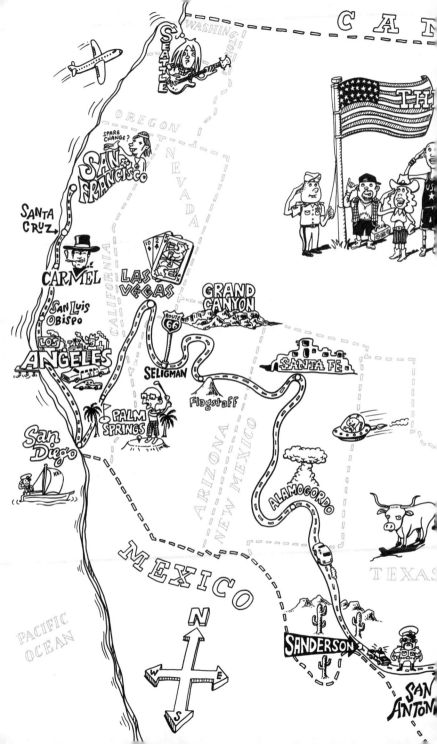

A Wicked Deception

In the middle of 1996 I was working as a copywriter at an advertising agency in Melbourne. I had my own office, with floor-to-ceiling windows and a terrific view of green parklands. I was earning decent dough, and even though I despised advertising, my overdeveloped hypocrisy allowed me to take the dough with my left hand and do the work with my right. My little life was just fine – but it wasn't going to stay that way for long.

One of my accounts was a large American video chain attempting to make a big splash in Australia. We agency clowns were instructed by the video marketing clowns to come up with a TV campaign to loudly announce the chain's arrival. 'We want something really . . . big,' they told us. 'Something really huge. Bigger than huge, something . . . hugely big.' Their parent company was an important player in Hollywood and they hoped to use its leverage to coerce 'hugely big' movie personalities into becoming TV hucksters for next to nothing.

It became my lamentable task to write literally hundreds of scripts for the Hollywood A-list. When we received the shocking news that no Arnolds, Toms, Jodies, Julias, Harrisons or Michelles would even consider *considering* the job for less than half a billion dollars, I was given a sheet of B-list types to work on: Bill Pullman, Christian Slater, Jeff Daniels, Jamie Lee Curtis, Cybill Shepherd and the like. Jerry Lewis apparently accepted an offer, but it was quickly withdrawn by the video company who felt he was 'too old and not big enough'. The rest of the B-list declined. I moved down the list to a group of Hollywood 'personalities' who were, presumably, desperate for cash and didn't give a good god damn where the money came from. I churned out scripts for Jim Belushi, Corey Feldman, Steve Guttenberg, Cybill Shepherd (who'd slipped to C-grade in just three weeks) and Henry Fonda, whom nobody would accept was dead. Eventually some sad hack accepted and preparations for the shoot in California were hastily made. I became increasingly excited about flying to America and meeting a real live Hollywood failure.

But there was a problem – my boss. He came loping and sweating into my office one dull but desperate Tuesday to tell me that there were a few 'issues' about who was going to America for the big shoot. The creative director was going, naturally. He was the creative director and you don't become the creative director without earning yourself a few free trips overseas.

'I have no problem with that,' I told my boss. 'I like the creative director. He's a nice guy.'

The producer was going, naturally. You can't have a smooth international shoot without a producer.

'Fine,' I said, looking into the blinking dimness behind my boss's glasses. 'She's going too. So what's the problem?'

'The problem,' he said, finally getting to the point, 'is who goes out of you and me.'

'Me,' I said. 'I wrote the script, so I go.'

'Yeah, well it's not as . . . simple as that,' he said, trying to think of a clever word for simple.

'Why isn't it simple?' I asked.

'It just isn't. Anyway, I've thought it all over. Going to America for this shoot will probably be the high point of your whole life, and in a couple of years I'll be living and working there as a screenwriter anyway, so I've decided that you can go.'

The following Monday he came into my office and said that he had to talk to me about 'all this overseas business'.

'Fine,' I said wearily. 'What is it?'

'Over the weekend I talked with my wife about who should be going overseas out of you and me. She said, "Look, Richard, the trip'll probably be the highlight of this Sean guy's life. And anyway, in a couple of years you'll be living and working over in America as a scriptwriter. So let him go." So I'm letting you go.'

I looked at him blankly. Clearly he had absolutely no recollection of our little chat the previous week; the cartoon script in his mind had been lost. He told me to be ready to leave on Friday, and headed out of my office feeling arch and clever – another fool deceived by his wicked brilliance.

My bags were packed, my visa was issued and I was all ready to go. On the Thursday, Richard strode into my office once again. He stood with his puffing red face just inches from mine (a cheap intimidatory tactic he'd learned at Boss School), and said that we had to talk about 'this America thing'.

13

'What is it *now*?' I asked.

'You're staying. I'm going.'

And that was the end of that.

I quit the agency two days later, free of my malignant boss and determined not to waste a perfectly good US visa.

The only problem was I didn't want to go to America alone. My girlfriend Sally couldn't leave her job in the cavalier and foolish manner with which I'd thrown away all hope for the future, so I called on someone who could. I visited my good friend David at his painting studio.

'Dave,' I said, handing him an influential beer, 'you're an artist, what are you doing for the next three months?'

'Well . . . nothing,' he said.

'Come with me to America. It'll be fun and we'll have some laughs.'

He sipped his beer silently and looked at the empty canvases that surrounded us. 'All right.'

Another fool deceived by my wicked brilliance . . .

East
Coast

A couple of swarthy types in off-the-rack suits held us down in metal chairs while electrodes were attached to our nipples . . .

Airport 1996. **Sean and David fly to Montreal – the beginning of a wild road trip across North America. Co-starring Joseph Cotten as 'the pilot'. Rated G (premiere).**

9.10 p.m. (Pacific Time)

I am wearing sunglasses and pretending to be blind. David is asleep a few rows behind me, exercising his almost superhuman capacity for relaxation. We are on a plane somewhere over the American Northwest, headed for Montreal. We've been flying for about twenty-eight hours now – as near as I can establish with any accuracy given the numerous time zones and the fact that we've been flying for about twenty-eight hours.

I'm dying for a cigarette. Sometime back in the international vapour trail of yesterday, I bought a pack of nicotine gum so I could chew my way to hypertension and heart trouble. They taste disgusting – worse if you inhale.

I've finally met someone apart from some stranger wanting to stamp me, x-ray me, feed me or seat me. She's a smart, pretty student named Jennifer, heading home after a holiday in California. I am enjoying her company immensely, but there is one problem: she thinks that I am blind. Pretending to be blind is an excellent way of avoiding annoying conversations with in-flight strangers about where they're headed and what they're going to do. Either pretending to be blind or a big fan of Sidney Sheldon, which I find far more difficult. But I was a little hasty in laying it on Jennifer, who is not at all annoying. Although I keep having to discourage her from asking me about the intricacies of Braille.

10.10 p.m. (Mountain Time)

My dining tray has been unfolded and a steaming, foil-covered meal sits on it. It's too late to backtrack now, so I reach forward and deliberately knock the cup of orange juice onto its side.

'Oh dear,' I say numbly. Jennifer is already dabbing at it with a napkin. 'I'm terribly sorry.' It seems that I'm also pretending to be well mannered and sophisticated.

'That's all right,' she says gently. 'Don't worry about it.'

'You're very kind.'

'Would you like me to feed you?'

I am shocked by this sudden intimacy, and almost gag. 'Oh no. No, I'm fine. I'm not really hungry.' Actually, I'm starving and very much enjoy plane food, but I'm trapped by my own stupid trick.

'I hope you don't mind my asking,' says Jennifer, 'but were you born blind?'

'No. An industrial accident when I was seventeen.' I'm getting a little carried away. 'I was an apprentice lathe-turner in a bicycle factory and one day I got careless,' I continue, getting careless. 'We had to turn four hundred cylinders each day to meet our quota. It was a lot of pressure. One afternoon I was a little tired, slightly hung over to tell you the absolute truth, and working too fast. I looked away from the capstan wheel for a moment, and the chisel caught on a snag and flew up into my head. Bang, I was blind.'

I hear Jennifer's sharp intake of breath. 'Oh God, I'm so sorry.' North Americans are always sorry for you, even if they don't know you. Even if you're a liar. It's a very endearing trait.

I am tempted to ask if I might touch her face, her fine skin, but realise that would be going way too far. Instead I decide to ask her to describe herself to me but it comes out wrong. The words 'Describe me to you' tumble out. I sneak a look at her and see that she is confused, perhaps even upset. The truth is always difficult – especially the truth about me.

'Well . . . you're pretty handsome, especially your eyelashes. Your nose is fine, there doesn't seem to be any scarring from the accident. Nice hair. I like the grey. You've got a good build and . . . and you're well dressed.'

'Thank you. You're a very kind girl,' I say, sounding like a movie nun. She may be kind, but she's a bigger liar than I am. The truth is I am overweight and sallow, and my grey hair is dry and wavy. She was right about the eyelashes, though. They're gorgeous.

'Do you remember what things look like?' Jennifer asks quietly. 'Cars and trees and sunlight and people?'

'Yes, I remember most things. The rest I just make up. It seems to work.'

11.10 p.m. (Central Time)

The lights have been dimmed and the faint, clean smell of sleep consumes the cabin. Jennifer's eyes are closed. I want to take a look at a magazine but it would be too risky. Anyway, I am very tired myself.

Dozing . . .

One night in 1974 my father came home from work and announced that we would be moving to Montreal, Canada. Being a bright and curious boy, I immediately got out an atlas and investigated the location of our future home, pinpointing Melbourne and Montreal with my thumb and little finger. 'Geez, it's far away,' I said, holding up my hand and stretching the fingers as far apart as they could go. 'Look.'

We spent two years in suburban Montreal, where I picked up a little French, chucked some snow at other kids and had a couple of second-hand pet salamanders named Starsky and Hutch. I loved Canada. Everybody had different accents and there were two boys called Aram in my class. *Two!* And Monie Mayer's mom made a dish with eggplant, a vegetable unheard of back in mid-70s East Doncaster. One time me and David Vienot and Terry Robinson (who had fluffy white hair and a pet boa constrictor, which I actually saw eat a live mouse, and whose crazy mother walked around all day topless) were stuck at the top of Mont Royal with no money for the bus fare home. Terry and David insisted that I be the one to approach strangers for money, '. . . because you've got sort of a British accent and people *fall* for it.' Our neighbours Ian Cockfield and his sister Brenda convinced me that they had the skeleton of three-titted Ann Boleyn in an upstairs cupboard. I asked their mother if it was true. 'Oh yes, it's true,' she told me. 'We're related.' My sister Julie came home from school one day crying, with frostbitten feet. We put the oven on low and told her to stick her legs inside it. As her feet thawed, her little toe snapped off. We kept it in a jar in a cupboard upstairs. My best friend was Alberto Gatti. One leafy afternoon we were hanging around in the park when we saw a grey Mercedes with four Italian guys in big suits and hats pull up outside Alberto's house. Three of the suits got out and went inside while the other one tapped his fat fingers on the leather steering wheel. I'd seen *The Godfather* and I knew what was what. I looked from Alberto to his house and back, saying nothing. Even today I wonder if 'Berto's dad was a made guy. And whether he now sleeps with the fishes.

We left in 1977. I was eleven years old, my voice unbroken, but a boy of the world nonetheless. And ever since the day we left, I have wanted to return.

Sleazes of Montreal. **David develops a messiah complex, foolishly mistaking Sean for a disciple. Robes by Edith Head.**

2.20 a.m. (Eastern Time) Westin Mont Royal Hotel

After a quick look in the mini bar, David and I decided to take a walk to get a beer and maybe something real to eat because all we'd had for the past thirty or so hours was plane food, which is not fit for human consumption, so naturally we really enjoyed it. There was a lot of angry-sounding French being spoken as we wandered the downtown area, none of which looked or sounded even remotely familiar to me. But I soon found something that brought back rich, smoky memories.

At a restaurant called Reubens on Sainte Catherine we sat in a red vinyl booth and drank our eagerly awaited Molsons, accompanied by Montreal's traditional dish – *viande fumée*, or smoked meat sandwich. This is what we got:

Meat slice–Bread slice ratio, 12 : 1
Fries–Sandwich ratio, 900 : 1
Fries–Gherkin ratio, 900 : 2
Sean–David ratio, 1 : 1

It was great stuff. The sweet, bright yellow mustard all over my face and hands especially reminded me of being ten years old. It was 1.15 a.m., and we'd been awake for about thirty-six hours; we were happy and lucid, having a great time giving ourselves heart disease with beer and meat in Montreal, a city just about as far from home as we could possibly get. The Great North American Fat Fest had begun.

Now, back at the hotel, I've got to try and sleep it off.

Slept for about four minutes then got up for breakfast.

Trying to embrace the half Gallic spirit of Montréal, David and I had *crêpes* for *petit déjeuner.* They were pretty horrible, all rough and square and brown. Soylent brown.

'I like 'em,' said David, through a dense mouthful.

'You like a lot of strange things though.'

'Such as?'

'Such as eating liver, the smell of Band-Aids, smoking dope but not cigarettes, pretending you're a surfer by having long blond hair and a mismatching goatee, sitting around doing nothing for hours on end, teasing people, doing air guitar solos to Al Stewart songs, drinking unflavoured milk, Neil Young –'

'Neil is not strange.'

'Remembering the details of everybody you went to school with, catching up with the aforementioned morons at reunions, bourbon and Coke, your insane dog Indy –'

'Leave her out of this!'

'Breakfast cereal toys from the 1970s, Roger Moore instead of Sean Connery, women wearing G-strings –'

'Aaah, butt floss,' he said dreamily. 'Yeah, well you're pretty strange and I don't like you much.'

Even though I am not in the least bit strange, I took it as a definite compliment.

Biography

David is one year older and a couple of inches taller than I am, so he likes to lord it over me. (I let him because I figure that anybody who spends a lot of time alone with me must have some sort of special powers which I'd hate them to use against me. Consequently, I'm usually on my best behaviour with people like David and Sally – in case they find out who I really am, what I'm really like.) Throughout our lives, our paths had crossed several times: we grew up in adjacent neighbourhoods far from the city, went to the same high school and eventually ended up working together at an advertising agency/slaughterhouse for a year or so. At every stage we hadn't liked each other. How and why we became friends is something of a mystery – fate or alcohol intervened somewhere along the line. A couple of years ago we drove around Australia together and discovered that even the close confines of travelling through our country in a small car didn't cause an irreparable rift. We're good friends, but I'm not sure *how* good. America could make all the difference.

6.15 p.m.

I'm thinking about calling Alberto, my childhood pal from Town of Mount Royal, the suburb where *la famille* Condon lived for most of the two years we spent in Montreal. I'll call as soon as I'm drunk enough, and can remember what I looked like in 1976.

My memory isn't up to it, so instead I call Jennifer and attempt to convince her that I am *not* blind by accurately describing what I look like in 1996. During our ten-minute conversation she goes through the whole Kübler-Ross deal: denial, anger, bargaining, depression, acceptance and then back to anger again. But she graciously agrees to come over anyway.

She arrives with a case of St Ambroise, a strong local beer which David and I befriend immediately.

'I can't believe you would trick somebody like that, Sean. It seems so stupid and pointless,' Jennifer says after a few minutes of avoiding my eye. 'I'm really disappointed in you. And I don't even *know* you.'

'I'm sorry, Jennifer, I really am. I was just fooling around and it got out of hand.' I'm trying to look contrite, but the soft roundness of her Montreal accent makes her admonishment sound delightful.

'If it's any consolation,' offers David, opening another beer and handing it to me, 'he'll probably end up blind tonight.'

'So David, how do you know Sean?' Jennifer asks.

'I answered an ad,' David replies dryly. 'In *Mad* magazine.'

'I was lonely,' I say. 'Looking for laffs. I sent in one of those fold-in pictures. Made me look a lot thinner.'

'We arranged to meet at Luna Park,' David continues. 'Sean was too scared to ride the Ghost Train, and he didn't even have enough money to buy fairy floss. The whole thing was a disaster.'

'What's fairy floss?' Jennifer wonders.

'Cotton candy,' I translate.

'This is when you were kids, right?' she says.

'Oh no.' David shakes his head. 'Last October.'

'Y'know something,' Jennifer says, 'you two are idiots.'

She's right. And after spending a few more hours with us, her opinion doesn't change.

Trying to Sleep
. . . What if I die right now in this bed? They'll have to do an autopsy.

They'll cut me wide open and sift through, trying to discover why I died and how I lived. They'll find all sorts of terrible crap. Stomach contents:· partially digested poutine *('What exactly is that, Doctor?' 'Sludgy French fries and gravy covered in lumps of mozzarella cheese. And damned if it doesn't look like it's from Celine Dion's restaurant downtown.'); an ineffective Australian sleeping pill; and about a gallon of Montreal beer and Swedish vodka. 'No wonder he's dead, Doctor. The fool's been committing suicide for years.'*

And what if they do an autopsy on my brain? What will they find there? 'The deceased's mind was in a state of extreme disarray and is coated with yellow anxiety. The Potential Cavity is virtually unexplored, while the Maths and Sciences Wing of the Frontal Lobe is completely closed off. Also notable is the fact that the entire brain is flooded with memories of what seems to be . . . I think it's the mid-70s. And the words "boyhood", "me" and "I" seem to be appearing everywhere.' . . .

So much for conquering jet lag. I thought I had it beat after just one day. But here I am, exhausted at 6.30 in the morning. God . . . David left the damn window open on his side of the room and some horrible industrial noise and fumes are coming in. I've gotta close it. But his head is facing that way. What if he wakes up just as I'm trying to shut the window? My round, white ass will be right in his face. I don't think either of us could continue the trip after an incident like that . . . Oh my God! David sleeps with his thumb in his mouth!! Wait till I tell everyone back home about this!!

S. C. – Phone Home

I give up trying to sleep, wander downstairs to the lobby phone and call Sally to check if we've been robbed since I left. We shoot the international breeze for a while until we both start crying. I spend a while sobbing around the hotel, then kill an hour chuckling away at the *New Yorker* over a large, solitary breakfast. It really should be the *Montrealer*, but who would invent a magazine called that? Nobody – it's just not that kind of a town.

Starsky and Hutch. **A trip into nostalgia gives Sean a headache. With Denzel Washington as Huggy Bear. Rated M (violence).**

In the lobby of the hotel is a mob of fifty-year-old men wearing black jeans, leather jackets and permanent, dilapidated smiles informed by years of cannabis use. David, who knows so much about these and a frightening array of other things, informs me that they are none other than 70s stadium rockers Styx, resurrected to commit noise pollution in Montreal over the weekend.

'Wanna stick around and see 'em, Seanina?'

'Yeah, David. I travelled halfway around the world so I could go back in time and check out Styx.'

'What if they were playing with ELP *and* Supertramp? At the Olympic Stadium?'

'Put Foreigner on the bill and I'm there, baby.'

'I wanna know what love is.'

'Well don't ask me.'

Irrepressed Memory Syndrome

We caught a teak-panelled, twenty-minute, $14 cab to Rockland Park Shopping Centre – mall of my youth. Naturally, twenty years later it bore little resemblance to my memories, but at least it was there. (Then again, long after humanity has disappeared malls will still be around. Malls and cockroaches.) We walked through the complex and out into the car park where I caught the first glimpse of my old street, Brittany Avenue. I felt incredibly excited – visiting my old house was one of the few things I'd wanted to achieve in my lifetime (apart from all that Nobel crap), and at the same time it was something I'd been almost sure I'd probably never do (like all that Nobel crap).

The neighbourhood is classic Mike Brady-designed North American upper-middle-class suburbia with an Eisenhower-ish touch of repressed immorality behind each neat facade. Detached and semi-detached houses with yard sales and basketball hoops, lawn mowers buzzing out front and barbecues smoking in back. The kids have all gone off to college and the wild, wife-swapping years are but a tingling memory. It's sedate and leafy with a pervasive air of security-enforced calm patrolling the streets. In fact, Town of Mount Royal is literally a 'gated' community. A cyclone fence separates it from the huge ethnic ghetto on the other side of the mall, which is filled with all sorts of people of disreputable colour and finance – that is, not white, and not enough.

I was shaking as I stood in front of our old town house, which hadn't changed at all except for the colour of the front door. I knocked on it, wondering what the hell I thought I was doing. A woman covering her mid-thirties with too much make-up opened the door and I began babbling while David stood to the side, grinning at me.

'Hi. I've come from Australia because . . . Hi. My name's Sean. I used to live here. In the 70s. I was a boy. Hi. Sorry. I'm from Australia. I came to look.'

'Oh . . . We just moved in.'

'D'you like it? It's a nice house isn't it? The door used to be blue.

Up there was my bedroom.'

'Really, you're from Australia? You sound British.'

'Yeah. But I used to live here. Right here, I mean.'

'We just moved in two weeks ago.'

There was a brief silence. 'Well . . . I hope you enjoy it. And if you happen to find a salamander, don't hurt him. His name is Starsky and he used to be mine. His partner Hutch died in 1977.'

And that was pretty much it. I don't know what I'd hoped to achieve by that stunt. Well, actually I do – I'd wanted her to invite me in so I could show her around the Old Condon Place. 'My mother sat right there in a bad mood after root canal work and . . . In this room every Christmas we would . . . This is where I vomited because of . . . And here's where me and Cathy Todd first . . .'

And like that. I'm sure she would've enjoyed it, too. But she'd just moved in.

We wandered further down Brittany Avenue, toward my old school. A few happy and many shameful memories clouded around me as we drew nearer . . .

Christmas Present Past

I'll never forget my first cruel Yule in Montreal. Along with a whole bunch of other greatly unfamiliar customs came a humiliation rite called Kris Kringle, whereby each kid in the class had to buy another kid some sort of Christmas gift. The little girl who had unfortunately drawn my name was Frances. She had a dark mop of hair which framed a white, wide and open face whose ingenuousness was further set off by the smear of food – jelly, peanut butter, ketchup – that always sat near her mouth. On a

27

prettier girl, you might have wanted to lick it off. But not on Frances, who you felt sure would grow up to be someone you'd never want to kiss – a librarian, a teacher, your mother. She wore cheap, dowdy clothes and was probably a little . . . simple. But there was no doubt about it – the Australian boy in the class was a whole lot simpler.

On Kris Kringle Day, Frances came running over to me through the slush and nervously explained that she'd made a mistake in the gift she'd bought for me.

'Why, what is it?' I demanded.

'This.' She held out a flimsily wrapped shape covered in bright thistle print. I tore off the paper to reveal a 30¢ peppermint candy cane. 'It's all broken. I'm so sorry, Sean,' Frances said, tears about to plop from her big grey eyes. 'What should I do?'

'Go down to Rockland and get me a book – the latest *Encyclopedia Brown* or *Great Brain*. They're only about two, three dollars. A book would be perfect,' I ordered, chomping on the candy. 'I like books.'

'Okay,' she said tremulously, her hands fidgeting with the zip on her puffy green parka. 'Okay then.'

When we all filed into the classroom, removing our warm, damp coats and wiping mud from our boots, I saw Frances sobbing in the corner with our teacher. Miss Chevastek was rubbing the little girl's heaving back and patting her bowed head, more like a parent than a schoolteacher. As her eyes caught mine they narrowed. I began to feel a little ill.

Once we were all at our desks, Miss Chevastek asked me to come up to the front of the class and stand beside Frances. 'Class,' Miss

Chevastek began, 'today I have heard a terrible, terrible, *terrible* story. It is a story that tells us what Christmas is *not* about. Christmas is *not* about greediness, selfishness and insensitivity. However, our Australian visitor, Mr Condon, doesn't see things that way at all.'

My face grew hot and I began to glow . . .

Back to School

David and I walked past the park, a familiar house, the corner store, heading ever closer to the schoolyard . . . But something was wrong – where Russell School should have been was a huge retirement village.

We got the inside dope on the educational razing from a couple of nice little old ladies who were residents of the mausoleum which now occupied the historical site.

'We like it here,' they told us.

'I'm sure you do,' I said, perhaps a little testily. 'And I'm very happy for you. But isn't there even a fucking plaque that says Sean Condon used to go to fucking school here?'

'Why the fuck should there be?' said the older of the two, a sprightly 97-year-old. Then she hit me in the eye with her cane and I started crying. For someone born last century, she was pretty strong. I had to leave after that.

Hair Today

Had my hair cut by Migyuel at Funky Torque on Saint Laurent, *the* bohemian Montreal boulevard. Migyuel was French and gay and didn't like me too much because I'm overweight, Australian and have too much brittle grey in my hair. Fair enough. He did a good job on my head though. Thirty dollars, plus tax. Dandruff tax. I had to take off my t-shirt and put on this kimono thing that let all the cut hairs in, which I didn't like too much. Undressing tax.

That's gilding the lily a bit, isn't it?
What's gilding the lily mean, exactly?
I'm not sure. It's probably an imported phrase.

White male and female, approx. 30

Montreal is a stunningly beautiful city – European in its relaxed, late-summer attitude and rich with a strong sense of its own history. There are restaurants, parks and gardens everywhere and a sweet atmosphere of lazy romanticism. But at the same time it is stylish, dynamic and modern; its close proximity to the US border ensures that, as does the almost palpable tension between the secessionists and Commonwealthers. I would very much like to live here. However, there are some distressing things I've noticed about the place:

- All the boys and girls my age are much younger and prettier than me. There seems to be very few fat, ugly people around. I hope the United States puts an end to that unhappiness.

- Most people think David and I are from England, which kind of annoys me. The fact is, I'd much rather *be* from England than Australia because you get a better accent and hairstyle.

- The population of Montreal is made up of a whole bunch of people who think they live in France and a whole bunch who wish the other half did.

MONOLINGUAL? CALL 1-800 PARLEZ-VOUS

7.26 p.m.

David is sitting by the window trimming his big, yellow toenails. The worrisome thing is I'm not all that bothered by it. He's cutting his toenails. So what? I'm smoking a cigarette. That's far more disgusting and he's not complaining.

Now David's saying that he's quite looking forward to staying in one of those 'Raymond Carver-ish one motel, one bar and one diner type towns'. I, on the other hand, am not. I'd prefer to read a nice short story about it.

Just tried to call Alberto. Some old woman told me she didn't speak English and hung up. See ya, Bert.

10.10 p.m.

As David chewed on his calamari and I ate filet mignon with shrimps at an outdoor restaurant, a scurrying junkie named Mickey drew caricatures of us – frizzy lines with eyes as David and fat lines with eyes pretending to be me. They were terrible and not worth even the two Canadian dollars I gave him. But seeing Mickey plying his trade brought to mind a striking thing about North America, as opposed to the bottom of the world David and I call home: there are many, many more beggars and panhandlers and homeless people here. Because I am not socially and financially inured to them, I am possibly the most popular tourist in town. 'Seanie Two Bucks' I'm called on the street. 'Here comes Seanie Two Bucks. Quick, pretend you can draw!'

Stars and Stripes

Tomorrow we're going to the United States. Our psychological training for that has come from years of assiduously watching American TV and Movies; reading Great American Literature; studying American Art; worshipfully tuning in to American Music; conceding to the American Point of View; following the American Example with weary haste; caring about the celebrated lives of Celebrated Americans; and being appalled and fascinated and moved by American History, American Crime and the American Flag.

I'm filled with a mixture of excitement, swaggering brashness and righteous conviction – a distinctly *American* feeling. There is, however, also quite a bit of Australian Dread which I'm trying to ignore. America is a very big country and apart from New York City we have no idea where the hell we're going. I'm tempted to nominate Route 66 but there are two problems with that – it's too corny and there's not much left of it on the map we're studying.

'So where would you like to go, David?'

'Down.'

'Down?'

'South.'

'Where south?'

'Down south.'

'Yeahuh. Anywhere in particular?'

'Wherever falls in the path of where we're going.'

'Where are we going?'

'Wherever.'

David O'Brien – Zen traveller.

The Out-of-Towners. **Tension when Sean tries to smuggle twenty pounds of fat strapped to his stomach across the US border. Rated .45.**

Midday

Master David and I are on a Greyhound bus about to leave for New York City. We're with all the freaks, fiends and fuck-ups of Montreal. Our driver is this tall, hoe-thin Shaft dude with Superfly wraparounds and a spinning green cocktail toothpick poking out of his teeth. He's the very essence of summer 96's hippest look, Bus Driver Cool. Outside my window a cop is making telephoning motions to his wife, who is sitting right behind me. A French-Canadian teenager just walked past, crying lightly after hugging and kissing his girlfriend for as long as they could until Shaft called her onto the bus and turned over the ignition. Poor little fella – reminds me of me (but bilingual). Somebody up the back has opened a tin of corned beef.

We've been rolling for about 45 minutes, along a freeway surrounded by very green fields and trees. *C'est tout.* Perhaps things will pick up at the border crossing. Maybe Warren Oates will be there and he'll shoot one of us. Or maybe the immigration guys will insist that I bear no resemblance to my passport photo, take me out back, search me and discover a hunk of Semtex strapped to my waist. Yeah, maybe. We'll see.

1.50 p.m. Canada

We're right on the border – I'm finished, man. This is it for Little Rico. I'll have to blast my way across. See ya on the other side!!

33

2.10 p.m. America

The crossing went all right, although clearly the pistol-packin'
public servant, Immigration Officer B. T. Phillips, was none too
fond of David and me. He was a cold, pink, stumpy guy (kind of
like a ham with a Walther) who looked at us hatefully, disinterestedly and suspiciously all at once. It was quite a feat of
physiognomy. I'd've given him some lip but he might've shot
me. Or worse – refused to let me into his great country. This is
how it would've gone:

BTP: Where are you going?

SPC: It's the border into the US – where the hell do you think I'm
going?

BTP: BLAM!! BLAM!! BLAM!!!

SPC [BLEEDING]: Is this the end of Little Rico . . . ?

2.25 p.m. Bordertown

The first town of any size we come to in America is Plattsburgh,
and it's pretty awful. 'Not to be confused with Pittsburgh,' a
pleasant Christian woman in a sterile bank tells me. 'That place
is the pits. We're the Platts.' She seems to be the type of person
who would like people to notice her shoes – which pair she's
chosen for a particular outfit and the care she always takes to
keep them neat and in good condition. But she's behind a counter
so I can't see them.

Plattsburgh appears to be mostly made up of car parts outlets and
a place called Friendly's Restaurant. *Friendly's*. Get forked! It's
all very prefabricated; the local mall, Consumer Square, was
clearly built in the 1980s to look like 1540s Tudor-influenced
1960s American suburbia. It works.

We've pulled into a Dairy Queen whose big feature is the Char-Broiled Brazier® Burger. I fantasised about eating a warm Wonderbra® once. Maybe it's something along those lines, but I'm not game enough to find out just yet. Besides, I have no American cash since B. T. Phillips took my last six bucks for his personal slush fund. I should've tried to pay for my visa on Visa but he probably would've detained me for being 'needlessly reflexive'.

Conversation Piece

'David, I have something important to tell you and you're not allowed to get mad at me, all right?'

'Why would I get mad? Is it something *Crying Game*-ish? Are you really a black woman?'

'No, it's far more shocking than that. You sleep with your thumb in your mouth.'

He raised his eyebrows as if to convey no more than passing interest in a notion so patently absurd. 'Oh really?'

I knew then beyond all doubt that he was only too aware of his shameful habit.

View from a Bus

I wish I was wearing a seatbelt. It doesn't feel very safe not being strapped in. The bus smells like oranges now. Could orange be the smell of death? The colour? Just saw a sign for Lake George, a famous holiday spot. My mother tried to murder me and my sisters there when we were kids. It's all forest-covered hills and smooth silver lakes. Sheer drops of rock cut the mountains as though they've been sliced like cakes. Nature as dessert. I'm looking for anything I might remember from family driving trips of twenty years ago. A couple of pine trees look vaguely familiar, but I can't be sure. Just crossed an American river – like the plug holes up here in the northern hemisphere, they flow in the opposite direction to Australian rivers. There are rolled-up hay bales in the fields, lying on the grass at random like a game the cows have abandoned – due to the inherent dullness of rolling up hay, as opposed to rolling in it. A woman walking her dog by the freeway. American woman. American dog. I'm in America. It's finally beginning to dawn on me. A flashing police car has pulled over a van up ahead. American cops. American van.

I'm in America. And I'm very excited.

David wakes me to point out Dutch Schultz emerging from the courthouse as we pass through Saratoga Springs. He is wearing a nice Homburg.

5.45 p.m. Albany

We've stopped for half an hour in the state capital's bus terminal: a hot concrete wasteland of torn wire fencing, rumbling freeway overpasses and wind-skittered litter. We're picking up more passengers, including a guy who wanders from one end of the bus to the other saying, 'Pawdonne, pawdonne, pawdonne me,' as he passes each row. He looks like a Hispanic Rupert Pupkin. The bus smells of popcorn, old flowers, oranges and corned beef. And although it shouldn't, it's making me hungry. The sun's beating down through the concrete overpass above the terminal, packing a mean heat even though it's late in the day. The hot light stills the scene and I feel listless and tawdry, as though I'm trapped in an Edward Hopper painting. The cop's wife, who turns out to be the popcorn, orange and corned beef eater, the very same woman who's kept the bus waiting every time we've stopped somewhere, is insisting on her exact seat back, forcing two black girlfriends to sit at opposite ends of the bus.

6.50 p.m. Poughkeepsie.

David is picking his feet. It's dark now and we still have a long way to go.

Breakfast at Tiffany's. Sean accidentally eats two pounds of uncut diamonds and gets indigestion. Co-starring Audrey Hepburn and Woody Allen as each other.

I too walk'd the streets of Manhattan island, and . . . felt the curious abrupt questionings stir within me.
Walt Whitman, *Leaves of Grass*, 1856

New York City

We arrived at the Hilton at around 10 p.m. Exhausted from sitting down all day, I sat on the bed, switched on the TV and became addicted to cable in about twelve seconds. There are sixty-six channels. So I lay there, ignoring the Chrysler Building and Central Park, the Empire State and Radio City, pumping the remote until about 2 a.m. God, it was beautiful.

I Can't Believe It's Not Not Coffee®

Had breakfast in the West Village at a cafe called French Roast. It offers about five hundred coffee-like drinks, most of which contain nothing poisonous or upsetting like actual caffeine because Americans seem to be frightened of the stuff. (I suppose a shot of real juice would put the already wired average New

Yorker into some sort of jangly stratosphere.) With some trepidation I tipped the waitress $5 off a $15 check. She seemed quite happy with it. This I gathered by the fact that she didn't spit in my eye or explain how difficult it was to be an actress/artiste in this city.

'Hey, David,' I said. 'Why do you think there are so few one-armed women in the world?'

'So few? Aren't there enough for your liking? To meet your needs?'

'No, it's just that the one-armed lady is a rare creature.'

'Of loveliness?'

'No, just rare. Look I'm not *in love* with one-armed women, I've never even met one. I just want to know why there are so few of them.'

'Maybe women don't drive Corvairs. Or operate heavy machinery. Or get drunk and walk into airplane propellers.'

'Yeah . . . If you only had one arm, would you pin your spare shirtsleeve up near the shoulder stump or just let it flop around?'

'I'd let it hang, man.'

'I *knew* you would! I'd pin it for sure. I'm too neat. God, I'd hate to have only one arm. Although you'd get to hear the sound of one hand clapping every time you went to the theatre. Did you go to the theatre last time you were here?'

'No, it's too expensive.'

'What did you do?'

'What tourists always do in New York City. Empire State, Statue of and all the galleries. There's a million galleries.'

'Where'd you stay?'

'The first two nights, I slept in an abandoned car. A Pontiac Grand Am.'

'Weren't you scared?'

'Not really. It had a doorman.'

I suppose you could call me a racist because I used to give money to
the black doorman in our building. Now we've got a white guy, I don't
give money.

White male, approx. 38

We wandered down a street composed entirely of shoe stores,
three-quarters of which were going out of business. (This, I
suppose, is a direct result of NYC's fondness for 'districts': the
Second-Hand Record District around Bleeker Street; the Art
District of SoHo; the Immigration District at Ellis Island, etc. I
guess it's convenient, but I'd sure hate to be a shoe guy tryna
make a buck in this city.) We were looking for clothes because
our slobby travel gear was making us feel insecure – doubly so
since most of the people we passed were pretty well dressed –
but I couldn't find anything not overpriced and in my size. So
we kept wandering aimlessly, ducking into alleys to sneak a look
at our tourist map to make sure we didn't end up like Sherman
McCoy – in the Bronx with Melanie Griffith, a sure-fire recipe
for trouble.

Down into a subway station where a black man did a terrific
version of 'I've Got You (Under My Skin)' accompanied by a
paradiddle of hand claps and finger clicks. I gave him a dollar
(no tax). He really was great. Into the subway car. Two stops
down the line a thin, haggard-bearded white guy got on and
announced that his right leg was crippled from a hernia and that
he lived at the YMCA (pointing to YMCA t-shirt) and needed to
pay his rent by 4 p.m. (displaying the rent form), that he didn't
use drugs (revealing his apparently trackless forearms) and that
it was a 'bad emergency'. I only gave him 75¢ because I'm not

39

sure if hernias can cripple your right leg.

Anonymous Autonomous

There is, sometimes, a ticklish feeling of anonymity in which the foreign traveller may wallow; a kind of sly rootlessness which allows you to be anyone from anywhere or nobody from nowhere. This is most particularly the case in New York City, where there are already so many people who are not interested in anybody else, that the presence of two more persons – even from as exotic a place as Melbourne, Australia – is of remarkably little interest to the general population. And, indeed, the particular population: the woman sitting next to David and me who cannot help but notice our distinctive accents and think to herself, 'Wow. Those two guys are British. I'll bet *they've* got some interesting stories to tell.' Or the guy in the bar who sees us drinking Victoria Bitter and wonders, 'Victoria . . . isn't that in South Africa? Are those two guys racists?' And so on.

This never happens. Nobody gives a damn. (Which is fair enough – I couldn't care less if I sat next to a Frenchman on a bus back home.) But when *you're* overseas, it seems somehow wrong that nobody's stopping you and saying, 'Hey, I haven't seen *you* around Manhattan before. Are you new in town? What do you think of the place? Come stay at my house. Here's some money.'

What all this boils down to is that while you're in a foreign country, you can be absolutely anything or anyone you wish to be. The problem for me is, I don't want to be anyone – I want to be someone. *I want to be me.* And in New York City, that's hard.

2.10 p.m.

I rang the NYPD, curious to see if it would be possible to spend a couple of hours in the back of a patrol car. 'Sorry, we don't do dat no more,' the officer told me.

'What if we get arrested?' I questioned abruptly. 'Could we do it then?'

'Don't be an asshole,' he said, and hung up.

I'm in our room making a cup of 'coffee' from Carnation Coffeemate® Non-Dairy Creamer Lite and Superior Sweet 'n Low® Sugar Substitute.

'Guess what, David?' The 'coffee' looks like river water.

'What?'

'I can see Woody and Mia waving to each other from their apartment windows across Central Park.' And tastes like an oil spill.

'They broke up ages ago.'

'This is an old hotel – the views are historical.' I pour the liquid down the sink.

Meet the Beats

Near Columbia University we see a cafe/bar called the Beating Place. We are drawn by the steady bongo music pouring out and the unsteady stream of stoned swingers and hepcats going in. The smoky, hazy, jazzy, crazy joint is crowded with tired poets and beaten writers (all men) trying to tame and give voice to their wild thoughts and ideas. *Everybody* is here: Norman Mailer, naked and dead looking; the yin and yang of Life and Art, Neal Cassady and Dean Moriarty; dopey Maynard G. Krebs the bongo beater, tapping out a bongo mantra; Charlie Parker on the nod;

41

rhyming Langston Hughes coming down with the blues; Williams Gaddis and Burroughs, sweating, puffing, arm wrestling on a bar stool; the man with the golden voice, Nelson Algren, singing a swinging song; Corso, Ginsberg, Ferlinghetti, Kerouac and 'Shopping Cart' Johnston all gathered around a single table and talking at once, quoting Baudelaire, Céline, Kafka, each other and themselves. Mostly themselves.

David and I hunch our shoulders and squeeze through the *je ne sais quoi de Weltschmerz* that engulfs the room. We order a pair of brandies while Allen Ginsberg, who looks like a hairy owl, cries out, 'I saw the best pair of shoes of my generation destroyed by inferior polish, peeling hysterical naked. Dragging themselves through the bleaker streets at dawn looking for a cobbler.' It's a hoot. Whereupon Gregory Corso announces that he'll recite a list of words 'inspired by too much caffeine'. 'Ragout!' he shouts. Everyone nods.

David and I find seats at the table Mailer shares with Neal and Dean. Up close, Stormin' Norman has a gruff, jowly face, although I am impressed by his dewlaps and fine head of hair.

'D'you wanna fuck me or fight me?' he asks, flexing his two favourite muscles.

'Neither,' David says.

'You?' Mailer asks, looking at me and downing an espresso. 'I knew Marilyn.'

'Lime!!' shouts Corso over at the beat seat.

'No, not really,' I tell Mailer, and he looks pissed. 'What was she *really* like?' I ask, hoping to pacify him.

'Frigid like an ice-cream ice-queen. Miller's prick must've been a fuckin' stalactite, you ask me.'

Corso shouts stentorian: 'Buttock! Snowjob! Pillock! Ham!

Auburn! Dope! Keg! Shatter! Speak! Fish! Mongoloid!' It's starting to sound good.

'Are you two twins?' David asks Neal and Dean. I kick him under the table. 'Ouch,' he cries at the same time as Greg Corso. 'What was that for?' Quietly, I tell him that Neal is the real deal but Dean is a wacky Kerouacian construction. 'Sorry,' he says to both of them. 'What's it like being fictional?' he asks Moriarty. 'You tell me. Your come will turn, man,' Moriarty says a little petulantly.

'Yuk,' says David.

Corso approves. 'Yuk! Bitch! Brain! Phantasm! Novocaine, help, bray, simper, whine!!'

'Shut up, Nunzio! Go back to San Francisco,' scream the Williams in unison.

'How do you like New York?' Neal asks me, smiling as though he just survived a car crash.

In a room where they fly like spit from a babbling man, words fail me: 'Well, it's very . . . New York,' I offer, lame-jawed.

He leans in close to me and I can smell the adrenalin as he speaks. 'It's all there is, man. Forget everything you ever knew, and know New York. Know her rhythms and pulses, her energy and secrets. Once she gets into your head, she'll never leave you. New York is Life itself. With a capital 'L'. There's nowhere else.'

'Except maybe Nebraska and Kansas,' offers Kerouac, who joins us as Mailer leaves in search of somebody to fight or fuck. 'Yam!'

The din is overwhelming – nobody can shut up. David is comparing skin tone with Dean Moriarty. 'I am the sub-editor of my own destiny. Writing about the self is all almost that matters,' states Kerouac. 'But even that passes, becomes so much historical, egotistical dust. When all's said and overdone, the only thing that ultimately matters is –'

Corso reaches a crescendo – 'CHAPERONE!' – and obscures Kerouac's final whispered words. I strain to hear and am almost sure that he says, 'The only thing that ultimately matters is . . . *the Emmys.*'

I Ate Andy Warhol. **Conspicuous consumption when Art and Food join forces. Directed by Sam Peckinpah.**

He was too romantic about Manhattan. He thrived on the hustle bustle of the crowds and the traffic. To him, New York meant beautiful women and street-smart guys who seemed to know all the angles . . . Ah, no. Corny, too corny for a man of my taste.

Woody Allen, *Manhattan*, 1979

We've moved to a groovy, younger person's hotel/hostel called the Gershwin on 27th and Fifth, where the staff are young, pretty, French, arrogant and hopeless. Where the lift doesn't really work and there's no air-conditioning in the rooms. Where the fourth floor is reserved for 'models only'. We were told that Miss Petite Texas is staying here (with her Ma) so we're keeping an eye out for a small, over made-up, twangy kid in a ten-gallon hat. But the only person even remotely model-like is the blonde on reception, who is more likely Miss Petite Bourgeoisie.

The lobby is infused with the Euro-gloom of tired backpackers fed up with the lift and their personal laundry problems. There are some bad, colourful sculptures lying around and a lesser Lichtenstein behind the front desk. The manager informs us that there is also 'an original de Kooning around here somewhere. We've sort of lost it.'

'We have to find it,' David whispers to me. 'We could pay for our entire trip with that.'

The Gershwin is influenced by Mr Warhol's Factory notion of the late 60s, a halcyon period which nobody around here seems to have quite gotten over yet. It's all 'Andy this' and 'Billy Name is our in-residence photographer and devout Catholic' that. 'Excuse me while I make Ultra Violet a cup of tea.' To one side of the lobby is a silver-painted bomb site that's used for 'happenings' and hanging Mr Name's artwork. There is also a signed-by-Andy Campbell's soup can in a glass box on a wall. IN CASE OF ART/HUNGER EMERGENCY, BREAK GLASS.

In fact they *so* worship the dead Popster at the Gershwin that on the most recent anniversary of his expiration they held a seance in the Silver Happening Space. They decked it out with votive candles (in deference to Billy's Catholicism) placed inside Campbell's chicken noodle soup cans (in honour of Andy's enduring appetite) and employed a gipsy to call upon the white-wigged spirit. When that failed they wheeled out a performance artist, named Eugene Calamari Jr, who lay on the floor chanting 'Don't be a doormat,' while being vacuumed by his partner in Art Crime. I am truly sorry I missed it, although I once had a very similar experience when I fainted in the soup aisle of a Safeway back home.

Mugging for the Camera

Our thoughts were elsewhere, busy trying to absorb the energy of the great metropolis of which we were just a tiny part. Trying to assert some slender sense of individuality in a city of towering personality. We were on our way to TriBeCa or SoHo or MoMA or SoMeWhere like that, just minding our own business and not

45

gawping up at the tall buildings like a couple of rubbernecking rube tourists, when this guy slipped out of a crack in a wall waving a sap and demanding money. Strangely, we weren't frightened. We were shocked, obviously, and stunned and alarmed and even discombobulated, but not frightened. Maybe if he'd had a gun ... but he didn't. He had one of those little black leather saps you whack people over the head with in old movies.

'Gimme all whatcha got,' he said. His gravelly voice seemed to come from somewhere near him, rather than from him. The mugging ventriloquist ... 'Stop thinking, bub, and hand over the handover.'

I looked at David. He was staring up at some tall building like a complete tourist. 'There's a guy down here wants to rob us, Dave,' I said.

'Well he's out of luck with me, I'm afraid. I haven't been to a bank yet,' David said to me.

'Me too,' I replied. 'I've got zip. Not even a subway token.' I pulled out my wallet. David took it, looked inside and shook his head. 'Yep, empty.'

'Can't do nothin' for ya, man,' I said to the mugger. He looked mighty pissed off, not so much about the lack of money, but the lack of attention. The fact was, he'd become something of a bit-player in our little scene.

'Credit cards!' he barked, and slapped the sap into the fat of his hand with a flat *splat!*

'Oh, you don't want those,' David said.

'They're Australian,' I added.

Meanwhile, a small but attentive crowd had gathered on the sidewalk around us – a gleaming phalanx of camera and video lenses, and slitted, peering eyes. One man was even taking notes. I nodded a polite greeting at the huddled mass, but in return received only slow blinks and the quiet whirr of zoom.

'Jewellery!' the mugger ordered. David and I couldn't help laughing. 'Whatsa gag?'

'Well come on, mate,' David said. 'Do we look like we're from Run DMC or the Gambino Family? We're just not jewellery guys. I'm sorry.'

'Aren't you wearing a toe-ring?' I asked David. 'From your surfer days?'

'Yeah, but it's covered in filth. I think it may even have become subcutaneous.'

'How do you spell that?' asked the note-taker in the crowd.

Somebody else piped up. 'When're we gonna see some action? This is no "New York-style" mugging.'

'Yeah,' said another voice. 'Are you guys performance artists or what?'

'Yes,' I said, smiling. 'My name's Eug–'

'Shut up, dickhead!' the mugger shouted, then hit me on the side of the head with the sap. Everything went black for a moment and I woke on the pavement, staring blurrily into a dozen lenses. I moaned, coughed, then moaned again.

'Was that real, or just part of the show?' somebody wanted to know.

I couldn't think of anything smart-alecky to say. I wanted desperately to get up and mouth off to the crowd, but nothing would come to me; no movement, no thought. Somehow, the mugger and his city had succeeded – together, they'd robbed me of my personality.

At MoMA

I was wearing headphones, listening loudly to the Undisputed Truth as I wandered among the Great Works of Modern Art.

David kept glaring at me and mouthing instructions along the lines of 'Turn that off, you bloody fool,' and I was happy to ignore him – after paying two bucks for a Coke at the MoMA SoDA stand, I felt I could pretty much do as I goddam liked.

And so I slid musically around admiring the gifts of genius, themselves the generous gifts of generously wealthy New Yorkers. *There's that Van Gogh flower painting. Oh, that's that Cézanne fruit job. Very nice. Hmm, another Munch with haunted, long-faced people in it* . . . In fact, I think *The Scream* is where little Mac Culkin got the idea for his famous aftershave gag in *Home Alone*. A classic example of art imitating Art . . .

The hot stuff, judging by the sweaty, whispering traffic jam of art-loving humanity, was a little corner in which hung that hairy-lipped self-portrait by Frida Kahlo and some dripping clock number by Salvador 'Big Sal' Dali. The paint hounds couldn't get enough of that action. I took off my headphones, shouldered my way through the crowd and started talking about how the pieces had a 'wonderful otherness' and 'negative capability'. Everybody nodded enthusiastically, especially this woman who looked like Diane 'Buster' Keaton. My work there was done.

Elsewhere, we saw lots more modern American art about America by Americans (or artists the museum *claims* as American, e.g. Marcel Duchamp [French], Philip Guston [born in Canada] and anyone else they think is pretty talented and could not possibly have come from Iowa, like the Bee Gees and Peter Allen). On still another floor was an exhibition called 'New York – City of Ambition'. And if there's one thing New Yorkers love more than America, it's New York City. It was good. Ambitious, but good.

City of Ambition

It was once my ambition to live in New York City. The notion of living in Manhattan really appealed to me: a slick young know-it-all at the peak of my breathless arrogance, working in some monstrous, gorgeous Madison Avenue corporate headquarters with a rent-controlled apartment and catwalk-model girlfriend. But I was too chicken to try it. Which is a shame, because at that age I might just have been able to adapt and thrive here. Maybe. The new me (that is, the old me) has just one word for this city: intimidating.

Manhattan isn't big, it's enormous. Central Park isn't a park, it's a territory (it really should have its own senator). The traffic isn't just a bunch of cars caught at the lights, it's an endless stream of grumbling metal, most of it the angry, battered yellow of cabs. There's not merely a hell of a lot of people here, there's a great swelling sea of humanity. They're loud and opinionated, and when they shout the world pricks up its ears and *listens*. The New York stock exchange is the one that *matters*. New York City's buildings aren't just many, tall and beautiful, they're a magnificent, sky-scraping swarm. There is here a greater concentration of everything than virtually anywhere else. If New York could speak, it would say, 'Well, how about me, huh?' Either that or 'What the fuck you lookin' at!?'

'How do you know so much?' Babette said.
'I'm from New York.'

Don DeLillo, *White Noise*, 1985

7.20 p.m. Hotel

David has just returned from looking for the (Kenny) Scharf·Shack. He couldn't find it, but stumbled on the Haring Hut, Koons's Kave and the Mapplethorpe Maisonette. He has brought back six Buds, some sushi and a can of Pringles. I'm drinking my first Budweiser, the self-proclaimed 'King of Beers'. I have to disagree though – because of its almost total lack of flavour and pathetic alcohol/volume content of 2.8, I'm calling it the 'Serf of Sodas'.

Artland

Through the hustle bustle of the crowds and traffic, we cabbed over to the lovely Meat Packing District to see my old pal Suzy, a journalist who lives in a loft/studio owned by a couple of artists. (The lady artist once made some wallpaper out of a year's worth of her menstrual blood, which I'm not even gonna go into lest I say something about how inspired and brilliant *that* whole idea is.)

Suzy took us to the Art Bar in the West Village. It was extremely dark and decorated like a New Orleans bordello – candles everywhere and a raging fireplace, even though it was daylight and 95° outside. The bar was filled with the 'after work' crowd, street-smart guys who seemed to know all the angles, including a young Roger McGuinn fan with a long blond fringe and black Raybans who smirked like he knew something nobody else did – a smirk I saw all too often on the human face of NYC. Next to him sat a boy of around sixteen trying to pass himself off as an adult and practically begging the waitress to beef up his Coke. 'Can'tcha stick a little rum in it or something?' he asked her very nicely. I kind of hoped she would, but she just rattled her curls in the negative. 'I can't sit in a corny place like this cold *sober*,' he pleaded. 'C'mon, can'tcha stick a little rum in it or something?'

I drew him aside and offered to buy him a drink with a little rum in it. 'What are ya, Mac?' he said. 'Some kind of goddam flit or something? Leave me the hell alone.'

Obviously he didn't rely on the kindness of strangers.

Tequila-drunk, David, Suzy and I left the Art Bar and trawled the wide, empty, dirty streets past abandoned warehouses and guys packing meat. At a diner-style restaurant called Florent we drank Rolling Rock (as drunk by Robert De Niro in *The Deer Hunter*) and ate hamburgers. I pretended to be a Polish/American steel worker, which the others found very unamusing because of my thick accent and frequent requests for 'pirogi'.

'Suzy,' I said, softening my accent, 'you've lived here for a couple of years now. What's it like?'

'I have to leave every six months and spend some time in Europe,' she replied, removing a ring of brown onion from her burger.

'Why's that?' said David, taking the onion from her plate.

'Mainly because people are always asking you how you like New York. Everybody does it. It's like giving progress reports on a disease. "Are you better yet? Is it getting worse? How much longer do you have?" It's a real doctor-patient relationship between the native New Yorkers and the immigrants. I'm quite sick of it.'

'How much longer do you have?' I wondered.

'I'm leaving next week.'

'For how long?'

'For as long as I can stand it. Somehow, you always get pulled back,' she sighed. 'For treatment, I suppose.'

Back at the Gershwin, David and I hunted everywhere for the misplaced de Kooning. We searched every closet, coolroom, storeroom, backroom and subroom; every inhouse, outhouse, henhouse and shithouse. No luck, but we chanced upon some old tins of Spaghetti-Os which David has signed and we may pawn later.

FOR MINT SNUFF YOU CAN CHEW, CALL 1-800 EAT MINT

The Bible. **An incident on a subway has far-reaching consequences. With Edward G. Robinson as 'Him'.**

'The men' believed it impossible to paint New York . . .
Joan Didion, *The White Album*, 1976

Gave my washing to a Korean lady who charges 75¢ a pound, which was a shock as my mother used to charge me by the stain. I had about eight pounds (roughly 21,000 stains).

Condon 1st. Hitler 2nd
David is trimming his goatee with the tiny pair of scissors on his Swiss Army knife. There are little red hairs all over the sink.
'How much are you gonna tip the maid for cleaning up *that*?' I ask.
'It's all part of the wonderful service here at the SoHo Grand, Mr Condon.'
'You'd make a great wealthy Arab.'
'I kill you,' he says, spitting all over the place.

'So what do you make of America so far?' I ask. He's finished with his beard and is now watching TV. Golf or yachting or something on ESPN.

'Hard to say, Seanie Boy. It's probably a bit early to say. It's a big place.'

'Do you get a kind of deathly feeling?'

'Deathly or deadly?'

'Either.'

'Neither.'

'Well, you should. It feels like the opportunities for being killed here are much greater and more varied than at home.'

'Well, there are more people in America.'

'Exactly.'

'You're a barrel of laughs to travel with, you know that? A real good-time Charlie.'

'Ah come on, David. Who would you rather be with?'

'Just about anyone, I think.'

'Hitler?'

'He's dead.'

'If he was alive.'

'If he was alive he'd be really old. I'd have to look after him.'

'Well, there you go.'

'Yeah. You're ahead of Adolf Hitler in the travelling partner stakes. Congratulations.'

New York was an inexhaustible labyrinth of endless steps . . .
Paul Auster, *City of Glass*, 1985

Dying for (their) Art

The intense heat of the previous few days had enervated the entire city, including David and me as we wound our way up the winding trail of African art exhibits at the Solomon R. Guggenheim Museum. Frank Lloyd Wright has created a great building in the Gug (as we New Yorkers affectionately know it). The long, slow, smooth single incline means that you don't have to waste time and footage going back and forth past stuff you've already seen. It's a clever, thoughtful concept, and beautifully executed. The big joke, however, is that the curved walls were designed by the Wright brother to make hanging paintings difficult in order to piss off the artists, for whom Frank apparently had little regard.

'It'd be superb for skateboarding down,' observed David, as we wandered ever upward in an art-stupor.

I found it kind of interesting and very ironic that we were gazing at all these ancient tombs and heads and stuff sculpted in honour of long-dead Africans inside a big museum, the various wings and levels of which were named after *American* dead. Still, if I was a dead guy, I'd probably rather have a museum than a piece of wood named after me. Not that I will have, of course. Then again, I don't plan on ever being dead either.

Afterwards we went looking for the Whitney Museum, which our map had inaccurately placed at the corner of 77th and Madison. We asked about twenty people for directions, mostly men in grey flannel suits or doddering ancients unleashed from the afternoon's social engagements and taking themselves out for a walk followed by some hunched lackey with a jewellery-scooper (we were right near Park Avenue). No-one seemed to have any idea where or even what the museum was. 'The whatney?'

When we finally found it the gallery was closed, but the gift shop was open so we bought some postcards of paintings and looked at them for a really long time. It was nearly the same. Better in some ways, because I know a lot about postcards and therefore know what I like.

Subway Story

We weren't really going anywhere in particular; we just wanted to catch subways as often as possible and see if anything happened. The re-taking of Pelham 123 or something like that. So we hopped on the first train that came along. The car was empty and we sat anywhere, opposite each other on the bright orange vinyl seats. I stared at David like a subway nutcase for a while, making him nervous until he told me to stop.

'What's that by your side?' he then said, pointing a long finger to my left.

I looked down and saw a heavy black book on the seat next to mine. I picked it up, ran my thumb across the thin pages and held the book up to my nose. It smelled old and reassuring and loved. I opened it, and pasted inside was a paper sticker the colour of turned milk. It had a school crest at the top, and a dedication typed in hard, lumpy letters below. The headmistress's indecipherable ink signature was a faded watery blue; a capital 'S' and a capital 'P' were all I could make out.

'Well?' asked David almost tersely. 'What is it?'

'It's a bible. A bible belonging to someone called Victoria Lucas.'

'Tricky Vicky,' said David, with an improper familiarity that annoyed me.

'Yeah. It's from 1967.' I couldn't take my eyes off the sticker.

55

To Victoria Lucas,

'Anything else? An address or anything?'

'No, that's all. I wish I could give it back to her.' *For excellence in English Composition.*

'I'll bet the subways have a fiendishly large Lost and Found department.'

'I want to return it to *her*, not some subway public servant,' I said, already shot with an almost missionary zeal. *Graduating Class of 1967.*

'This is New York City – you'll never find her.'

'There's a small clue.' *Charlotte Hughes High School.*

'Good luck.'

We ended up in the cramped and busy streets of the China-town/Little Italy district, eating noodles or pasta. I can't remember too well, because I was too busy wondering how many women in America were named Victoria Lucas. And how many places had a Charlotte Hughes High School. I couldn't stop thinking about her, and what had led to the strange intersection of our lives.

I imagined her whole life, the early years rich in cliché. Born around 1950, Victoria was the only child of decent, hard-working parents. A bright, pretty girl, she'd matured early and dated a few local boys before leaving town after graduation to live in New York City, where she'd studied anthropology and become a beautiful professor. She earned enough money but wasn't showy with it – she bought good wine and rare jazz records – and was popular on the Manhattan social scene. Ironically, this was mainly due to her firm sincerity and lack of ostentation. She spoke quietly, almost duskily, and moved with graceful purpose. Naturally, there had been lovers – a few men, perhaps some women – but she remained elusive, even to those she moved deeply. Somehow almost everybody had managed to disappoint her in some way: a quiet lie; a small, neat deception; a lingering, wistful glance into a future she instinctively knew did not include her. Striding beyond her mid-forties with confidence and style, she was still single and still breathtaking, living alone in a three-storey brownstone in Brooklyn. Last night she'd gone to a party where she'd gracefully fended off advances from Jimmy Breslin, Rudy Giuliani, Harrison Ford and Sandra Bernhard. The martini-fuelled merriment had lasted until dawn, so she was a little tired when she'd decided to journey into Manhattan to buy a replacement stylus for her Bang & Olufsen turntable. Heading out of her house, she'd grabbed the bible on a whim from a bookshelf by the door, deciding that she'd take a look to pass the time on the subway. But the late night had taken its toll. She was heavy-lidded as she waded through Genesis and when she woke with a start and hurried out at the Spring Street station, she absent-mindedly left her bible on the seat.

By the time I'd finished, I couldn't wait to meet Miss Lucas. I was *in love* with her.

Barechested in the Park

No visit to New York City would be complete without a visit to Central Park (the same goes for being mugged, and we're attempting to do everything the guidebook recommends), so we have found ourselves in the great wilderness of trees and ice-cream carts. The park is full of baby-strollers, professional dog-walkers with packs of hounds straining at webs of leather

57

leashes, smug roller-bladers and generally shirtless individuals all enjoying the warm sun in 'the people's backyard'.

'Wanna go feed the ducks?' asks David.

'Sure. Where do you suppose the ducks go in winter?' I ask him. We are over on the west side of the park in the looming shadow of the Dakota Building, where there is a small garden called 'Strawberry Fields', in honour of John Lennon.

'There's not even any strawberries in it,' remarks David.

'A little marijuana crop would be more appropriate for old Lennon,' I suggest. 'It'd certainly be more popular.'

'Or vegetables. Maybe they should give peas a chance.'

Later, as we pass by the zoo, I see the kid from the bar the other night, the guy urging the waitress to put a little rum in his Coke. He's sitting on a bench waving to a little girl called Phoebe riding a beat-up old horse on the carousel opposite him. There is a broken record in pieces at his feet and I think he may be crying. Music from the carousel is playing – 'Smoke Gets in Your Eyes' – all jazzy and funny. It is a depressing scene, but oddly beautiful and strangely familiar.

God, I wish you could've been there.

Back in SoHo, we saw *Basquiat*, SoHo Art Under-Boss/Disrespector of Crockery Julian Schnabel's biopic about SoHo Art Genius Boy Jean-Michel Basquiat, which starred 70s Rock Transvestite David Bowie as SoHo Art God Andy 'Andy' Warhol. It wasn't very good. Samo (J-MB's street tag) was a cool artist but the film didn't really get to grips with him as a human being. And it was full of sly references to the SoHo art scene in the 80s, which you don't really give much of a damn about unless you were connected to it. And everybody connected to it was *in*

58

the movie (except all the dead guys) so they'd already seen it in real life. Still and all, it was interesting to *be* in SoHo, seeing a film *set* in SoHo about something *so* SoHo.

Which one was Basket?
The one wit' de hair.

Hispanic males, approx. 41, in cinema foyer

7.15 p.m.

Collected the washing. I can now hold my head high with the confidence of the 'stain-free' traveller. We're watching a great documentary about New York mob boss John Gotti – right here on his turf. Wow. This is followed by a movie about him. We're watching that too. Can't get enough of Gotti. Or cable.

867 5309

Using a telephone card, this is the number I called to speak with Sally: 9180066947731591538510116139510666l. Thirty-five numbers I know off by heart and sometimes speak aloud in my sleep. I asked her whether our apartment had caught fire since I'd been away. A little huffily, she told me that it hadn't.

Dental Hero. Sean becomes an idol to some pre-teens when he fails to realise there is some parsley caught in his teeth, while David rescues some people in a plane crash. Notable mainly for its excellent catering.

And New York is the most beautiful city in the world? It is not far from it.

Ezra Pound, *Patra Mia*, 1950

The financial relationship between me and beggars, bums and showmen so far:

- The *I've Got You* singer – $1.
- The Bad Emergency with a Hernia guy – 75¢.
- The guy who claimed to be 'a friend of the band' and promised to introduce me for $5 – 60¢ and a subway token.
- The guy who claimed to be organising a spaghetti and meatball dinner for 10,000 homeless people the next day and showed us an old letter from Fiorello La Guardia to prove it – $1 and a recipe for a very nice tomato sauce.
- The fella who came up to me and asked for change while I was talking on a telephone at Coney Island – 45¢ (a small reward for such temerity).
- The guy with no legs in a wheelchair with a 'Vietnam Veteran' sign resting on his stomach – $2.
- The thin, thirty-year-old Canadian who looked sad and scared and non-bilingual – $1.80 (Canadian) and five cigarettes (duty-free Dunhills).
- The ridiculous six-year-old squawking her way through 'Unchained Melody' whilst resting her forearms patronisingly on the heads of two small Chinese kids – 50¢ (a small amount because she was gonna get a whole lot more from the crowd of admiring tourists – and because she sucked).

Grand total – $8.10 and an invaluable sense of holiness.

10.15 a.m. SoHo

Right now, I'm spending an hour 'on line' at a post office. The service is terrible. I thought it was the postal workers who were supposed to be disgruntled, not the customers. In fact the employees look extremely gruntled. It takes about three bullet-proof hours to send a shoebox full of books to Australia by sea mail. 'It's not *sealed*, Sir,' the mail guy muffles at me through four inches of Uzi-resistant glass. 'The package is not *sealed* properly.' He is referring to a box of paper within another box, covered in plastic bubble wrap, not some chemical weapons I have stumbled upon and am sending home for Sally to put on the mantelpiece. I can't understand it – does he want the parcel welded shut or something? I whack on more tape, put the slightly better sealed package in the bullet-proof package-receiving chamber and close the door. He presses a button, opens his door of the chamber, glances at the package, then at me and says, 'It's not *addressed* properly, Sir. You have to *address* it properly. You're not doing this very well.' And so the bullet-proof exchange continues. When was the last time anybody robbed a goddam post office anyway? The Depression?

Hero Sandwich

For lunch, I had an authentic New York 'hero sandwich'. It'll probably be dinner as well. The beast was longer than my arm – thicker too – and a real slop-fest: French bread injected with bloody red peppers, sausage and onions. David had a 'slice' (of pizza). You only have to say 'Gimme a slice' around here and they know what. It all came from a semi-famous joint called Big Nick's. They have a picture of 'Iron' Mike Tyson sexually harassing some pizza dough in there.

For dessert we went to the Museum of Natural History, as we were keen to see its collection of 1.5 million spiders and insects. I hate spiders like death but quite like the experience of having glass between me and them. Even the dead ones.

61

While David waited in line for the tickets I stood outside smoking and was soon joined by a museum employee.

'S'up?' he said.

'Nuttin',' I said, pretending to be from around here. 'Waitin' tuh see da spiders.'

'Spiders is closed. Dey're rebuildin' it.'

'Aw fuck.'

'Here,' he said, handing me two tickets. 'Dey're tickets to da Skyshow in da Planetarium. It's a good show. You'll like it.'

I thanked him as he gave me directions to a different entrance with no queues.

'Dat line's for suckers,' he said, pointing to where David stood, still in the same spot. 'Total suckeroos.' Then he stamped on his cigarette and ground it into the concrete. 'Bam!'

David and I stood in awe in front of the brilliant dioramas of creatures from all around the world. Expertly taxidermied animals were set against rich, vividly painted backdrops with real trees and dirt and grass and snow (well, the snow was fake). It was all terrifically well done. And incredibly lifelike and dynamic – frozen in action until the end of time (or when they rebuild it). It was so much better than a zoo, where the animals are barely more alive, mournfully wandering around 18 square feet of lime-washed concrete. These displays were made back in the 1940s, which was especially lucky, because today they'd do it with computer-generated backgrounds and animastupidtronics instead of the lovingly detailed paintings. Electronic beavers would mechanically thump their tails and gnaw like over-revved tooth engines. The old way is more exact and respectful.

Later I pretended to be chased by 1.5 million escaped spiders, running down a big hallway shouting 'No! No! Noooo!' The guard didn't like it. Neither did David, who stood by shaking his head. But a bunch of schoolkids standing side by side in a long, schoolkiddish row, led by a woman with 'Miss Aigletinger' written on her lapel, stared at me as though I was their hero. It must have been my lunch.

4 p.m. In hotel room

David's gone off to Fire Island to see Neil Young. I was tempted to go – but Fire Island, y'know, I wouldn't want to accidentally 'discover' myself or anything. And there'd be all that primal screaming for the encore. Besides, I had an urgent matter to attend to.

I opened the bible, lay it on the desk and read again.

To Victoria Lucas,
For excellence in English Composition.
Graduating Class of 1967.
Charlotte Hughes High School.

I started with the phone books but gave up that folly after a micro-second when a glance told me there were about five thousand people named Lucas in Manhattan alone. I decided I'd have to wade through muddy bureaucracy and the slime of officialdom to see if I could somehow obtain a list of all the Charlotte Hughes High Schools in New York State (and possibly in all of America). After about ninety minutes and thirty phone calls I had a list comprising the only known Charlotte Hughes High School in the United States. It was in a town called Good Hope, near Jackson in rural Mississippi. Twelve hundred miles away.

I called the national telephone directory and asked for the

numbers of all the Lucases listed in Good Hope. There were three, and I called them all. The first two were dead ends but with the third I hit paydirt, as we say in the private investigation business. An old man answered after a few rings.

'Yes, hello there,' he said.

'Good evening, Sir,' I began. 'I'm sorry to bother you, but is this Mr Lucas of Good Hope, Mississippi?'

'Yes, it is. Who am I speaking to?'

'My name is Sean Condon, Sir. Do you have a daughter named Victoria?'

'Vicky, yes. Who is this please?'

'I'm calling from up north, Sir, New York City. I have your daughter's bible and I want to return it to her.'

'Oh dear, here it comes again,' he said to himself, tiredly. 'She's long gone from New York, Son. She's down here with us.'

'Oh . . .' So much for the beautiful professor of anthropology. She was probably a tubby, disinterested schoolmarm with lank hair and twenty-two children. 'Did Victoria go to Charlotte Hughes High School, Sir?'

'Yessir, she did. Class of 67.'

It was definitely her bible. I decided to go for broke. 'It so happens that I'm going to be in Good Hope soon, Sir. I could drop by.'

Mr Lucas breathed down the line noncommitally for a while. 'Well, yes, I suppose you could, but –'

'I'd really like to give the bible back to your daughter, Mr Lucas.' There was more emphysemic sighing. 'All right.'

He gave me his address and I told him to expect me in around ten days, maybe twenty. I hung up feeling excited, wondering if I could make a living as a private detective: Returning Bibles a Specialty.

David comes back shortly afterwards, his long hair even longer. 'Man,' he says, 'like it was the grooviest, most way-out mind trip I've had. Neil was beautiful, the crowd was beautiful . . . Everything was beautiful.'

'Are you sure you didn't accidentally go to a Grateful Dead concert?' I say.

He just looks at me peacefully and goes to shower off his body-paint.

There's a copy of the *New Yorker* lying on the floor of our hotel room. I flick to the 'Talk of the Town' section and read the following item.

The recent arrival (shortly to be followed by the eagerly antici-pated departure) of two antipodean visitors to the Big Cliché has certainly set a number of sharp tongues a-waggle. S. and D. have wandered the city streets leaving a trail of inanity and scraps of 'litter'-ature wherever the tourist map has taken them. At Coney Island, for example, 'the lads' (as they are fond of calling them-selves) were overheard making disparaging remarks about not being allowed on the Astrodome, as well as about the size of Nathan's Famous. Tom Wolfe, on learning of the comments, quipped, 'The hot dogs weren't big enough for them, yet they themselves were too big for the roller coaster!' Continuing their wayward path of deconstruction, the pair made repeated calls to Rudolph 'the reigning deer' Giuliani's office, trying to make an appointment to see what they sniggeringly called 'Ed's Koch'. President Truman Capote then mordaciously suggested that neither could tell the difference between a mayor and a gelding! It remains to be seen what further acts of foolishness will be committed by S. and/or D. whilst in the US, but it is hoped that they find a city more inclined toward their style of stupidity – Boise, for instance. Or anywhere in California.

With a burning sense of shock and outrage, I wonder who these imposters are.

My Shout

It was David's birthday, so as a special treat I took him to a restaurant called Lemon. Well, they *say* it's called Lemon but the name's not actually written anywhere – there's only this graphic of an angry citrus sucking on a stogie. Très chic.

You're not allowed to smoke at the tables, so I was forced to spend a fair amount of time clinging to the bar while David waved to me from across the room. There was no ashtray in which to deposit the filthy by-product of my filthy habit, so I signalled politely and unobtrusively and undemandingly to the tall peroxide head dancing with a cocktail shaker at the other end of the bar. He glared at me hard, put down the shaker, strutted all the way down to my end of the bar and told me loudly and vexatiously that he couldn't just drop everything to come down here to give me an ashtray. He made me sort of indignant. 'But you *can* drop everything to come all the way down here to tell me that you can't drop everything to come down here to give me an ashtray, can you, YOU FUCKING IDIOT!?' I shouted, not even blushing. I skimped a little on the tip for dinner, too.

How art thou out of breath when thou hast breath to say to me that thou art out of breath?

William Shakespeare, *Romeo and Juliet*

All up, I'm becoming quite the New Yorker. I'm almost ready to ask someone how they like the city.

Empire State of Confusion

As we walked back to the hotel, David and I argued about whether 'that building up there' was the Empire State. I said that it wasn't because there was no ape shimmying up its face (*King Kong*,

1933) or any bombers crashing into it (Real Life, 1945). Plus, for a Wonder of the Modern World, it was too small. David insisted that, despite my very foolish protests, it was. He was right.

After dark, the wrong New York streets carry in their shadows only a suggestion of life: an ankle disappearing around a corner; the low moan of an unseen car; the closing umbrella of the steamless hot dog cart; a whispered conversation on a tenement staircase. But at midnight, the streets open up and secrete from the darkness smugglers, scramblers, burglars, gamblers, pickpockets, pedlars, even panhandlers.

'The unemployed or non-void,' says David, continuing the song.
'Walking around like they're Pretty Boy Floyd,' I say, rapping it up.

Hair. A funky time in Harlem. (Black & white)

No one as yet has approached the management of New York in a proper spirit; that is to say, regarding it as the shiftless outcome of squalid barbarism and reckless extravagance. No one is likely to do so, because reflections on the long, narrow pig-trough are construed as malevolent attacks against the spirit and majesty of the Great American People.
Rudyard Kipling, *From Tideway to Tideway*, 1892

I won't go into too much detail. Let me just say this – I'm lost on a subway right now, trying to get to Harlem, and I look like a Nazi skinhead. An *ugly* skinhead. (I *know* it's a tautology.) Also, I am alone as David has snuck back to the Gershwin to try and find the missing de Kooning.

How It Happened

I got Marko – an Italian/Siberian/Albanian/Romanian/American

67

who didn't learn his cutting skills in the Army (he was 4F when it came to the old scissors, so it seems he developed the craft of ruining young men's prospects in the National Guard or the Boy Scouts). The display window featured dozens of snapshots of happy customers like Bruce Willis, George Clooney and one of the lesser Baldwins with their arms resting fondly on the shoulder of their personally favoured tonsorial artiste. Styles included 'The Brooder', 'The Homosexual (includes bushy moustache)' and 'The "Who Me?"' In the only photo of Marko I could see, he was standing sheepishly beside Telly Savalas, who was sporting a do called 'The Wig'. Many of the barbers had small, crowded areas packed with people waiting for a session with their preferred head man. Marko's area was empty. I got Marko.

1.05 p.m.

I have found myself in Queens – a whole other, different and wrong borough from Harlem, and, for that matter, from the island of Manhattan. I'm in a subway car full of black kids arguing about what cassette to play. I think they hate me. I only suggested Mr Barry Manilow once.

2.30 p.m. Somewhere

Still nowhere. Man, am I confused. My innate and finely tuned cartographic interpretation (map reading) skills failed me as soon as I so much as glanced at the subway guide in the train that was taking me from Queens to where I am now – wherever the hell that is. At least my hair has grown a little longer – but will I ever see daylight again? A young guy is singing some absolutely brilliant ballads to a karaoke-style backing tape, sweating down here in the dankness and singing about the shining sun as he wipes his committed brow with a wet cloth. 'Thank you ladies and gentlemen, thank you very much. Now I'd like to do another song by Mr Al Green, and if you'd care to sing along, that'd be just great.' I give him a dollar. I'd like to give him two, but don't want to seem like I am showing off. God, I'm lost. Where the hell is Harlem?

Heaven in Harlem

It was well worth the two hundred subways it took to get to Harlem. I took off my headphones and sunglasses so I could hear and see everything. Lots of 'Yo's, 'S'up?'s and 'Hey girl!'s. Hustlers everywhere. Dinah Washington's 'Salty Papa Blues' floating down from a window. I'm not claiming that I saw the *real* Harlem – all I did was walk about a mile along 125th Street, a hot, noisy, crowded technicolour bazaar selling greasy chicken, cheap clothing, electrical goods and general crappy stuff. I figured I ought to contribute to the Harlem sub-economy (my small attempt to slow the US National Debt Clock and help alleviate financial suffering in the Land of the Opportunity), so I bought some horribly sweet lemonade and a hip-hop tape (I couldn't find any Manilow).

Right underneath the el-train station I discovered a sort of heaven: a huge stall of about ten million records – one for $3, two for $5. As soon as I started rifling through the crates, I knew I was gonna *stop* that Debt Clock. There was everything funky, souly, jazzy, disco-ey and groovy. While sorting through the first few thousand, I began chatting with a fellow enthusiast in his early forties. He was wearing a hair-net and had a discoloured yellow glass eye that kept looking wildly off to the left.
'Have you ever heard this?' I asked, holding up a copy of *Movin'*

69

On, a Commodores record from 1975. 'It's fantastic. You should pick it up.'

' "Hold On" was the single, right?'

'Yeah, I think so.'

'Okay, I'll give it a try. I gotta do a party tonight.'

'What's your name?' I asked.

'Ervin.'

'Hey, Ervin, what would you do if you found a bible on a subway?'

'I would consider myself lucky and that the Lord was grooving kindly on me that day.'

He was a funky *and* religious guy. 'So you'd keep it?'

'Sure. Finders keepers. That's in the bible, ain't it?'

'Uh maybe. Probably in the New Testament.'

We continued to pick away at the records, making recommendations and observations about this group and that. Willie Bobo, Brass Construction, Larry Graham, Ripple, Les McCann. It was great – there we were, two music fans, one older and one younger, one black, one white, one American, one Australian, both having a good time spending our dough on the stuff we loved. The only problem was he had kind of bad breath. But who knows, maybe I did too.

And Harlem was Seventh Heaven.
> Malcolm X, *The Autobiography of Malcolm X*, 1965

6.25 p.m.

On my way back from Harlem, I collected the photos I've taken so far. All forty-eight of them are awful. I'm such a bad photographer. After seeing all that stuff at the Whitney and MoMA, it's especially depressing to realise that I have no talent for photography. None at all. I'll have to get a better camera.

Back at the hotel I showed them to David. 'Who's that?' he asked, pointing to an egg-coloured blur.

'You . . . or me. Or someone else.'

'Where was it taken?'

'Here. Or in Montreal. Maybe on the plane. I'm not sure. I think it's an art shot.'

'I couldn't find that de-fucking Kooning anywhere,' he told me unhappily. David rarely swears, so he must have been quite upset. 'Although I came across some Jeff Koons porcelains in a thrift store in Chelsea. Four for a dollar.'

'Did you buy 'em?' I asked excitedly.

'Are you kidding? His work is terrible. The only reason I'd ever buy his pieces would be to smash them.'

'Then they'd turn into Schnabels.'

'You can't win. It's impossible to destroy New York art.'

We went on to discuss whether Farrah (Fawcett) and Lee (Majors) were the Jack (Kennedy) and Jackie (Kennedy) of the 70s. Watching cable TV raises these sorts of questions that one simply cannot ignore. My personal opinion (and as a temporary New Yorker, I'm sure as hell gonna give it to you) is that if Farrah had married Burt Reynolds, there'd have been nothing those two couldn't have achieved.

Night

After a couple of drinks at the Algonquin with Dot Parker (mumbling whiner of *bon mots*), Al Woollcott (Man Who Came to Dinner) and Bob Benchley (grandfather of *Jaws* author, Peter), David and I went to the very glamorous, expensive and

71

icy-cool Tenth St Lounge, where the new intelligentsia like to hang out and trade quips. Right from the start, the place was weird: we paid $5 each at the door, walked into the club and were handed back our money. It brought a whole new meaning to the idea of short-term investment.

While we were waiting at the bar we got talking to two engaging women: Cassis, a French import, and her friend Jane, an American. Both of them worked in advertising, but I was happy to ignore that unfortunate detail since they were about the friendliest New Yorkers we'd met. And they were female. The four of us crowded around three chairs and a table until I got in trouble from a bouncer for *kneeling* next to the others. Evidently they had a standing 'standing' policy at the bar.

'So what do you two 'ope to learn from America?' asked Cassis, h-lessly.

'That's a good question. I have no idea,' I told her stupidly. 'What have you learned?'

'Not to get lost. But is 'ard,' she said. 'I drove across the desert alone last year. I am not sure yet if I 'ave left it.'

She was *so* French. I loved it.

'What about you?' David asked Jane.

'Oh, I live in Connecticut,' she said brightly. 'It's easy over there. They teach us everything we need to know. I wish they'd make it a borough of New York City though. It'd be better for everybody's taxes.'

'Were you born there?' I asked.

'Yeah, I guess so. Sometimes.'

In order to understand Jane's conversation I decided to get even further out of my mind than I already was by drinking

Stolichnaya Cristall vodka on the rocks. This was foolish (40% proof) and very expensive (500% mark-up). And it led me to try and weasel in on two Ramones-looking guys who were talking about hair and 'The Flintstones'.

'Yabba dabba doooo . . .' I blurted, by way of introduction. 'D'you think Betty and Fred and Barney and Wilma were wife-swappers? They looked like swingers to me. Whaddaya reckon?'

'Are you British?' asked Joey.

'No. 'Stralian.'

'Then fuck off,' said Dee-Dee.

I fucked off back to Jane, Cassis and David. 'Jane,' I slurred, 'I'm not sure I understood what you were saying before.'

'That's okay,' she said warmly. 'You're not from Connecticut.'

'I've made passes at girls who wore glasses, so y'know, Dorothy Parker can go to hell.' Boy, was I drunk.

'Have you ever made contact with a girl who contacts?' David asked. The girls laughed wildly. Boy, was he witty. 'Come on Seanarama, we'd better go,' he said, scooping me out of a chair. 'We have to travel across the country tomorrow.'

'Just remember not to get lost,' Cassis said again as we left. 'If you look 'ard enough, you will see that the truth is out there.'

What truth? Out where?

The Philadelphia Short Story. Sean slugs Katharine Hepburn. Unrated.

<u>12.03 p.m.</u>

Thanks to a cab speeding across town to the New York Port

Authority, we made the midday Greyhound to Philly.
'So how do you like New York City?' I asked the reservations
clerk as I picked up my ticket.
'The fuck you talking 'bout, Jack?' he said.
'Nothing . . . I'm Australian.'

We should be in Philadelphia in about two hours. Meanwhile,
may I remind you that this is a non-smoking coach, including
the restroom. You are free to smoke when we stop, however we
will not be stopping. If you are listening to headphones, please
keep them at a reasonable volume in consideration of your fellow
passengers. There are no alcoholic beverages allowed on board
and there is a restroom located at the rear of the coach for your
convenience. Thank you. Please enjoy the trip.

We're flashing through the fluorescent light of the Holland
Tunnel – it's long and goes deep beneath the Hudson River. And
when you get to the other side, everybody's Dutch! In fact I think
I see Sally (Van Es) smoking a Wee Willem on a park bench
surrounded by tulips, reading a book about Rembrandt while
wearing clogs, eating rollmops and tilting at windmills.
'Isn't tilting at windmills a Spanish pastime?' David asks.
'Yeah, could be.'
'You want to get your facts straight before you start shooting
your mouth off, Sean Quixote.'
'Si.'

In the seat directly in front of mine is a guy in his mid-twenties
doodling around with an Apple Newton (the Edsel of digital
technology); behind me is a constant phlegmy sniffing noise;
opposite me is David, yawning, rubbing his eyes and listening

to Ted Hawkins on his Walkman. Down the back of the bus is a trio of Hispanics making jokes about the smell of the restroom. But there was nothing funny about it when I went there.

Near Secaucus, New Jersey
It's flat and industrial and ugly, but looking back the other way you can see the Manhattan skyline, the Chrysler Building glinting in the sun, reminding you that you don't live there, you haven't made it.

Gas plants, refineries, train yards, power lines, turnpikes, freeways, airports, billboards advertising Nude Go-Go and couch and shower dancing, traffic, weeds, warehouses, storage tanks, gas stations, generators, superstores, smoke stacks, smog, heat haze, containers, cars, trucks and other Greyhound buses. That's the New Jersey Turnpike from the man on the ground.

We are passing a bunch of ragged trees. It's been a long while since I saw trees by the side of a road. They look amazing, primeval almost. After barely a week in Manhattan, David and I are both glad to be getting out of the city, out to where there's trees and breeze and birdies and space. NYC is so relentlessly urban. Being able to see more than two hundred feet in any direction other than up is quite a privilege. It really is. I'm no Henri Rousseau Nature Boy but it's wonderful to see hills, grass and yards. I feel like a guy who's been cooped up on a luxury liner and has finally ended up on the deserted tropical island he's long yearned for.

A fool sees not the same tree that a wise man sees.
William Blake, *The Marriage of Heaven and Hell*, 1793

1.50 p.m. Pennsylvania

Washington crossed the Delaware somewhere around here in 1776. Then he checked into the Travelodge for a rest. The outskirts of Philadelphia (the City of Brotherly Brothers) look pretty broken down, deserted and scary. I wonder what the second-hand cars are like.

$10 per Night

We'd heard you could get super cheap accommodation in out-of-season university dorms, so here we are in a dorm room at the University of Pennsylvania. We've arrived right at the end of summer vacation and the place is crawling with students and their parents, driving up in wood-panelled station wagons crammed with crappy old furniture from the basement for the young PHI BETA KAPPAs to put in their dorms and frat houses. Judging by the quality of our digs, U of P (as we temporary alumni call it) is no Ivy League institution. Or perhaps we're in some sort of circus midget scholarship room. It's about seven feet wide and fifteen feet long, and contains two tiny mattresses with encrusted sleeping bags, a small desk and, mercifully, a TV with cable. The previous residents must have been English hopheads or tripped-out fantasists because there are posters for Hawkwind, Marillion and Pink Floyd all over the walls. The floor is covered in spilled bongwater Rorschach patterns the colour of cheap meat and the beds stink of deep hashish dreams involving trolls and sword fights.

'It's kind of charming though, isn't it?' says David.

'It's the distillation of the first half-dozen rooms I had after I left home. Pokey little holes where I tried to seduce girls who felt a kind domestic pity for me. So, no, not really.'

'Imagine the fiendish sex that's gone on in here,' he says, with a sour look.

'I think it's more of a masturbator's room.'

'Some bearded little freak who majored in Onanism 101.'

'And loved to sit around mentally undressing Bilbo Baggins.'

Down in the university administration building I picked up a brochure for a course entitled 'A Tabloid History of America'.

A Tabloid History of America

1492 – COLUMBUS DISCOVERS LAND GOING CHEAP!!

1620 – IT'S WAR – PILGRIMS VS. TURKEYS!!

1775 – IT'S WAR – WITH THE BRITISH!!

1812 – IT'S WAR – IN CANADA!!

1861 – IT'S WAR – WITH OURSELVES!!

1898 – IT'S WAR – WITH THE SPANISH (IN CUBA)!!

1917 – IT'S WAR – WITH THE HUN!!

1941 – IT'S WAR – WITH NEARLY EVERYONE!!

1946 – IT'S WAR – AND IT'S COLD!!

1950 – IT'S A POLICE ACTION – IN KOREA!!

1959 – IT'S WAR – IN VIETNAM!!

1983 – IT'S WAR – WITH GRENADA!!

1991 – IT'S WAR – IN THE GULF!!

1992 – IT'S WAR – ON DRUGS!!

It sounds fun!!

6.50 p.m.

David's gone to make a few calls and check out the hygiene at a nearby singles bar, Smart Alex. I'm staring out at the university quadrangle where a few hundred poor, sad, eager and hungry students are lined up to receive a plate of free barbecue. If you ask me, there are few more pathetic sights than people lined up for free food – all those desperate, watering mouths, and sphincters fiercely clenching and unclenching as they pray with their stomachs that there'll still be plenty left when they finally reach the holy grill. That's how it is for me anyway, because – Oh my God! I think I see David waving up at me from the end of the line!

'The mighty Hawks got into the finals at the G – by a point. And Jason kicked ten goals, including his hundredth,' David tells me, back from the barbecue and a chat with his Dad on the phone. 'The who did what where?' Boy, it's been a long time.

7.30 p.m. Watching Nickleodeon on Cable

'Cheers' was the 'M*A*S*H' of the 80s. 'Seinfeld' is the 'Cheers'/'M*A*S*H' of the 90s. Either 'The Mary Tyler Moore Show' or 'The Dick Van Dyke Show' was the 'M*A*S*H' of the 60s. 'The Honeymooners' was the 'M*A*S*H' of the 50s and before that they had the radio and a world war for entertainment.

Round Midnight

We hung around the student hangouts but were pretty much hung out to dry when it was revealed that we weren't freshmen. That in fact our 'student bodies' were pudgy, white and Australian.

'Ever been inside a frat house?' David asked me, over a pre-mixed Whiskey Sour.

'I've never even seen *Animal House*.' I lifted a maraschino cherry out of my drink. 'These things are revolting.' David took it from me and ate it. 'Nobody round here's heard of the O'Jays,' I said with a little disgust.

'Why should they have?'

'They're a very famous Philly band. And they're brilliant.'

'Virtually every city in the States has its famous sons and daughters. Songs about the place, movies set there, all sorts of cultural history. You can't expect people to keep up. Especially teenagers.'

'It seems a shame though, don't you think? To be part of so much culture and not even be aware of it. I'll bet everybody in Chicago knows what Motown is.'

'You mean Detroit. It's not worth seeing anyway.'

'Detroit?'

'*Animal House.*'

Crash! And they don't even have a car yet. Rated a write-off.

Hey.
Hey.
What's up?
Nuttin'.
. . . Cool.
White male and white female, approx. 19, outside a Burger King

Here's the dope on realising the great Australian/American dream of buying a beat-up old car and driving it across the country – you can't do it. Renting is prohibitively expensive, even if you *can* find a rental company that will let you drive the car more than five miles from where you picked it up. And forget *buying* a car – if you don't have a permanent address in the state of purchase you can't register the vehicle or get it insured, and you have to get it insured because if you have an uninsured smash in America, your financial life is over. And David and I are too gutless, law-abiding and poor to risk it.

To gather this information, it's taken us four visits to the American Auto Association, appearances at seven different insurance offices, tyre-kicking at twenty-two car dealerships and being kept on hold for up to a day by several other institutions which seemed to think that hearing an Australian voice on the phone was the cue to take lunch. At various stages, we've considered stealing a car, risking death by hitchhiking or pretending that we *live* over in Pittsburgh with a woman called Cindy.

'Land of the Free, my international driver's licence,' snorts David.

Our great dream has stalled and broken down in the City of Brotherly Bureaucracy.

5.48 p.m. The Marriott Hotel

To our great relief we were only allowed one night at the university and have now moved somewhere a tad more salubrious. David is in the bathroom singing 'Que Sera Sera' in an absurdly high contralto while he shaves. I'm lying on my bed thinking about jumping onto flatcars, wondering if my luggage will fit into a handkerchief tied onto the end of a stick and whether hobo stew comes in a can.

6.44 p.m.

On the news tonight were Al Cwanger and Misty Stepp (she posed with weasels). America the Beautiful. We're catching a bus to Washington DC tomorrow to see if we can borrow a car from the Clintons. We've heard they have a few spares and the mileage on them is pretty good. The White House is there. It's the capital of the United States.

Our last night in the City of Sisterly Brotherness is spent eating soggy and maudlin Chinese food (part of my continuing investigation into exactly what TV Americans mean by Egg Foo Yung, Mu Shu Pork, Chop Suey, etc – at this stage, a tragic and deeply unhealthy journey of gastro-intestinal discovery). Over the click of bowls, the slurp of green tea and the sizzle of hot platter, a little chopstick chat makes its way across the table.

'Don't you think that life is mostly a disgusting rip-off? That there should be a way for decent folks like us to make good money in our chosen field, as long as we're not, y'know, completely hopeless at it?' I ask David, over the *ching-dao* of beer.

'No, I'm just happy doing what I do, making my own way and seeing what Life in the World has to offer,' he says, hovering cross-legged above his chair. Bastard.

Back at the hotel we watch a brilliant documentary on TNT about Mohammad Ali, the Black Superman. I love old Cassius Clay. He was a great fighter and a funny, cheeky guy. I wish I was him. Or James Brown. Or even one of the O'Jays.

CALL 1-800 MACY BED

SNORE NO MORE. CALL 1-800 ZZZZ

Mr Condon Goes to Washington. **The title says it all. Rated Capra-esque.**

Repro Man

There was an hour to kill before the bus left so we paid a visit to the Norman Rockwell Museum and Gift Shop. Well, they got the last part right. The rest of it is a shiny, noisy linoleum floor and a fluorescent ceiling in the basement of an anonymous civic building. Down there in the boweldom of art you come face to face with the art of boweldom – a hideous plaster representation of Paintin' Norman, who looks like Truman Capote with a meerschaum pipe poking out of his face. He's dressed in a flannel shirt with a cravat, striking the cavalier pose of a debonair, yet bohemian, artiste. Then you're in for a framed and faded *reproduction* of every picture, portrait, advertisement, *Saturday Evening Post* cover and cereal box Norman the Brush ever painted. There's even a framed jigsaw puzzle of two kids doing something unbearably cute one sunny afternoon in the ideal America of Rockwell's mind. Don't get me wrong – I like his stuff, it's fine. But if a place is going to call itself the Rockwell *Museum*, then just one original wouldn't be a bad idea. Even a fake one.

On a Greyhound bus – again. Sean & David's Long Experiment with Public Transport. This is some bumpy highway to DC. I'd call it the rocky path to democracy if I was feeling politically poetic. Luckily, I'm not.

The Jones (by Elmore Leonard)

'Sir, could you put the air down please? Sir, *the air!?*' cries a thin black man in the seat over to my right. Ten minutes later, the whole bus is freezing. He's constantly spinning around, changing positions, getting foetal then quickly frustrated, pulling his t-shirt sleeves down over his elbows, covering his eyes with his hands, shivering and sweating, winding and curving his wiry body every which way in search of relief that won't come until sometime after the end of the line. He's got some big jones going on. 'Sir! Could you *please* put the air down? Sir, please! The air! *The air!*' But it's already down as low as it's gonna go.

Later he gets up and wanders the aisle for a time, pacing up and down with these frail, timid little steps, muttering at people. Sort of hopping along. He sells another guy, a white guy he calls Slick, an imitation Dunhill watch for $2. I observe the deal with a little envy, because even though I know the watch is a piece of junk – stolen junk or a dead guy's junk – it still seems like a bargain. And my own watch is nothing special. Imitation leather crap, with green mould under the glass. The Jones offered me the watch first but I didn't want anything to do with it. Scared, I guess. So now it sits clunky and heavy on Slick's wrist, ticking time as we highway through the afternoon.

1.52 p.m. Maryland

We've just crossed into a new state. Through the tinted bus window, everything looks smoky and thick. Maybe it is. But if you don't get off the bus, you can never know. Maryland isn't famous for anything, although it is sometimes known as the Oyster State, and I guess that's something to be proud of. I wonder if Chicken Maryland was invented here. If so, why, and what does it taste like?

Passed a truck with 'Mayflower Transportation' written on the side. I'll bet there are dozens of Pilgrims in buckle shoes and hats huddled inside eating turkey sandwiches. Or maybe Hoagies.

It's raining. We're driving through Baltimore – home of the Orioles (baseball team), 'Homicide – Life on the Streets' (the

best TV cop show ever made) and the early films of Barry
Levinson (like *Diner* and *Tin Men* but not *Good Morning,
Vietnam* which was set in Vietnam).

Rest Stop

The exhaust fumes of a dozen idling buses fill the parking bay,
all dense and sweated from the rain. Like a song I can't get out
of my head, the Jones keeps shuffling around. Now he's trying
to sell a tube of toothpaste, while Slick, a big blond guy with a
touch of the Finnish cowboy about him, is staring at his wrist,
like he's trying to decide if the new watch goes with his outfit or
whether it works. Wondering whose it was, maybe. I suck on my
cigarette trying to look hard, like I don't want to be bothered.
Nobody bothers me. I may as well be an American. The Jones
still can't sell the toothpaste. 'Hey lady, you wanna buy some
Colgate? It's good stuff. Gimme a dollar. C'mon.' I buy an
orange juice from a vending machine, give the Jones the change,
refuse the toothpaste and get back on the bus.

3.28 p.m. Heading out of Baltimore

A few rows ahead of me a Japanese salaryman in a grey suit is
clutching a mobile phone. He's wearing a completely undetect-
able toupee and huge black, square sunglasses, like he's in
disguise as a cartoon. He probably owns Sony.

It's increasingly clammy and humid the closer we get to Washington, a city built next to an enormous swamp. And our driver's
forgotten to hit the air-conditioner switch. 'The air, mister! Turn
on *the air!*' Only this time it's me calling out. The Jones is back
in Baltimore, gone but not forgotten.

4.45 p.m. Suburban DC

The cab driver who took us to our hotel was very surprised to hear of my interest in seeing Chuck Brown, a brilliant black Go-Go musician. He warned me not to venture out to the neighbourhood where old Chuck was Go-Go-ing. 'Guns is everywhere over there,' he said. 'You look at somebody wrongways, they gonna kill you.' I was quite disappointed, since I like both Go-Go and handguns but am not willing to risk death in pursuit of either.

'I can tell we're in Washington,' I say to David, 'because of all the dark-windowed stretch limos everywhere.'
'I'll bet they're all bullet-proof too.'
'Can we get a bullet-proof car? We might accidentally get in a drive-by.'
'They shoot *from* the cars in drive-bys, not *at* them.'
'Is it drive-bys, or drives-by?'

Few people would live in Washington . . . who were not obliged to reside there; and the tides of emigration and speculation, those rapid and regardless currents, are little likely to flow at any time towards such dull and sluggish water.

Charles Dickens, *American Notes*, 1842

Two of the President's Men. **Sean and David become media darlings when they find that all is well at the White House. Rated R (genitals).**

'Y'all together?' the waitress asked, waving her finger between David and me.
'How do you mean?' I said.

85

'Are you two *together*?'

'We're friends,' said David, 'but we're not *together*.'

'We're not good-looking enough to be gay, Ma'am,' I told her.

She was still laughing when we finished our coffees and left.

Outside the White House fence (the one which separates 'we the people' from 'they the government'), we peered over the pink polo shirts, cream slacks and white heads of dozens of fence-gripping tourists to stare up at Abe Lincoln's former home; the old Kennedy place; chez Nixon; the Roosevelt[2] spread.

'Well, this is pretty boring. I'd much rather live there,' I said.

'Yeah,' agreed David. 'It'd be better if you could see the Prez and a couple of his mates playing kick-to-kick on the other side of that rose bush.'

'They'd be playing touch football, not kick-to-kick.'

'Or chucking a frisbee . . . in the nude.'

'Yeah! We could see little Chelsea's budding womanhood and –'

Then some Secret Service guys showed up all of a sudden and whisked us away.

In a cool cell somewhere beneath the Capitol Building a couple of swarthy types in off-the-rack suits held us down in metal chairs while electrodes were attached to our nipples and genitals. (I'd always wondered what that would feel like and, without wanting to sound either tough or lewd, it's really not as bad as you'd think. I mean it's not exactly *pleasant*, but I've felt worse.) We were then informed that making lewd and suggestive remarks about the First Daughter's 'budding womanhood' was a federal offence and that if we wanted to stay in the country we'd better watch our 'goddam dirty mouths'. Then they disconnected us and let us go.

As we walked away David remarked sorrowfully, 'It seems a shame to go to all the trouble of taking our shirts off and pulling our pants down and then not even electrocuting us.'
I couldn't help but agree. If nothing else, it's a waste of the taxpayer's money.

Institutionalised

Visited three of the Smithsonia. At number one (US History) we saw Edith and Archie Bunker's chairs, Arthur Fonzarelli's leather jacket, a wry martini glass from the set of 'M*A*S*H' and a bunch of other stuff that wasn't from TV.

At number two (Natural History) we had close encounters with several fat, *live* tarantulas, which made me quite ill. The hairy beasts reminded me of a story about Watergate personality G. Gordon Liddy. Apparently, while he was doing some scandal-related corrective institution time, he forced himself to overcome his fear of spiders by eating a large one in a sandwich. Or maybe it was a rat. I'm not sure. Liddy went on to become a talkback radio host, which, if you ask me, seems not inappropriate. I sometimes think about eating a Howard Stern sandwich. The King of All Sandwiches.

At number three (Air and Space) we checked out the rockets and planes, including that beautiful but infamous destroyer of worlds, the B-17 *Enola Gay*. I thought about naming my future daughter Enola Gay but decided that anyone called Enola Gay Condon would end up living in a trailer park wearing oversize housedresses.

The Vietnam Wall

At the first Smithsonian we had seen a very moving display of the gifts for the dead that have been collected from the Wall over the years – flak jackets, helmets, dog tags, cans of beer, cartons of cigarettes, bottles of alcohol and tear-stained letters ('Sleep my brother, sleep . . .'). The thousands of names carved into the great black memorial possessed that much more life for our having seen the hard evidence of the way they are remembered – in the gifts, the good thoughts and the tears.

Continuing our ever longer walk through the expansive DC parklands, we stared up at the great spire that is the Washington Monument, reflected on why the long lake that leads up to the Lincoln Memorial is called the Reflective Pool and eavesdropped on some hick in a hat named Jeff Smith chatting about justice with that huge statue of Honest Abe Lincoln.

In Washington Today . . .

We've decided to hold a press conference to set the record straight about precisely what is going on – why we're here and what colour car we've decided on. It's not strictly necessary for us to do this, but with so much of the powerful US media concentrated in one small city, it's very hard to resist.

A great flashing, poking, jostling, questioning, probing, prodding, buzzing press gang has gathered in the hotel ballroom, where David and I are sitting behind a large table, smartly dressed and be-sunglassed, flanked by jugs of water, plates of mints and a couple of C-grade PR flacks we've hired for the afternoon. We're about to call for quiet from the five hundred or so assorted hacks, before taking questions, one at a time, for the next seven hours.

JEROME ST JACQUES (CNN): Precisely what is going on?

DAVID: We have no firm idea at this point in time. Next!

ANNA-BELLE CHERRY (ABC): Why are you here?

SEAN [CHARMINGLY KENNEDY-ESQUE]: Good question, Anna-Belle [WINKING AND SHOWING PLENTY OF TEETH], but I'm gonna have to take the Fifth on it, darlin'. [SOTTO VOCE TO PR TYPE] Get me her hotel room number. Next!

FORD HENRY FORD (AUTO EROTICA MAGAZINE): What colour car have you decided on?

DAVID: What I can tell you at the moment is that we *have* chosen a colour, a very popular colour. But exactly *which* colour cannot be revealed until tomorrow. Next please!

CARL BERNSTEIN (ex-WASHINGTON POST): I feel I've been treated unfairly by my former wife. What do you think?

DAVID: Try this – Ignoragate. Next! Up the back in the brown culottes!

GLORIA STEINEM (MS MAGAZINE): Why isn't one of you a woman?

SEAN: In the film version of this trip, David will be played by Winona Ryder. Or Willie Aames in a dress. Next!

WILLIAM PALEY (CBS): What do you think of America?

SEAN: America is the greatest country on earth. Her people are the best people on earth. National security is superb – if there's even a slight bump, the whole country goes off like a cheap car alarm. Your food could stand a little help, though. Next!

E. GRAYDON CARTER (VANITY FAIR): Why should we give a . . . a . . . hoot what you think?

DAVID: I think you'd be wise not to.

BEN HECHT (THE FRONT PAGE): I'm dead, aren't I?

SEAN: Correct. Next!

ANONYMOUS (JOE KLEIN): Will you be publishing this book under your own name?

SEAN: Sadly, yes.

W. S. (NEW YORK TIMES): Is this trip an intellectual or aesthetic exercise?

DAVID: A combination of the two, but I should warn you that we'll be either drunk or hung over most of the time, so most of the exercise will be spent drinking or vomiting. Next! You in the Chanel sunglasses.

ANNA WINTOUR (VOGUE): What will you be wearing? Mostly?

SEAN: Clothes. Mostly.

GORE VIDAL (SELF): Will you be making any grand pronouncements or incisive observations about this country?

SEAN: I seriously doubt it, Gore. I'm too weak, lazy and stupid. Besides which, I think that the best observations about the self come from within the self. As sly, fun-loving Earl Butz might say, 'If you no liva here, you no maka da wisecracks.'

GORE VIDAL: Now wait just a moment, *I* said that!

SEAN: Exactly. Next!

11.37 p.m. Hotel room

We've retired early, exhausted after our ordeal with the media. Tomorrow we're supposed to pick up a rental car and begin driving across the country. But knowing America as I do, I'm sure it won't be that easy. They'll probably want to do a pathology study and an IQ test first. We'll pass the IQ test and that will only lead to trouble.

The South

Three-wheeled Piggly Wiggly shopping carts, grease-caked engine blocks, baby strollers with shredded black hoods, Soviet rocket parts, human skulls on spikes and orange-eyed Rottweilers on heavy chains breathing fire . . .

Dead Men Driving. **Based on the novel by Sister Helen Prejean and James Dickey. Rated X.**

9.50 a.m.

Hurricane Fran is sabotaging our travel plans by flooding all the places we'd thought of going to. Also, I've developed a hideous cold. Spent a feverish night listening to the Geiger-counter weirdness of my tapping nose and having strange delusions – a Commodores guitar riff came alive and took me shopping on Fifth Avenue. It was very expensive.

12.35 p.m.

At last, we're in 'our own' car – a white Chrysler Neon with stereo air bags, an economical 2-litre engine and electric windows. It's a real nerd-mobile and, just to take the sense of automotive anaemia that one step further, it's registered in Maine – WASP headquarters of these en-tire U-nited States. Interestingly, our first moments of independent motoring take us along Interstate 66. It's *almost* Route 66.

David has agreed to do all the driving on this trip. Actually, he more or less *insisted* on it because I've had my licence for less than six months and in that time have reversed into many trees. With David behind the wheel, I'm freed up to worry about on-coming traffic, momentary loss of control, wild spinning, hospitals, traction, cracked ribs, punctured lungs, rupturings, traumas, catheters, facial reconstruction, amputation, paralysation, permanent coma and chips in the paint job of our rental.

There's debris blown all over the highway by Fran, who has so far killed twelve people with her windy ways. And after just fifteen minutes' driving, David has run his first red light. I can't help but think that this is a highly inauspicious beginning to 'being our own men'.

12.58 p.m.

Leaving the wet, clotted grey of DC behind us, we take a wrong turn and get off the freeway about 120 miles too early. And we don't even have a particular destination in mind – anywhere with cable will do I guess (my travel attitude is a happy confluence of TV and second-hand Zen). There's a constant hot rain, like we're driving through somebody's bathroom. Whenever a truck passes, the wall of water it leaves in its wake prevents us from seeing anything at all and we must rely on our memory of what lay immediately ahead.

The radio says: *When everything's been taken into account and every-thing don't add up to much, why not try Chemical Bank?*

1.44 p.m.

Now it's like we're driving through somebody's lake. It's terri-fying. We can't see anything at all – not even the hood of the car. We know that the wipers are on only because a dash light tells us so. These are the worst driving conditions I've ever sat through. And David's been doing the 'wrong side of the road' deal for less than 90 minutes! I feel pretty sure we'll die soon. How can the tyres possibly stay on the road? We must be out of our minds. Most of the other cars have stopped underneath overpasses or bridges. The smart cars. 'Don't worry, Seanella,' David says calmly. 'I'm a professional.'

A professional what, though?

Road Cliché-O-Meter

'Driving really fast down the wrong side of the road when there's a fuel-laden semi coming at you at eighty miles per hour, and screaming ecstatically to show how crazy and unbridled and in love with life you are, then swerving back into your lane just before the truck hits. Then you turn to each other panting and laughing as though you've just had the most brilliant orgasm.'

'Excellent. A real classic. Stupidity, danger, excitement and sex all in one. I'll give that a 9.2. How about this. You see a long-haired hitch-hiker up ahead, covered in dust. You pick him up. He throws his duffel bag in the back. You say, "Where you headed, man?" You have to say, man. He says, "Anywhere." Just too cool. You have a long conversation with him and it turns out he's insane and kills you. Or you're insane and you kill him.'

'Very good. The homicidal stranger – but *who's* the stranger? I'll give it an even nine. Here's another. You break down in the middle of nowhere at dusk. You don't know what's wrong with the car. You start talking about *The Texas Chainsaw Massacre* – even though you're in Maine. Two gorgeous chicks pull up, wearing bikinis. They're mechanics. They fix your car and invite you to stay with them in the next town. Sex follows. The next day you get married in a double wedding held by a "crazy" preacher who smiles at the four of you with witless benevolence.'

'Not bad. The happy ending sucks a bit.'

'You get divorced seventeen months later.'

'Okay, 7.6. What about going to the doctor complaining of "white line fever"?'

'Good one. I'll give it an 8.5. How about this one: while you're away, you keep an obsessively detailed diary which forms the basis of a book about your crazy adventures on the road.'

'Absolutely superb. I'll give it a nine. Ten if it's packed with clichés and self-reference.'

6.37 p.m. Virginia

We cruise through Front Royal (population: the Dukes of Hazzard meet the Confederate Army). There's little to see, all of it absolutely soaked by rain – auto shops and auto parts, gas stations, and a few sad wooden houses with coloured plastic furniture overturned by the wind on their porches. The town numbers barely 12,000 but they have McDonald's, Hardee's, Taco Bell, Pizza Hut, Popeyes, HoJo's and four 7-11s (which is why the town smells like old, cheap cologne).

We stop at Sandy's Diner, a real old-fashioned diner with hostile patrons, cantankerous waitresses and rancid food, all of it doused in the 'ole Virginny-style' country music coming from the little jukeboxes on every table. A small group of men and women all fattened by thick layers of flannel keep barking and snapping and yelling and laughing as though they can repel the gloom by overstating their blitheness. David and I sit in a booth way up the back and talk in low voices. Neither of us order the liver and onion sandwich, thrice-boiled haddock, fried squirrel or pig's heart goulash that the menu offers. With a gruff country snarl, our burned but rare hare burgers are plonked in front of us; we take a few quick bites, leave a big tip and get the hell out of there. Friday night, Front Royal, Virginia, USA.

Tie a Yellow Ribbon. (**Round the Roanoke tree.) Rated MIA (colorised).**

A whole new day with all new weather – clear blue skies and

chilled sunshine. Delightful. It turns out that Front Royal proper (as opposed to the outskirts, where we had inadvertently holed up) is in fact quite a lovely old town. Sorry.

But all is not good. We'd planned to take the Skyline Drive through the Shenandoah National Park but Freakin' Fran has caused the closure of the road. And the alternative road. And the other alternative road. Curse you Fran, and your mother, Nature.

Have a bless-ed day.

White female motel clerk, approx. 34

9.17 a.m.

Ran over a previously run over skunk on the slippery Stonewall Jackson Highway. Passed a campground completely submerged beneath water; only the roof of a hut and a detumescent American flag flopped above the waterline. Drove by a storm-damaged sports oval, now lake. I've never been caught in the immediate aftermath of a natural disaster before. It's pretty distressing.
'I'd sure hate to have owned anything around here,' I say, 'except possibly a boat store.'
'Or a Sandbags R Us outlet.'

We're driving along a thin highway, the Jackson-Lee, with fields and a great many small, two-storey wooden mansionettes on either side. Bonsai antebellum. It's very green, but strangely uninteresting. One hundred and thirty-five years ago there would have been plenty of action though. Some cannonfire and screaming.
It's quite God-fearing around here. This I'm assuming from the hundreds of mainly Baptist churches we pass every few feet. In the reception area of yesterday's motel was a list of all the service

times in all the churches in Warren County. It was a long list. Thank the Lord for cable – it covers all denominations.

The radio says: . . . *if you look at it in that light, the problems of three people don't add up to a hill of beans in this crazy old suburb. And in local news, Old Man Treadwell has finally admitted that pop star Michael Jackson is a better dancer than he is.*

Commerce around here seems to consist of lawn ornaments and fireworks. Everybody drives a 4WD, wears a John Deere cap and looks at us suspiciously – they think we're a couple of faggots from up north. We are two men travelling together, we talk funny and we drive that nancy boy car with Maine plates, so I cain't hardly blame them.

Coming into Harrisonburg

'Another papilloma on the sole of America,' says David. Actually it's pretty nice, but I understand what he means. It's hard not to feel sick about a place when you enter it from the outskirts – which, unless you travel by chopper, is mostly unavoidable. That's the hard thing about going to a new city: the physical process of *entering* it. You have to see all the ragged, peripheral stuff. It would be so much better to be dropped in the middle, to immediately be able to look outward from within. But, in a way, that would be like being born and instantly turning eighteen.

FOR CHILLI & CHIPS CALL 1-800 PETROFRY

Musical Interlude

We're listening to Underworld, ultra techno, through the green hills of Virginia. If the locals could hear it they'd shoot us, even though it's better driving music than the calf-killin' bluegrass that's so popular around here. At least, it is in a Chrysler Neon. It'd sound damn silly coming from a rickety pick-up truck.

We've had to detour again for about the twentieth time today. Oooh, that Fran! Boy, are we ever on the backroads now. Even our map has given up on this spider trail. This is it. We're gonna be hog-tied, humiliated and killed right here. Fact is, if'n I wuz a hillbilly 'n I chanced 'pon a coupla fancy city slickers and they smart-assy opines on bluegrass and vittles, I'd kill us fer sure. And they's not a jury in the whole county'd convict me neither. 'Did you ever see *Southern Comfort*?' I ask David, winding up my window and ducking.

'Yeah. But that was set in the Louisiana bayous, not round here.'

'Doesn't matter. We're in the South. Anywhere below DC is the South. It's a huge area. I don't understand how they lost the war.'

'They were drunk most of the time. Probably *on* Southern Comfort.'

'I was drunk when I first saw it. But on beer. At war with my liver.'

Somehow we've ended up in a mountain range, motoring through tall trees in glorious sunlight with a spectacular view presenting itself for mile after twisting mile. Some Burt Bacharach on the radio is lifting my spirits even higher. Sadly, we'll lose the reception soon because there are too many competing radio stations in America and they all have broadcast bands of about six feet. 'What the world needs now is bigger radio towers.'

Two for the Road
A short play set in a small car travelling at 60 mph on a scenic Virginia

parkway. Behind the steering wheel is DAVID, *a hirsute blond, aloof and mysterious behind sunglasses. In the passenger seat is* SEAN, *smoking a cigarette and staring out the window. There is a moment's silence.* SEAN *puts out his cigarette before lifting his t-shirt to reveal his stomach – so fat, white and hairy that the first sound we hear is the collective gasp of the audience.*

SEAN: I think I might die of a heart attack when I'm forty-eight. If I keep up this fatness and drinking and smoking.

DAVID: You forgot stress and lack of exercise. But yeah, if you maintain the others you've got a pretty good chance.

SEAN: Don't worry, I'll keep 'em up. I'm very committed.

DAVID: Why don't you try the Israeli Army diet?

SEAN: What's that?

DAVID: Everybody's mother was on it in the 70s.

SEAN: Not mine. She was a fiend for fondue, that woman. What was in the diet?

DAVID: Two days of apples, followed by two days of boiled chicken, two days of cheese and then two more days of something else . . . ice-cream maybe.

SEAN: Yuk. I'd rather go on the Mossad diet.

DAVID: ?

SEAN: They kidnap and starve you.

CURTAIN/WINDSCREEN WIPERS

In Search Of

In 1587 a group of 121 men and women led by Governor John White set out from England to found a settlement in the New World. They settled on Roanoke Island in North Carolina and seemed to have a fine time. In fact the first child of English parents to be born in America was born there – little Virginia

Dare, granddaughter of Governor White. But what became of Virginia no-one knows . . . Soon after her birth, her grandfather sailed back to England for supplies and was detained there for three years (apparently he'd left his passport in his other pants and this caused no end of trouble with Immigration). When he finally returned to the New World there was not a single person to be found on Roanoke Island!

It had been previously arranged that if the colony moved away while the Governor was gone, they should carve the name of their destination on a tree. And if they went away in distress they were to carve a sign to tell him so. Sure enough, he found a word carved on a tree: 'Croatoan', the scary and haunting name of a tribe of – ironically – friendly Indians who lived nearby. There was no sign of distress or struggle to be found in the few traces of the settlement that were left. The Governor was comforted by this, but never determined what exactly had become of the colonists – he'd left the kettle on back in England and had to set sail at once.

Many believe that, hard pressed for food, the colony had taken refuge with the Croatoan and eventually intermarried with them. It was noticed that a tribe of Indians living in the area had blue eyes and showed other traces of white blood (e.g. they couldn't dance – even to Manilow). Whether this is true or not, no-one can say. So don't ask. Still, it's a great story.

'But why tell me all that if it's not even the same Roanoke as the one we're going to?' David asks.

'Because it gives me a chance to do my Leonard Nimoy impression.'

'Yeah? Well you forgot this!' he says, leaning over and squeezing the top of my left ear into a painful Vulcan point.

7.10 p.m.
We're at the Jefferson Lodge Motor Inn in downtown Roanoke. The *other* Roanoke. Plenty of down, but not much town, I'm afraid. Maybe this *is* the lost colony of Roanoke ('Missing since 1590') and they don't know it. I shout the word 'Croatoan!' out the motel window a few times, but nobody shows up.

Uncannily, in layout, design, decor and size, our room is a precise replica of last night's place – right down to the exact same TV remote control bolted to the table. Except this one controls a measly six channels, compared with last night's fifty-two. That's why this joint is only $43.18 (incl. tax).

Endured another distressing middle-American meal at a restaurant called Dad's (Dad, you motherfucker), which was decked out in 'old timey' knick-knackery like hoes, gas cans and Grover Cleveland. David had a half-rack of baby back ribs while I pecked at some chicken 'tenders' (oversized nuggets of reconstituted chicken which are ideal for small children and Virginia's many toothless adults) with gravy and mash plus a side order of decobbed corn. It reminded me of the sort of food served in mental institutions – colourful, easily digested and non-lethal if used in hand-to-hand combat. The 'insane' food was probably no accident, as most of the customers looked demented – a bunch of withered arms, shrunken spines and babies with soft skulls. And me in the middle of it all, sniffing and burbling and spooning in the mushy forkfuls, being 'howdy'-ed and limply waved at by my brothers and sisters (most of them sons and daughters of brothers and sisters). David, my keeper, wiping my mouth every

101

now and then, making sure I didn't make a fuss.

At a bar (sorry, *the* bar) downtown, we met a jug-eared guitarist named Cyrus Pace. As well as grabbable ears, Cyrus had a puddin' bowl haircut and close-together eyes; he slouched forward when he spoke, making him look lazy but inquisitive. Somehow he pulled it all together and was easily the coolest person in Roanoke. He told us that he played for two years in a Navy band stationed in Guam, where he met quite a few Australians. 'And man, they were the craziest people I ever knew. I mean they were crazy. And man, could they drink. We just couldn't keep up, they were so drunk and crazy.'

'Yeah,' I said. 'I'd be out of my mind right now myself if I didn't have a cold.'

'Heh heh heh,' heh-ed Cyrus. 'That's funny. So what the hell're you doin' in Roanoke, man? I hope you ain't expectin' much, because we ain't got but a whole lotta nothin'.'

'This is fine,' said David. 'We were in Front Royal last night.'

'Oh wow!! I was born in Front Royal, man. And that place is a hole! Oh God, what the hell were you doin' there?'

There was a long silence. It was an impossible question.

Back at the motel David and I had a drunken conversation about whether the Beatles were as brilliant as history and the Apple shareholders want us to believe. Obviously, you must consider the Stones, but what about Creedence, the Doors, J. M. Hendrix and the 1910 Fruitgum Company? You have to be pretty oiled to discuss this age-old and sadly pointless question, so it wasn't long before we both fell asleep, with the TV on, dribbling into the morrow.

City Slickers. **Sean and David watch people abusing cattle. Rated Grade A.**

We were about to leave when I jumped out of the car. 'Sorry, I forgot something.' David looked kind of steamed, but it had to be done.

Breakfast Sandwich

We were out of Roanoke by 10 a.m. for a bless-ed day's driving. Just had a Hardee's Texas Breakfast Sandwich®: two fat-soaked hunks of square white bread (like Momma used to bake) clapped around a thin omelette (like Grandma used to batter) and slices of ham and bacon (like the hogs Poppa used to slaughter). The taste was not unpleasant, but my heart is seizing up already, so I wouldn't recommend more than one of these Slabs of Death® per year.

We're driving along the Blue Ridge Parkway (again) and listening to old soul stuff on the radio (again). It's very green and lovely – except for these huge spiderweb cocoon things that hang off the trees. They're extremely creepy and God only knows what's going on inside them. It's real 50s sci-fi movie territory.

How many de-commissioned yellow school buses does one family need parked in their yard? The place we just passed had seven. Seven! I think I saw Charlie Brown and Lucy waving for help in the back of number five.

Plot Summary

After a freakish radioactive accident, huge mutant spiders learn how to drive and take over the school buses, kidnapping the

103

school kids and turning them into spider children who eat their parents and teachers. They go on a rampage, spreading an enormous suffocating web over everything as they creep up, ever closer, to Washington. The Army is called in and tries everything to stop the arachnoid menace – mortars, missiles, rockets and nuclear weapons. But the nuclear weapons only make the spiders stronger! It's like food for them! A couple of thin, determined teenagers, Sean and David, decide that they must act. Armed only with four bottles of Coke and a copy of 'Rock Around the Clock', they climb into their souped-up jalopy and speed spiderward. On the Virginia/DC border they come face to face with the monsters! Just as they're about to be eaten, the plucky teens spray Coke in the boss spider's face, causing it to dissolve, hideously. They blast out the rock 'n roll record, and all the other spiders shrivel up and die. Sean and David are heroes – but the harrowing memories mean that they can never drink leading-brand cola or listen to rock 'n roll ever again.

'What do you think, Dave?'

'Not bad. Who's the lead teen?'

'Me.'

He shakes his head.

'You?'

He nods.

County Fair

A busted, faded sign in nausea green paint advertises the Franklin County Fair. The sign was painted during the war of Northern Aggression (as we Southerners call it); the fair, however, is happening right here and right now. Gathered on a large field is a swirling sea of heavy plaid, John Deere caps and overalls. Before we get out of the car, and with some difficulty, David and

I change into our disguises: jeans, boots and t-shirts that say 'We're from round here'. And into the fair we walk, bow-legged and sniffin'.

Most of the 'attractions' have a distinctly agrarian bent – brand-new threshers and tractors in roped-off squares being stroked and teased by comely farmers' daughters in designer bibs 'n braces; the very latest in sexy irrigation equipment and gleaming power generators on lovely velvet mounts.

'Thet thar shure is purty, ain't it Cletus?' I drawl at David, a dribble of spit lending theatrical verisimilitude to my remark.

'It shure iyus, Otis,' responds David, sardonically.

'Look over yonny, Cletus,' I point. 'A reg'lar ole-fashioned cow tippin'.'

'I hope yew ain't pore-mouthin'. I gots me a real sof' spot fer topplin' cow critters.'

'I ain't. Let's us git on over.'

Over yonder, a crowded roped-off area contains a large heifer named Clover and a sinewy little guy whose cap reads 'Ralphie'. Ralphie circles Clover for a while, as she stands impassively chewing her tobacco. He paces slowly, carefully, his tiny eyes never leaving the cow. Suddenly, he darts forward and connects with Clover's distended gut. He pushes and strains at the beef, digging his heels into the moist ground. Clover bellows once and falls onto her side, her legs sticking out like toppled furniture. The crowd goes crazy – me and Cletus too. We're a-stompin' an' a-hollerin' like there ain't no tomorry. People are even clapping us on the back. With the help of the gentle art of bovine bashing, we've finally found a home in America.

Back in the Neon, approaching a one-room town called Floyd, we pass Slaughter's Supermarket, right next door to a large tin shed that advertises 'Holy Ghost Revival. Here today. 3 p.m.' Outside the shed, a casually dressed man is holding a baby up toward heaven. Both he and the baby are crying. I fear the God-fearers.

The talkback radio says: *I seen it, an' she seen it while she was wearin' her lavender dressing gown, but if Uncle Charlie didn't see it and he was standing right 'neath it, well who's gonna believe me an' Anna-May? Nobody. I seen it all before, an' it were just like this ever' time, flashing green an' music like from a callyope . . .*

North Carolina

We're on the sleek Interstate 40 heading south to Statesville, a couple of hours away. Painted on the back of a transporter truck is a big sign: 'Start the week off right. Attend the church of your choice.' A pro-choice truck. I, however, prefer to start the week off with fourteen tons of grease coagulating in my guts. That's *my* choice. If the Catholic Church invented some sort of tasty Host Sandwich®, I might pop along.

Gettin' Religion

We stopped at a roadside picnic spot for lunch. At a table near ours was a man whose clean, radiant joy was palpably religious: Baptist probably, but it might have been Jehovahian, Quaker-esque or perhaps even Anabaptist (although I'm not sure how fired with the old missionary zeal Anabaptists were. Weren't they the people who eschewed buttons?). He was with his wife, a slow-limbed, overtly peaceful looking woman who I imagined took a perverse delight in devilling eggs – the name alone giving her a clipped, sacrilegious tickle.

'Keep them away from us,' David said firmly, buttering his bread with a fixed intensity.

'What can I do?' I asked, slicing a soft and sun-warm tomato. 'If they come over, they come over.'

The man came over; tall, confident, a blow-wave of majestic grey up top, like a sentencing judge. 'It's a beautiful afternoon,' he said, his face smiling up to the sky. So far, so good. 'God's looking out for us today.' Oh dear. 'It's most difficult to bring Armageddon into our thoughts on a day like today.' Oh no . . .

As David very obviously concentrated on a copy of *USA Today*, our fellow picnicker told us that he and his wife were Gideons on a hotel/motel bible-placing mission. 'It brings us together and there are fresh glasses wherever we go.' Then he asked me to describe the end of the world. 'Using your own words,' he said. 'Can't I use the Bible's words? All the good ones are in there. Scourge. Pestilence. Apocalypse. Loathsome and malignant ulcers.'

The Gideon nodded his head eagerly. 'Yes, indeed. Hard to believe on a day like this, isn't it? But God has a plan. Pardon me, Sir,' he said over to David. 'Are your thoughts with God today?'

'No,' David said, looking up and past the Gideon. 'They're with the *USA Today*.'

The Gideon laughed heartily and sincerely. 'Well, they're much the same thing, wouldn't you say?'

'Yes,' David agreed. 'I would. But I could be reading *Soldier of Fortune* and say the same thing.'

The Gideon's face eclipsed and he skulked off in a stiff-backed huff as David snapped the spine of the newspaper with a sharp crack.

Forsyth County

This here is tobacco country – Winston-Salem and Chesterfield are nearby places. There's even a tobacco town called Needmore. Brilliant. I'm keeping my eye out for Kool and Dunhill Blue Twenty-Fives. In celebration of the fact that I am travelling through a kind of personal heaven, I light up an American Length (long) Marlboro and puff lovingly.

'I'm trying to give up passive smoking,' says David, electro-winding down his window.

'You should smoke, y'know,' I tell him, releasing a lungful of North Carolina's finest. 'It's a good habit. You'd like it.'

'It's stupid, it stinks, it gives you bad breath and costs lots of money. And you die from it.'

'All the good people smoke.'

'Like who?'

'Well . . . Hitler didn't smoke.'

'What *is* it with you and Hitler?'

'He's an excellent benchmark.'

'For what?'

'Evil and general badness. He was a real Nazi.'

'I think he *did* smoke.'

'No way. He was too short.'

'Well, that just about proves it.'

'No way. Plus I think he had asthma. All those Nazis were sickly types. Goebbels had a club foot. Goering was fat. Himmler was practically blind and had shocking dandruff. Oh, they were a bunch of saps, all right.'

'Not an Aryan amongst them.'

'Nope. Just a bunch of bullies and fetishists.'

Took a quick stroll around the small, Sunday-quiet town of

Statesville. There were a few barbers and clothes stores advertising 'New York Styles' – of late last century, judging by the few people we saw, spats and top-coats on every one of them. David bought a pair of Rayban Wayfarers for 53¢. And he hasn't stopped pretending to be Tom Cruise in *Risky Business* since. Right now he's driving along in nothing but boxer shorts and socks, searching in vain for a cassette with Bob Seger on it. I bought some cheap paperbacks and am reading quietly, fully clothed for safety reasons.

I've got to hand it to the radio stations around here. What we're listening to now is very funky – Roy Ayers, the Staple Singers, BT Express and the Chi-lites. 'It's probably one o' them coloured stations,' remarks David 'Duke' O'Brien, turning off the Tom Cruise control for a moment, and spitting a wad of tobacco out the window.

Human Nature

Lining much of the freeway, soaring high above the treeline, is a striking sight – dozens and dozens of signs and billboards on tall poles advertising hotels, restaurants and gas stations. It's a desperately ugly vision: the adman competing with, and beating the hell out of, Nature. It seems a shame that Fran's grey funnel didn't pass through and teach the men in grey flannel a thing or two.

SHONEY'S CLASSIC AMERICAN FOOD. SALLY JO'S KITCHEN. BOJANGLE'S FAMOUS CHICKEN BISCUITS. MOM'S COUNTRY STORE 'N RESTAURANT. INTERNATIONAL HOUSE OF PANCAKES. HOWARD JOHNSON'S. LONG JOHN SILVER'S FISH SHRIMP & CHICKEN. AWFUL ARTHUR'S SEAFOOD. TASTEE FREEZ. QUINCY'S STEAKHOUSE. SAGE-

BRUSH STEAKHOUSE. CAMPFIRE STEAKS AND BUFFET.

In the mid-1920s, the good people of Burma Shave began a memorable and entertaining billboard advertising campaign to promote their brushless shaving cream. The signs, erected along America's highways, consisted of clever little rhymes or auto-poetry like: SHAVING BRUSHES / YOU'LL SOON SEE 'EM / WAY DOWN EAST / IN SOME MUSEUM / BURMA SHAVE (1930); and HE PLAYED A SAX / HAD NO B.O. / BUT HIS WHISKERS SCRATCHED / SO SHE LET HIM GO / BURMA SHAVE (1933). Later they even held national contests looking for new verses and received offerings such as: HER CHARIOT / RACED AT 80 PER / THEY HAULED AWAY / WHAT HAD BEN HUR; and the equally gruesome HE LIT A MATCH / TO CHECK GAS TANK / THAT'S WHY / THEY CALL HIM / SKINLESS FRANK. Despite their morbid brilliance, I don't think these last two made it to the roadside. Anyway, by the early 60s, with two-lane highways disappearing and the costs of rent and maintenance increasing, the last of the Burma Shave signs were gone. In fact the only reason *I* know about them is not because we've taken a left turn into 'The Twilight Zone', but because I'm reading about them in Bill Bryson's marvellous book *Made in America* as we drive. Like so much of American culture, all the really neat stuff is gone.

SEAN AND DAVID / FROM DOWN UNDER / DRIVE THRU AMERICA / WITH FEAR AND WONDER

We're just outside Waynesville (one of about five hundred towns in America called Waynesville or Wayneburg or Waynesboro. I even saw a couple called Waynesworld). Moonshine and dulci-mer country. It's not very comforting, because homemade rotgut and twangy 'musical' instruments are two things I associate with toothless old men who shoot you – or worse.

We're really high up now, over 6000 feet above sea level. Way up on the Blue Ridge Parkway, heading for the Great Smoky Mountains. If our car tipped over the edge, we'd really die. It's all foggy and misty for hundreds of miles around; beautiful, but eerie and unsettling nonetheless. If I hear the sound of a drunken dulcimer, I'll scream.

'Do you even know what a dulcimer sounds like?' asks David.

'I'll know one when I hear one, baby.'

6.10 p.m. Tennessee

We've found ourselves in a monstrosity of a town called Pigeon Forge, just a few minutes' drive from the peace, tranquillity and solitude of the Smokies. Just to ensure that you don't overdose on nature, you can whip back to PF, eat some syrup-soaked waffles, throw them back up on a Ferris wheel, nauseously play some dinosaur mini-golf, hit the pinball arcade or Skycoaster and finish up in a sweating thrill at the Elvis museum or Ms Parton's sickening shot at self-financed deification, Dollywood. The weird thing is, people *actually* come to PF for their holidays. They're not just passing through on the way to getting the hell out of here.

The truly sad thing about our being in Pigeon Forge is that the Comedy Barn has closed down. It had a 'mind reading' pig and a humorous fiddler. I think I could outsmart a pig.

The Emmy Awards are on television tonight, and mindful of what I believe Jackie Kerouac told me back in New York City, I will be watching very, very closely for the sweet secrets of life to be revealed during TV's night of nights when the stars come out to shine.

'It's just a bunch of stiffs in rented outfits cracking lame jokes,' David comments halfway though the show. 'What do they know?'

'They know stuff, David. They're from *TV*,' I explain, but he is not convinced.

'They know how to rake in the dough, that's what they know.'

Three hours later, I understand no more about life than I did this morning. Except this – the Emmy statuette has two very sharp points on it. You could kill a person with an Emmy.

*N*A*S*H*. Directed by Robert Altman. Rated C & W.

Just before we left the motel, I told David that I had to make a final check of our room. He shook his head and looked grim, but it had to be done. I was gone for just ninety seconds and returned pleased.

Had breakfast at a place called the Breakfast Place where they offered forty-five different types of breakfast – all with free cholesterol. I ordered juice, coffee, cereal, pancakes, waffles, muffins, hash browns, sausage, ham, scrambled eggs, cremated bacon and two robins on toast. But I'm relieved to report that I ate less than half.

Among the Forge's delightful attractions are the sprawling malls of Famous Brand factory outlets. Because we're white trash cheapskates at heart (and let's be honest, who ain't?), we spent about two hours trying on every pair of cut-price, busted, torn, stained or otherwise 'irregular' jeans we could find inside the converted military base that is the broken Levis HQ of Tennessee. For me, the only consolation in trying on four hundred different pairs and not buying any (because no jeans ever fit me right) was that I did it all without underpants. David bought plenty, though – he has lean legs, a thinnish waist and a positively anorexic wallet.

The last thing we saw as we left PF was a big tanker truck painting the roadside dirt a delirious sea blue/green colour. It was that Tennessee aesthetic again. If it was up to me, I'd spray the town some kind of agent orange.

The radio says: . . . *and contrary to popular thought, the to-do betwixt the Hatfields and the McCoys occurred just over the border in Pike County, Kentucky. Not here in Tennessee as many mistakenly believe. And buried in the middle of that complex, bloody, internecine tale is the story of two star-crossed lovers, Johnson Hatfield and Roseanna McCoy . . .*

11.50 a.m.

We've just been to the Fireworks Supermarket®, the world's largest fireworks store. We're both very excited because it's been over twenty years since we had the opportunity to dabble in this kind of good, clean mayhem. Also, given our situation at home, where fireworks are very banned, it feels as though we're getting into something highly illegal. And childish.

Complaints Dept

Tennessee radio sucks – it's all either country (the worst musical form the world has ever known) or country-rock (the worst

113

musical marriage the world has ever known – except of course Michael and Lisa-Marie).

There's always traffic on US roads. No matter where you are, or at what time, there will always be other cars and trucks right there with you, going the same way. It somewhat diminishes that 'Lewis and Martin' feeling of slapstick/exploration. As does the fact that we're travelling on a highway in the first place.

BEANPOT RESTAURANTS. O'CHARLEY'S RESTAURANTS. CRACKER BARREL OLD STYLE RESTAURANTS. COREY'S COWBOY CENTRE. EXECUTIVE INNS. HERITAGE INNS. SCOTTISH INNS. HUDDLE HOUSE RESTAURANTS. RAMADA INN. QUALITY INN. COMFORT INN. FAMILY INNS OF AMERICA. HOLIDAY INN. APPLEBEE'S NEIGHBOURHOOD GRILL. RED LOBSTER.

I wonder what it'd be like to die around here. Are funeral arrangements swift and reliable, clean and affordable?
'D'you want to be buried or cremated?' I ask David.
'Definitely buried. If I rise again, I don't want to get blown all over the place.'

Obituary

Initially the symptoms indicated he was suffering from a common – but painful – cold. He was feverish, weak and unhappy, and things grew quickly worse. As he sat slumped in the passenger seat of a rented Chrysler Neon snaking up a mountainside, bringing him closer to God and obvious metaphors, his temperature reached 108° and he began hallucinating, insisting to the car's driver, Mr David O'Brien (artiste, bum), that he'd inadvertently consumed Jesus in a taco the previous evening. By the time they reached Nashville, Condon, 30, of Melbourne, had died of pneumonia. And a brain aneurism. He will be buried in a pair of ill-fitting jeans on Thursday.

Res-erection

In the tiny town of Baxter we pulled into a service station. In the men's can was an ancient machine that dispensed coloured condoms and other novelties. For 50¢ I got a Lucky Nudie coin and some Stay-Hard cream. (Directions: Tear off end. Apply to area of organ covered by foreskin and massage in. Wait five minutes before intercourse. Enjoy.) Pretty good value, but if only we could find the factory outlet.

3.02 p.m.

We've had to pull over – it's another wall of water. Unbelievably, it's even worse than the hurricane stuff of a few days ago. This time we cannot see *anything*, including each other. The rain is pounding onto the car in flat sheets. Noise, wind and water, and no light. Death weather.

3.04 p.m.

It's over. The sun is out, and we're on our way again. It may as well have never happened, except there are dozens of tiny holes in the paint job on the roof of the car, which looks as though it's been pecked by metal birds. We're not paying the car rental people for Acts of God though. No way. With the suddenly clear weather, I'm in a pretty good mood. I'd be positively joyous if not for my cold and seeing Sally running nude through the trees.
'Why is she nude?' asks David.
'I don't know. She just popped into my head that way, which is strange because she rarely runs around nude at home.'

'Do you ever fantasise about having sex with Bigfoot? Maybe that's it. He's nude.'

'No. Vampires I do, but not Bigfoot. Bigfoot's not real anyway.'

'But vampires are?'

'I guess not, but they're sexier.'

'Werewolves?'

'Too hairy.'

'Mummies?'

'Too Oedipal. Almost though. I used to have a sort of sub-Oedipal complex, where I wanted to take my mother out dancing and whip my father at bridge while he had an eye infection.'

4.10 p.m. Nashville

Finally we've reached the 'Ville (population: 500,000 soon-to-be-discovered C & W stars). In keeping with my moronically clichéd impression of America, I'd expected Nashville to be the epitome of a small country town. Full of little wooden houses, wide muddy streets, and guys tipping their cowboy hats and saying 'Howdy, Ma'am.' I even thought there might be a brawl-filled saloon down on Main Street, a star-shirted sheriff sitting on a palomino out front. I guess you could say I wasn't expecting a real city at all, but a country and western theme park. (I'm quite ashamed of myself. It's the same simple-mindedness that expects Melbourne to be full of kangaroos hopping up and down the city streets. And even though my father *did* ride a kangaroo to work every day, things have changed mightily since the late 70s. We even have calculators in Australia now.)

Nashville does, however, live up to expectations in that almost every single bar, restaurant and cafe in the very modern and sophisticated downtown area advertises some sort of musical entertainment within: country and/or western; blue and/or grass; rock and/or roll; hip and/or hop; tech and/or no. And the city was of course the home of that infamous house of warble, the Grand Ole Opry, which was relocated in 1971 and turned into an all-singing, all-dancing theme park called Opryland. This comes as no surprise to me.

Nashville also boasts hundreds of record stores and about four thousand recording studios, most of which proudly advertise the fact that some star or other made his/her first hit there. In fact, no other city in the States (probably on earth) can claim to be the launching place of so many infamous pluckers, twangers and yodellers. Since David and I happen to be a little short on cash at the moment, we may even cut a disc ourselves while we're here.

You're Australian? Oh I love Australians. I was with Australians in Vietnam, in the Mekong Delta. I love 'em. I can do the kangaroo hop.
Spruiker, approx. 55

Life's Little Intrusion Book

Nashville is home to H. Jackson Little Brown Jr, the author of the pompous, pious, patronising five-volume billion-selling *Life's Little Instruction Book*. The slender (and bizarrely tartan-print covered) books offer dopey, homey, aw shucks-style aphorisms to help you achieve a kind of suburban saint-like holiness if, for instance, you:

- every once in a while let your children play in the rain
- ask permission before you take somebody's photograph
- mow the lawn next door once a year

- put $5 more than usual in the church collection plate
- buy 10,000 copies of this evil book and distribute it amongst your soft-headed friends

About the only thing that H. Jackson doesn't pat us on the head and gently remind us to do is to 'stop and smell the roses', 'quit beating the crap out of your wife' and 'never chew on your neighbour's testicle after you've eaten garlic' (or perhaps they're in Volume Four, which I haven't completely memorised yet).

Obviously, I'm a great admirer of H. Jackson's work and am keen to look him up and share a few NauseaHomilies© of my own. He's not listed in the local telephone directory, but I'm sure that the rich, sweet odour of SanctiMoney® will lead me right to his door.

True Story

At a downtown poolroom we met this pair of nutcases, Crazy Chris the chef and Showgirl Leigh. We talked with them, played pool with them and then went back to our hotel with them, where the insanity started. David was in the lobby being taught the macarena by Leigh while low-talker Chris was running this rap into my ear about his ability to 'shine' and how in 1994 he was beaten to death (yes, death) outside a bus station in DC. When he was brought back to life he found himself in 1999 and single-handedly saved the world (he declined to say exactly how). After which he'd gone *back* to 1994, having decided that he didn't want to be the next Saviour. 'Just because I inher'ted special powers from my Granny don't mean I'm obligated to save the rotten soul of every sorry-assed motherfucker in this world.'

Right after he told me all that I asked him to leave. And not to come back in three day's time.

My Beautiful Laundrette. **No racism or homosexuality, just plenty of good, clean washing. Rated OMO.**

<u>12.50 p.m.</u>

We took some wrong turns and ended up in the bad part of town, where the laundromats are. Immersed in the soapy hum of two dozen washing machines, serenaded by the thin, tinny radio and the pinball machine that will not be silent, even though nobody is playing it. There's a copy of the *Watchtower* on the formica table in front of me. David is reading the *National Enquirer* and not laughing. We're using Cheer Ultra with advanced colour guard, an all-temperature detergent that costs just 50¢ per load.

The radio says: *From a distance, God is watching us.*

On the pavement outside, a white guy dressed like a Native American is explaining something complicated to a black woman. As he talks he is gesticulating quickly, and I can see that the top joint of every finger on both his hands is missing. David shows me an article in the *Enquirer* about a woman in Tallahassee who was struck by lightning and can only write backwards now. I wonder what it would be like to grow up in Nashville. Would they teach the dulcimer in grade school?

<u>No Coughing</u>

We took a look inside the Museum of Tobacco Art and History (No Smoking). Boy, did that place make me proud to be an

119

addict. The paraphernalia that accompanied 'the gentle art' back before there was anything else to do (watch TV, visit Opryland, etc) is staggeringly beautiful. As were the pipes themselves: meerschaums carved into skulls, mermaids, elephants, horses, dogs, gods (minor ones), roses, bears, boars, ladies and anything else they felt like. There was even one enormous three-footer from 1880 depicting Napoleon's retreat from Moscow, humiliation and all. At the back of the museum was a display devoted to cigar smoking – humidors, cutters, holders and George Burns. My only complaint was that, according to the museum, cigarette smoking virtually doesn't exist. There were no fag accoutrements, not so much as an ashtray, and they didn't even *sell* cigarettes there! So I bought a corncob pipe instead and stuck it in my mouth immediately.

'This is a great place,' I told the attendant. 'I shall return.'

'See ya, Mac,' he said.

Makin' a Recud

For sixty bucks we booked an hour's recording and mixing time in a tiny studio on Music Row: Fat Bob's – the place where Jim 'Slim Jim' Slimson recorded his legendary lament about infidelity, 'My Cheatin' Penis'. Bob himself was indeed fat and probably a little short-sighted – when we walked in, he tipped his cowboy hat at David and said 'Howdy, Ma'am.' But he was one damn fine engineer, and we nailed my tune, 'Them Ole Nashville Blues', on the very first take. Me on drums and sobbing, David on vocals and Fat Bob himself picking up the bass, slide-guitar and fiddle. Since the song lasts only two and a half minutes, we had ample time for mixing, which also went well except for Fat Bob's poor hygiene and lack of social skills. His ceaseless sweating, burping and farting created a rich and fetid air in the control room – but one that I believe added a necessary note of C & W authenticity to the song, which was an instant classic.

Them Ole Nashville Blues

Well I've been lonesome an' I've been blue,
I've dropped tears on my pillow and into my stew.
I've cried in my sleep and cried in my wake,
I've bawled me a river and wept me a lake.

Oh baby I miss you,
Oh baby I do.
I sure need a tissue,
My face is red with the blues.

Well I've been drivin', I've been on the road.
Along the highways and bi-ways, I've weeped what I've sowed.
My nose is a-runnin' and so is the car,
My only friend out here's a six-string guitar.

(Repeat chorus)

I'm comin' home baby, down through 'Sippi.
In a little ole Neon with a long-haired hippy.
It's sure 'nuff pretty down in the South,
But you'd never know it from my cryin' mouth.

(words and music © Sean 'Salty Blues' Condon)

Driving Miss Issippi. **David acts as a chauffeur while Sean pretends to be a feisty old woman. Rated 45 mph.**

11.20 a.m.

It's lucky I went to Map Folding School (a correspondence course) and learned to unfold and refold a flapping map in a small car full of highway breeze without a colourful chunk whapping

121

into the driver's face and causing a spine-snapping smash. I am in fact qualified to teach map-folding (or carto-gami) but there's not much call for it these days. I blame the Internet.

Dropped by a K-Mart in outer Nashville, where we bought a dozen cans of Coke for $2.99!! And a packet of cigarettes for $1.83!! God bless America – this truly is the Land of Opportunity.

SIGN: WHEN GOD CALLS DOES HE GET A BUSY SIGNAL?

DAVID: Or are you just sitting around hoping He'll ring and invite you out for a couple of beers?

SEAN: Or do you record Him on the answering machine and sell the tapes to the *Enquirer*?

SIGN: DO YOU BOYS WISH TO SPEND ETERNITY IN HELL WITH YOUR JOKES AND LAMPOONERY?

SEAN & DAVID: . . . no . . .

12.18 p.m.

We're on the Natchez Trace Parkway, as smoothly curved and perfectly flat as a Scalextric track. Astro-grass, giant trees and old wooden fences zig-zagging on either side of us. It's an incredibly well maintained highway – we've actually seen people mowing the grass. No signs for Exxon or Citigo or Shell or Phillips 66 or Texaco or Amoco or Sunoco or Conoco or BP or Mobil or Esso or Caltex or 76 or Chevron or Fina or Golden Fleece. Which is nice. 'It's like driving through a golf course,' observes David. I've played golf about twice and I agree. We're making for Tupelo, Mississippi, birthplace of E. A. Presley, the rock 'n roll singer. But I don't like the look of the sinister van with tinted windows heading toward us . . .

Inside the Van

Martin is proud of the fact that he doesn't fit the profile: he's not some tightened-up obsessive loner who lives with his mother and used to kill animals when he was a teenager. Well, a few squirrels and some neighbourhood cats, but nothing more. He changes his MO each time. And yeah, he's meticulous, but not fastidious. He likes things clean and won't make a mistake, is all. 'The FBI serial killer profile can go to hell as far as this bear is concerned,' he says aloud. He sometimes likes to think of himself in the third person, but not as a cartoon bear. He's real flesh and blood and muscle. The bear thing is just his little joke. 'He cannot bear no bear talk.' The sentence sits at the forefront of his thoughts. Small jokes, double negatives and referring to himself in the third person: these are the things Martin likes.

He whistles while he works. Old Civil War tunes because they have a grimness and strange gaiety that suits the business of strangulation, bludgeoning or whatever. 'Lookaway, lookaway . . .'

He sees a white Neon coming toward him a quarter of a mile away. Blonde girl with long hair behind the wheel and someone else, he can't tell if it's male or female, sitting beside her. If it's another girl he might swing the van to the left and block the empty road. Closer now and Martin's heart sinks as he realises it's two men in the small car. He raises a hand as the car passes his van and drives on, wondering who's next . . .

The radio says: . . . *the reason disasters – flood, fire, hurricane, tornado, you name it – the reason they look more vivid on television than when you're standing in the middle of one is because the best and most natural state of human perception is one of detachment. When we become involved, we lose perspective . . .*

'I think I'd quite like to see Bruce Springsteen in acoustic concert,'says David.

'Yeah, me too. I like that Tom Joad stuff. But I tell ya, I don't think the Boss'd be nearly as famous if his name was Bruce Goldstein.'

'Or Herman Goldstein. He wouldn't've had a chance.'

'No. The Spring factor made all the difference. It was his *spring*steen to fame and fortune.'

'Then again, if he was called Herman Springsteen . . .'

'True enough, he wouldn't have got far. Especially if it was Hermann – with two n's.'

And so on for another thirty miles.

We're off the Parkway for a while and passing shacks with tons of rusted, broken crap spilled all over the front yard – three-wheeled Piggly Wiggly shopping carts, grease-caked engine blocks, baby strollers with shredded black hoods, Soviet rocket parts, human skulls on spikes and orange-eyed Rottweilers on heavy chains breathing fire – like a permanent yard sale with all proceeds going to Lucifer's Comeback Fund.

'Wanna pull over and have a look?' asks David, accelerating.

'Why, yes,' I say, spinning my neck 180 degrees and snapping a mental picture. 'I'd love to knock on the door and ask to take a look around, but unfortunately we'd be killed.'

Maine Man

I'm eating a steam-heated (the Tennessee equivalent of a microwave) ham and cheese roll I bought at a gas station in Lawrenceburg in Lawrence County. It doesn't taste as nice as you'd think. While I was buying it, a youngish Tennessean with a scraggly beard came in, calling to me, 'Maine? Maine!? Is that you? Are y'all from *Maine*?' It sounded urgent, as though he wanted to report a traffic accident.

'No,' I told him. 'It's a rental car. They have plates from everywhere.'

'Aw shoot!' he said, stamping his foot with bitter disappointment. 'That's somewheres I'd sure lahk to visit someday.'

If only he knew how *much* we're not from Maine.

With one hand David removes the lid from a bottle of Anacin, flicking his eyes up at the road every so often, and washes two pills down with Gatorade.

'Why didn't you want to talk to that Gideon guy the other day?' I ask him.

'I try to avoid any sort of zealous types. Their agenda is too strong to have any sort of conversation. They're always *telling* you how it is.'

I nodded. 'They have a weird sort of aura. Sometimes even a smell. The smell of self-assuredness. It's kind of musky and important.'

'Didn't Reverend Stockdale from school annoy you the way he always stood up close so he could place his hands on your shoulders in that way?'

'I guess. He and my father once wore identical suits at a chapel service. You should've seen 'em laughing it up afterward. I found it a bit creepy myself.'

'I'm not against religion. I'm against most religious people. They never stop.'

'Often their whole life is about preparing for death.'

'And that's no way to live.'

'But possibly a very good way to die.'

2.43 p.m. Tennessee

We'll be driving through a small corner of Alabama in a few minutes.

125

<u>2.47 p.m. Alabama</u>

So far it looks the same as Tennessee, except possibly a little more ugly and more Godforsaken. This *couldn't* be where Lynyrd Skynyrd are from. We're saying 'Alabammy' and 'Bammy' all over the place like a couple of idiots. It's sorta fun though.

<u>Later. Alabama</u>

Still the same. On the way into Muscle Shoals, we pass through a place that seems to be called Una.

'Where the Unabomber's from,' calls David, over the very loud Apollo 440 tape.

'And Una Thurman,' I shout back.

'Actually, it's probably just the University of North Alabama,' screams David.

'Damn!' I cry.

Stopped at a shopping strip in Muscle Shoals: Adam's Christian Resource Centre (carpentry tools available upon request), Kane's Hong Kong Karate (everything you've learned goes back to the Chinese in 1997), Sharon's Sensational Hair! ('Sharon, your hair looks sensational!') and Quincy's Steakhouse (you perform an autopsy on the rib eye and when you cut into it people nearby start fainting). All the shops in America are named after someone: Ted's Shoe Repair, Jimmy's Transmission, Ray's Hair Styling, Edna's Flea Market, Bob's Tires. They think it's friendlier that way. Sean doesn't.

Passed the Alabama Music Hall of Fame. Contents: Lynyrd Skynyrd and Alabama. Maybe an old dulcimer.

126

As an idiotic gesture to their southerness, almost all the houses around here, no matter how small and old or brand spanking new, have porticoes and columns out front. The other strange thing is the way the houses, prefab churches, gas stations and auto shops are just plonked anywhere, next to nothing in particular or everything at once. People in Alabammy must think that zoning is some sort of Communist idea. I don't. I think zoning's good. It'd be a crazy world without zoning.

4.17 p.m. Mississippi
We've left all the random craziness and ugliness behind us and are back on the Natchez Trace Parkway. Ella Fitzgerald and Louis Armstrong are along with us for the ride, fifty-nine miles to Tupelo. What a shame it doesn't snow there, that it doesn't get to two below in Tupelo. Humorous weathermen could have some fun with that.

We have had to let Ella and Louis go. We're in Mississippi now – and everybody knows what happens to a car full of blacks and whites travelling together down here.

Delta Blues
'We should be listening to some blues,' David says as we drive through flat, wet, cotton-picking country, the birthplace of the blues, the poor, sweet, sad, soul-thumpin' blues. 'Robert Johnson was born around here,' he continues, 'and he died around here too. Poisoned or stabbed at a country juke-joint in 1938.' It's a melancholy, essentially bluesy story, made just that much more heartbreaking when you consider what Johnson might have been able to bring to my own blues number.

127

BRAD, PLEASE GIVE JESSICA BACK HER MEMORIES

What the hell is that billboard supposed to mean? I'm stunned and mystified by the simple, odd words. They're so full of portent. Is it part of some local divorce settlement? The exposure of a bizarre and fiendish cult?

6.50 p.m. Tupelo

Walking down the concrete hallway at the Holiday Inn Express, I saw a thin, blonde woman in a safari short-suit, followed by her son. They both looked hunted and depressed. What were they running from? Was it Jessica? Was the little fellow Brad?

Tomorrow is the big day – we should be in Good Hope by late afternoon to give Victoria back her bible. I wonder if she'll have a firm handshake; big, horsey teeth; a lovely, mellifluous voice; long hair with split ends. Will she be a likeable woman? Will she like me? I still think she will be beautiful. And she *could* still be an anthropologist. I wonder what she wrote about in her excellent English compositions. Suddenly a dreadful thought occurs to me – what if she *meant* to leave her bible on the subway? What if it is a memory that she does not want back?

A Night in Tupelo

I asked the desk clerk about the Brad and Jessica deal. He told me that it was the name of a floorshow at the Ramada. 'Some name, huh?'

'Yeah,' I said. 'What's it about?'

'Some guy called Brad giving some dame called Jessica back her memories.'

There didn't seem to be any actual restaurants in Tupelo, just various chains, so it's not real hard to see where Elvis developed his love of the burger. We ate at a Mexican chain. Behind us was a loud and raucous table of male and female rednecks, off their sweating heads on margaritas, wittily asking all the Mexican waiters if they had Green Cards. They were a riot, old Bubba, Slick, Sarah-Sue and Fanny-Jo. We scarfed our burritos and necked our Dos Equis in a hurry and got the hell out of there.

'Only women bleed' – Alice Cooper said that.
Not when they' that young.
Buht they will, little bitches.

White male and female diners, approx. 37

We concluded our hysteric night in historic Tupelo by watching some porno movies (which had somehow got through the hotel pay TV system and into our room for free) and discussed what it'd be like licking other people for a living.

'It seems like a great job when you're a teenager, doubled over with horniness all the time,' I said. 'But now I'm not so sure. You'd have to hang around a lot of depraved people.'

'What do you mean? You hang around sleazy dickheads all day in advertising. And they're always talking about their balls. "The client's got me by the balls." '

'Stands out like dog's balls.'

'Ball-tearer.'

'Complete balls up.'

'Got my balls in a vice. Yep, they're ball crazy in your world.'

'Yeah, witty too. But it's not my world any more – I didn't have the balls. And they never talked about *licking* anybody's balls.'

'You never made it to senior management, did you?'

'No.'

129

'It's different up there, Seanesque. *Very* different.'

'Well, I'm definitely not going back now.'

'What'll you do?'

'Dunno. Be a porno star, maybe.'

David spent a while falling about the room laughing. Once he'd calmed down, I asked him a question. 'If you grew up in Mississippi in the 50s, d'you think you'd be a racist redneck?'

'I hope not.'

'But you can't be sure?'

'How can I be sure? It's a very hypothetical situation. Are my parents racists? My cousins? Am I mean and fat? These all seem like prerequisites.'

'You're enormous. And a real bastard. You love rifles, cars and your cousin Lisa-Lou, who refers to black people as "niggers". Your great-grandparents owned one hundred and seventy slaves and fought with the Confederate Army, and your brother's the tobacco-spitting sheriff. So what are you?'

'Not everyone who grew up like that was a racist. I'm one of them. I'm Elvis. What are you?'

'What are my circumstances?'

'You're a dirt-poor turnip farmer with a sub-normal IQ. Your name's Lester Ballard and you've had sex with animals.'

'I have not!'

'You laughed when you heard JFK was dead, but you didn't find out until 1967.'

'Some life you've given me. Is there *any* joy in it?'

'You like to get drunk on moonshine and sit on the porch playing the dulcimer.'

'No!'

'And you're *really* good at it!'

'No way!!'

Mississippi Burning. **Sean's virulent anti-bellumism creates tension with David as they set off to return the bible. (King James version)**

'Y'all come back now.'
'Why?'

10.30 a.m.

We're on our way out of Tupelo, having done the only thing we came for – indeed the only thing anybody comes for – a visit to the birthshack of the king of rock 'n roll. What an architecturally inauspicious beginning the Pelvis had – it's smaller than a poolside cabana at Graceland. You couldn't fit two fried peanut butter sandwiches into this bad-cheque-passing-father-built sub-cottagelet. There's a tiny front room (the communal bedroom) and a tiny back room (the communal kitchen), four tiny windows from which to shoot tourists – and that's it. And that really *is* it as far as authenticity goes. For your entry dollar, the only legitimate Elvisania you get is the floor, walls and ceiling. 'The rest of the stuff,' the small, lipsticked guide in the bra-hugging *Chevy 55* t-shirt tells me, 'is jest props 'n such. T'wasn't really theirs.'

'So whose was it?' I ask her.

'Don't rightly know. Other people's, I guess.'

'Other famous people's?'

'I don't *know*, Sir.'

'So where's his first huntin' rifle? His rattle, his git-tar?'

'I don't know, Sir. Have y'all been to Graceland?'

'Don't wanna. It's too gaudy.'

'Well we cain't he'p you with artyfacts and the like. All we is is his house.'

131

'Ma'am, at a dollar a pop I'd have thought you could at least afford his baby bottle or something. How 'bout that linoleum, is that real? Did the Pres ever cool his cheeks on that?'

'Here's your dollar back, Sir. Now git!'

We got – and now it's the Natchez Parkway again, through the pines and firs and corn crops, western sunlight strobing through the trees and hitting David as he drives us away from the Tupe to Good Hope and on to Jackson.

CHESTER FRIED – THE CRISPY, MOISTURISED CHICKEN

2.59 p.m.

Detoured through a lovely Ole Miss town called Williamsville in Attala County. Its decaying town hall stood in the middle of a mossy town square surrounded by ancient, crumbling stores advertising bankruptcy and going-out-of-business sales. The smoke store, however, was still doing a brisk trade. I bought a carton of cigarettes, some snuff and some chewin' tobaccy. The town was full of beautiful antebellum homes, slow, winding streets and people strolling 'neath the shade of stately trees. It was hard to believe that the heart of racial hatred once lurked in places like this. And perhaps still does.

'I'm anti-antebellum,' I tell David, as we cut out of town, with me sneezing snuff spatters all over the inside of the windscreen, thus causing both poor visibility and nostril cancer.

'So you're pro-bellum?'

'That's correct, yes.'

The road opens up and we are closing in on Good Hope, flanked by the rich green of rural Mississippi. We slow down to watch two deer standing in a field. They look like a mother and daughter.

'Deers always look like females,' comments David.

'It's deer. I'm sick with nerves about this whole bible business. What if they murder us?'

Songs from a Room

We arrived in Good Hope in the middle of the queer, sultry summer afternoon, the heat of the day slowing the sleepy town to near stupor. The main street deserted but for a couple of dogs dazed and swaying in the dry wind; stale signs in dust-coated store windows. We pulled over outside a barbershop and asked for directions to the Lucas residence. They were given with languid forbearance and a suspicious eye on our Northern plates. We took off again, driving gently and smoothly so as not to upset the balance of the town; its tired dogs and barber's silent scissors.

We found the Lucas home beyond a tangled forest a little way out of town, past the local cemetery. It was an old clapboard place that looked like it was waiting to be picked up and undone by a hurricane. In the enveloping quiet, the noise of our car sounded like the arrival of God.

We crossed the dirt yard and clomped up the stairs onto the porch. I knocked timidly on the screen door, sending a woody clattering into the shadows of the house. We heard footfalls; the door opened slowly and we both stepped back.

'Yes, hello there?' a man said. He wore heavy boots, ragged pants and a rough shirt, loose and flapping like a scarecrow's clothes. I swallowed dryly. 'Mr Lucas?'

'Yes, you're the boy from New York City?' He opened the screen door and stepped onto the porch. We took another step back, almost toppling into the yard.

'Sort of. I mean, yes. My name's Sean and this is my friend David.'

'Pleased to meet you,' said David, thrusting out his hand.

'Likewise,' said Mr Lucas, shaking our hands. 'Come on now.'

'Set down boys,' he said, as we reached the living room, a surprisingly bright and open space. David and I perched side by side on the couch, fearful of crumpling the antimacassars drooping behind our heads. 'Would you like some lemonade? My wife's just made a fresh batch.'

'That would be lovely thanks, Mr Lucas,' said David, much more relaxed than me.

'Mr Lucas?' I said.

'Yes?'

'Where should I put this?' I asked, offering him the bible on damp, upturned palms, like I was presenting a cake.

'Just set it down on the table.'

Mrs Lucas came into the room swamped by a large apron, followed almost visibly by the scent of baked apples. A puff of flour on her forehead mingled with her tight grey curls.

'These are the boys from New York City,' said Mr Lucas.

'Yes, I had an inkling.' She held out a delicate hand and smiled. There was silence for a moment while she poured us each a glass of lemonade.

'You've come a long way,' said Mr Lucas, wiping pulp from his upper lip. 'And we appreciate it greatly, it's very kind of you. But boys,' he went on, looking at the floor, 'you should know, our daughter Victoria is dead.'

My hand tightened around my glass as my throat closed. David made a noise that sounded like a cross between a moan and a small yelp.

'But . . .'

'She died a long, long time ago. In 1972,' Mr Lucas said.

Mrs Lucas wiped her hands on the apron. There were small rolls of flour sticking to the fabric. 'She . . . she took her own life.'

'But the . . . the bible,' I stammered, stupidly pointing to the table. 'I think you'd better take a look upstairs,' said Mr Lucas, standing up. 'Come along now.'

Stunned, and strangely embarrassed, we followed the stooped old man up the stairs. Mrs Lucas remained in her armchair, tinkling the jug of lemonade with a glass stirrer, the sound fading as we ascended. We made our way down a hall and stopped outside a closed door. 'This here is Victoria's room. You can take a look inside,' Mr Lucas said flatly. 'Go on now.' He turned the handle, pushed open the door and left us alone.

In the middle of the room was a freshly made up single bed. On a table beside it was a framed picture of a young, pretty black woman. Shelves and cabinets displayed a neat array of objects: an acoustic guitar, a small sculpture of a red-eyed bull, a copy of *The Bell Jar*, an Art Deco lamp, a glittering gold football helmet, a Statue of Liberty paperweight, a grade school exercise book with Victoria's name in bold handwriting on the cover, a silk scarf patterned with autumn leaves and two records, *New Morning* by Bob Dylan and Leonard Cohen's *Songs from a Room*.

Beside each item was a small placard with names and dates written neatly in the middle of it. There were letters placed next

135

to some objects while others were accompanied by photos of people holding the item: an uncertain half smile on the woman with the football helmet; a look of miserable shock on the couple clutching the lamp.

After a while, we went back downstairs, where Mr and Mrs Lucas were talking softly. 'Do you see?' Mr Lucas asked, raising his eyebrows.

'I think so, Sir,' I said. 'They're Victoria's belongings and they've been returned to you by the people who found them.'

'Yes, that's right,' said Mr Lucas, wiping his dark brow with a white handkerchief. 'Those people in the photographs and the ones who wrote the letters are all strangers. They found Victoria's things, just like you did, in subways or on street corners or left behind on restaurant tables. And somehow, they've determined who they belonged to and returned them to us. It's happened ten times since 1973, a year after she passed.'

'But how do they get here?' asked David.

'Her boyfriend, the man she was seeing when she . . .' Mrs Lucas took a deep breath, a slender finger playing with her hair, 'when she jumped from the subway platform. Each September, probably on the anniversary of her death, he leaves something that was hers for a stranger to find. And now with the bible, it's happened eleven times. You're very kind to have come all this way.'

Mr Lucas picked up an old camera from the large radiogram in the corner of the living room and asked us to bring the bible out on to the porch. The sun was in our eyes, silhouetting the old man as he took the photograph of David and me grimly addressing the camera. I handed him the bible and shook his hand as he thanked us once again for our trouble.

'It's . . . that's fine,' I said. 'But there's just one thing, Sir. When I spoke to you on the phone, you said that Victoria was down here with you.'

'She is, my boy. Vicky's buried here and she's in our hearts with us wherever we are.'

We waved goodbye to Mr Lucas and his wife, and got back in the car, turning around slowly and heading back down the long road to the highway.

I tried hard to remember what my impression of Victoria Lucas had been before this afternoon, but could not. This struck me as being a little like our trip across America – every idea and expectation I had being overrun with each passing mile. I'm pretty sure some scrawny cartoon character – Bart, Beavis, Butthead – must have said it before me, but reality sucks, man.

5.20 p.m.

We're at the Sun-n-Sand Downtown Motor Hotel in Jackson. It's an ultra-50s orange-n-aqua job, complete with Polynesian function rooms, on-site Beauty Salon and kidney-shaped swimming pool. Cool.

Jackson is the capital of Mississippi. We are in the heart of the old South: Civil War monuments stand on every corner (most of them not exactly thrilled with the result of said war); ancient, towering oak trees line the wide streets; the state capitol building, a huge domed and pillared structure completed in 1903, rivals its Washington counterpart in grandeur and stern import. Jackson is not a large city but it has a powerful presence, as though there is still a strong, simmering resentment at being made part of the Union. We have seen more than a few Rebel flag bumper stickers and our Maine plates do not attract many happy waves.

Spewing Tobacco

I am about to take my love of tobacco one step further than ever before – by eating some. I have a paramedic (David dressed entirely in white) and a glass of Coke standing by in case anything goes wrong with my heart or mouth. The terbacher ahm about to start a-chewin' is called Cannon Ball. There are no instructions on the pack, so I'm unsure how much to break off and shove in my face. It smells quite sweet and is cool and moist to the touch, like a fruit brownie that gives you cancer . . .

. . . I ripped off a matchbox-sized chunk, happily popped it into my mouth and began chomping away. Almost immediately my palate was swamped by a rich, revolting sweetness that spread like a honeyed virus into my head and chest. My eyes began watering and I had trouble breathing. I felt hot and started hiccupping and pulling faces like an angry mountain man – a Hatfield sighting a McCoy. My stomach began to spasm and I lurched as I stood up and pushed open the motel room door. Outside at last, my face a wild orchestra of sharp tics and bad notes, I spat great gobs of thick brown sludge into a nearby hedge. Many minutes later, as I lay on my back in the car park, I began to appreciate the only possible pleasure to be gained from chewing tobacco – spitting the stuff out. I think it's how they discovered the infamous rebel yell.

A security guard driving a blue golf buggy cruised up beside me as I tried to lift myself off the asphalt.
'How you doin' there?'
'Okay. I'm getting better.'

He looked over at the car. 'So you're from Maine? All the way down from Maine?'

'No, we're from Australia. The car's from Maine.'

'Australia? How is it?'

'Umm . . . good thanks.'

'Fine. Now lissen, Son. The manager sent me over to ask you to stop vomitising in the hedge. D'you mind?'

'No. Sorry. It's not vomit, it's tobacco.'

'Uh huh.'

'Not cigarettes, chewing tobacco. You're *supposed* to eat it.'

'Uh huh.'

Uh huh.

THE VIRGIN MARY SPEAKS TO AMERICA. CALL 1-800 MARYTALK

Two of the King's Men. **David runs for governor of Louisiana but is compromised by his hair. Directed by Jon Peters.**

We're on the very bumpy I-55 heading south from Jackson, listening to the Fatback Band out of New York City. The only traffic is big, empty logging trucks, the steel ribs on their sides shuddering and wavering like great metal fingers. We break the tedium of the drive with weak puns about places we've passed through lately. Eupora. 'You poora sucker.' Ackerman. 'Nice acker, man.' McComb. 'There's mc dandruff in my mc comb.' And other such intellectual marvels. Dreary chatter, unending blacktop and bleak, featureless roadside, from sea to shining sea.

1.48 p.m. Louisiana

For lunch outside Ponchatoula it was either a burger or a 'catfish

139

dinner', and I won't eat anything that has whiskers and swims. It's a policy that's got me where I am today.

I'm very reluctant to bring this matter up, but the fact that we're both pretending it never happened seems strange, even a little ridiculous, so I clear my throat and try to sound oh-so-casual. 'Well, how about that Victoria Lucas thing, huh?' My voice cracks at the end.

'I'm trying to think of it as a vivid dream,' David says, pausing at a tree-shrouded intersection.

'Which began when? In New York on the subway or yesterday afternoon?'

He looks left, right, left. 'Maybe at the very moment our passports were stamped at the US border. Maybe none of this is happening at all. Maybe we're both still asleep in Montreal.'

'Do you want me to pinch you on the arm? Is that what you're saying? I'll do it, but it won't make any difference. You'll get a bruise is all.'

After a while David says, 'Hmmmm,' and focuses on driving, swathing himself in the air of calm he carries with him wherever he goes. He doesn't ever lose his temper; he's not judgmental or insistent or arrogant or loud. He's not like the rest of us and he's especially not like me. He has this strange way of being there with you, but at the same time being removed from you; as though he's already looking back on the situation and telling someone an anecdote about it – leaving out the boring bits and enlivening things with new material. Maybe in his version he doesn't slow down at the intersection and there's a near-smash, and I end up with a broken jaw, my mouth wired shut for the next two months. Would he do that to me? Even in the hazy realm of anecdotal fiction?

The light from the low sky is grey and diffuse, the air heavy with rain and heat. We're a few miles outside N'Awlins and all the Lou'siana clichés have gotten together to greet us – it's swampy, there are shacks teetering by the 'gator-filled water and plenty of those trees with that green stuff drooping off them. Swelling clouds of mosquitoes swarm around the dead cypress trees and sand bogs in amongst the network of canals and inlets and bayous of Lake Pontchartrain. A breeze lifts small white caps on the lake, and the stench of stagnant water and rotting leaves wafts into the car. It's a relief for perception and reality to finally come together, but boy, does it stink.

3 p.m.

New Orleans is drenched with rain, great warm drops that pelt and puddle the steaming cobblestone streets, sending people scuttering into doorways or huddling beneath dripping balconies. I am sitting on the rain-protected balcony of our room looking up and down Chartres Street. We're staying at the most magnificent hotel I've ever seen in my entire life – the Soniat House in the French Quarter. Sitting at the wood and marble desk in our room, I can hear the clip-clop of hooves, the jangling of bells and bridles and the snap of reins as the tourist carriages pass below our window. Tonight I will be sleeping under my very own skylight on a hundred-year-old day bed with a great big muslin cover. There are two verdant courtyards where drinks are served each night at six. Brad Pitt stayed here once, so it has celebrity endorsement. I want to live here. And die here. I am in heaven.

Popular thought: It's not so much the heat, it's the humidity.
Popular t-shirt: It's not so much the heat, it's the stupidity.
Populist O'Brien: It's not so much the heat, it's the hotness.

141

Bourbon Street

A little drunk on Australian wine, we took a short walk along Bourbon Street – a terrible mistake. It was an assault of live music, strip shows, street performers, souvenir stores, bars, clubs, pubs, discos, dealers and deadbeats – and thousands of tourists feeding into and out of the mouths of it all. Gangs of college boys mostly, spilling out of the bars with their plastic cups of beer, a bright, hormonal glaze of perspiration on every smiling face. Through the throng, walking against the flow, isolating himself and lit by purpose, was a man calling loudly through the side of his mouth, 'Eeeeecstasy!' But I didn't want ecstasy; I've had it before and I spewed foam like a chemical-fire extinguisher. I turned around and cocked my head. He came over and said, not quite to me, 'You wanna buy?'

'You got any coke?'

He nodded and said, 'I gotta see m'man.' So me, him and his man did some wandering up and down Bourbon Street, this way and that. M'man passed it to my man, who shook my hand and slipped me a wodge of Saran Wrap. I passed a fifty back his way and we all quickly disappeared into the crowd of dope dealers and dopier tourists.

As we walked back to the hotel David interrogated me. 'Why do you waste your money like that?'

'This is how society is now. It takes drugs. It needs drugs. I like drugs.'

'But you don't. You're frightened of them.'

'That's true. I'm taking them to get over my fear of them.'

'It won't work.'

'Why not?'

'You just bought a bag of powder off a guy in the street, you great idiot. What do you think's in it?'

'Cocaine?'

David looked at the ground and shook his head. 'I doubt it.'

'He seemed like a pretty nice guy. He wouldn't rip me off.'

David laughed. 'You've got a lot to learn about being a tourist.'

'I don't want to be a tourist. I want to be a regular guy.'

'You have to work your way up to that. And giving fifty bucks to a stranger for drugs proves that you're a pretty long way down, I'm afraid.'

The French Quarter Connection. **David 'Olive Oyle' O'Brien courts disaster by pretending to be a rogue cop. Rated PG (barometric references).**

Post Office

Just after midday, David and I popped into the New Orleans Postal Emporium. While buying postal stuff we mentioned that we were planning on visiting the cemetery.

'Be very, very careful,' the clerk advised us. 'It's a popular mugging spot.'

'Oh,' I said, feeling for my wallet. 'But is it worth visiting?'

'Sure. Just be careful. How many of you are there?'

'Just me and him.'

'We're Australian,' added David, rather pointlessly.

'You should be all right then.'

Detour

Nevertheless, we went back to the hotel and deposited our money, cameras, credit cards, passports and jewellery, keeping just $5 in singles so that if we did meet any muggers they

143

wouldn't get angry and kill us. Plus I had some cigarettes, and muggers love a free smoke.

Cemetery

A sign posted in front of St Louis Cemetery No. 1 ('Burying the dead and near-dead since 1789') warns that the Catholic Archdiocese takes no responsibility for damage or loss to persons and property entering the graveyard. I felt that this was a discouraging announcement, but then again, Sally and I have a similar plaque at the entrance to our apartment.

'So what do you think so far, Sean-Paul?' David asked.

Because New Orleans is built pretty much right in the middle of a swamp, the coffins used to keep floating to the surface. (Initially, this problem – and it *is* a problem – was tackled by drilling holes in the coffins, producing an unhappy and fearful gurgling sound which the living found distressing when burying their loved ones.) So now all the graves are above-ground tombs, many of which look like tiny houses with pitched roofs and neat little wrought-iron fences and balconies. Most are crumbling into the ground, wearied as they are by the years of wet heat and being stared at. Some are so decrepit that they are simply piles of old red brick with a mere stain of mortar holding a wall or two in place. But I guess it's hard to find good help when you're dead.

'It looked a lot creepier from above when we were speeding past in the car,' I answered David. 'Sometimes things lose their mystique and lustre when you see them up close.'

In front of an enormous tomb I saw a woman in an LA Dodgers

baseball cap on her knees collecting mud and putting it into a test tube. Then she leaned back and began praying with her palms held out flat, skyward. Once she'd finished rolling her eyes and moaning, I took a closer look and saw that the grave was in fact that of notorious voodoo queen Marie Laveau. It was covered in a frenzy of rust-coloured X's that had been scratched into it by fans of Marie's very influential work. Scattered beneath the Greek Revival studio apartment Marie now calls home were a couple of cigars placed to form an X, a lollipop, some plastic flowers, lots of small change and the strong smell of cheap booze and vomit.

'I know what you mean,' David said, sketching a concrete angel so disintegrated she was little more than rough, rusted armature desperately clutching a harp.

If the Cap Fits . . .

I was dressed in a green hunting cap with earlaps that stuck out; voluminous tweed trousers rumbling with pockets of warm, stale air; a plaid flannel shirt; and a muffler. It was an outfit acceptable by any theological and geometrical standards and one that suggested a rich inner life. But, boy, it was hot and my valve was killing me.

I was sitting opposite the clock at the D. H. Holmes department store, a bag of sheet music and a lute string at my feet. I had been planning to buy a lute but could only afford to purchase one in instalments. Suddenly, a sad-eyed policeman stood above me. 'You got any identification, mister?' he asked, kicking at the bag of paper music. 'Let me see your driver's licence.'
'I don't drive. Will you kindly go away? I'm waiting for my

mother – I mean, my friend.'

'You a troublemaker, ain'tcha?'

'This city is famous for its gamblers, prostitutes, exhibitionists, anti-Christs, alcoholics, sodomites, drug addicts, fetishists, onanists, pornographers, frauds, jades, litterbugs and lesbians, all of whom are only too well protected by graft. And you make the mistake of bothering *me*.' I was a little surprised by my outburst, but put it down to the heat (or the humidity).

The cop lifted me by the arm. 'All right, Chubs,' he said, thumping me in the chest. 'Show me some ID now!'

I handed him my wallet. He pulled out a credit card and read aloud. 'Ignatius J. Reilly. What the hell kindofa name is that?'

'It's not mine,' I said.

'It's *my* name, and I'd like it back *immediately*, if you please!' A fat, moustached man dressed exactly like me waddled up and made a grab for the wallet. He was even carrying a bag of sheet music as I was, only there was a pair of drumsticks poking out the top instead of a lute string.

'And who're you?' the cop asked.

'I am Ignatius J. Reilly, you brute fascist!'

'Let's see some identification.'

The fat man handed the cop a wallet. 'It says here that you're Sean P. Condon.'

'Don't be absurd,' retorted the fat one, spittily. 'I couldn't walk the streets of any civilised city with such a ridiculous name.'

'Hey!' I shouted. The cop and my twin stared at me, their four eyebrows arching to form two question marks. 'Oh . . . nothing.'

'My mother will be here shortly,' said Reilly/Condon to the cop. 'I should like my identity returned to me by then or I shall invoke my great capacity for fuss.' He turned and whacked me on the shoulder. 'And may I ask why you are dressed in the fashion of

146

my own unique styling? Are you some sort of impudent prank-ster?'

'It's a conspiracy,' I told him. 'A conspiracy of punches.'

'Oh my that's poor. Are you aware that my creator *died* for me?'

'Well, it was his choice.'

Ignatius/Sean slapped me across the face. 'How *dare* you?' I was getting tired of being abused by fictional characters – those one-dimensional types can really hurt. He continued. 'John Kennedy Toole was a genius! A Pulitzer Prize-winning artiste of singular order too long ignored by the benighted fools in the Publishing-Literary Complex! How dare you muddy his name, you young imposter!' Then he released a noisy gust from the seat of his pants. 'Ooohhh-aaahhh, my valve,' he moaned. 'Sweet relief!'

'Good God,' gagged the policeman.

'Mater approaches,' said the fat man.

I looked over and saw a tall blonde woman marching out of the department store. As she approached us, I saw that she had a gathering of ginger facial hair around her mouth. Like a goatee . . .

I close the book as David joins me. He screws up his face. 'What the hell is that smell?'

'Something blew in off the bay.'

'Sure. What are you reading?' he asks.

'*A Confederacy of Dunces*,' I tell him. 'It's all set around here in New Orleans.'

'What's it like?'

'The main character is overweight and annoying. He talks a lot.'

'So you're empathising too much, huh?'

'No, not at all.'

As we walk back toward the Quarter, David says, 'By the way, where'd you get the hunting cap?'

<u>6.30 p.m.</u>

I love New Orleans. The food, the music, the heat, the swamp, the great porticoed mansions, gardens and oak trees of St Charles Avenue and the crumbling French Quarter have a distinctive grace, style and charm. On the other hand, the 'cocaine' I bought last night turned out to be $50 worth of icing sugar. I've been stung like a tourist! David was right. Double stung – it's not even good sugar. He's always right.

At the ACME Oyster Bar (Wile E. Coyote has their food mailed to him because it's so good), David 'Oyster Boy' O'Brien had a dozen slops of slime on the half shell while I had creole jambalaya, which is rice with chicken, shrimp and smoked sausage mixed in. It's called paella in Spain. And in East Doncaster, it's known as leftovers.

<u>No Votes for Sharon</u>

We've walked the close streets of the French Quarter trying to spot Anne Rice, but all we've seen so far are a few young Goths draped in lace and velvet, almost fainting from the wet heat. Now we're back from several hours of pointless drinking (that's where it costs but you don't get drunk) in a fantastic bar called the Napoleon Arms. It's small, dark and woody and there are fewer tourists because of the classical music they play. David is lying on his bed watching 'The Gossip Show' on MTV. He reports that there was a party for A. Morisette, the popular Canadian ironist, at Lemon (David's birthday restaurant) last week. Sharon Stone and Gwyneth Paltrow were there looking for us, but they were too late. Damn!

'Who do you prefer,' David asks, 'Alanis, Gwyneth or Sharon?'

'Gwyneth by a mile. Her mother's Blythe Danner. She was in "M*A*S*H" once, as a woman Hawkeye was in love with but too scared to marry. I would've married her, I tell ya. That husky voice.'

' "M*A*S*H" has had quite an influence on you, hasn't it?'

'I know. It's weird. I don't even *like* it that much. I just know about it. Who do you prefer?'

'Alanis. Mainly because I like saying her name. I'd love to say it to her face. "Hey, Alanis, pass the peas." "Want another jagged little pill, Alanis?" '

'That irony song was so stupid. All those things she mentioned – a fly in her glass of wine, getting a free ride after she'd already bought her ticket – they weren't ironic, they were just bad luck. It really annoyed me.'

'You're pretty easily annoyed though, aren't you?'

'And she sang as though she was giving birth to some sort of sea creature. I wonder if Brad Pitt stayed in this very room. That'd be a coincidence, wouldn't it? Or would it be *ironic*?'

No votes for Sharon Stone. Society's changed quite a bit over the last few years.

Final Thought

In the bathroom of the Napoleon Arms was a scrawled message: *I have a brother born minutes after me.* That's all. It's a very strange thing to proclaim. It's haunted me all night. I have two sisters born several years after me, but so what?

I Put a Spell on You. **Sean and David pooh-pooh voodoo. Rated F.**

Showered off the subconscious grime of dream-infected sleep and am now having café au lait and beignets at the open-air Café Du Monde with Dave 'Robicheaux' O'Brien. Café au lait is coffee with lait and beignets are lumps of dough generously covered with cocaine. It's raining. On the sidewalk a guy is playing a terrifically mournful version of 'Harlem Nocturne' on his trumpet.

'Say, David, you hear the song that guy out there's playing?'

'Yeah,' he says, turning to watch the trumpet player. 'It's nice. What about it?'

'The guy who wrote it, Earle Hagen, also wrote the theme to "The Andy Griffith Show", "Mod Squad" *and* "Eight is Enough". He covered the 50s, 60s, 70s and 80s. Amazing, huh?'

A few minutes later, the rain has become almost torrential and the trumpeter has changed to a Glenn Miller tune. 'Say, Sean, you hear the song that guy out there's playing?' says David, repetitively.

'Yeah. "String of Pearls." What about it?'

'The guy who wrote it, Glenn Miller, was thought to have disappeared in a military plane over the English Channel in 1944. But, in fact, it was recently claimed that he died in the arms of a prostitute. Amazing, huh?'

'Yeah. Boy, talk about an American patrol in the mood.'

We wander out of the cafe and see a trio of little black kids doing tap routines on the watery sidewalk. What's especially appealing about them is that their 'taps' are big pairs of running shoes with tin lids nailed to the soles. They're all really fluid, rhythmic dancers doing fine routines and being very demanding about getting money from us tourists. The great thing is, none of their moves can go for more than about eight seconds before they have to stop and reattach their taps. It's pretty funny.

'What you kids need is a manager,' says some Floridian fathead pointing a video camera at them.

'Yeah, and a cobbler,' I mutter, dropping $2 into the hat.

Is it gonna rain all day?
How the fuck do I know?
I don't know. I just thought you might know.
Am I the weatherman?
> White female, approx. 19, and black male, approx. 55

Bah Humfo!

The Voodoo Museum is not at all worthy of the cult and culture that has made New Orleans the US capital of the black arts (and cheap plastic beads). It consists of two rooms and a hallway full of bad paintings and badder junk: dead frogs floating upside down in filthy jars of formalin, scabby old alligator skeletons, horrible carvings of nothing resembling anything, two thousand empty booze bottles with candles stuck in the top and other regular stuff deemed to have special powers by dint of its inclusion amongst the detritus. Like a live python in a glass case sliding around a plastic skull. Oh no! And Marie Laveau's 'kneeling bench' (a lump of old wood). Aaaagh! And a *humfo* – some voodoo sub-cult thing – prayer altar (more kneeled-on wood) right beneath a *humfo* air-conditioner made by General Electric (in their Haiti plant, presumably) pumping out cool *humfo* air all day long.

151

The adjacent Voodoo Museum Gift Shop sells talismans and charms and 'spells that really work'. I bought a 'spell that really works with bonus un-hexer' for $3 (plus voodoo tax of 23¢). I was expecting to find some powdered rat skull, a dried chicken's foot and maybe a mysterious herb or two inside the envelope, but all I got was a photocopied sheet of paper carrying on about La Grande Zombie this and Papa Laba that, advising who's a good Loa (spirit) to buddy up to and instructing you to paint every ceiling in your house sky blue, put a bayleaf in the corner of each room and get yourself plenty of candles, incense, roots and a boa constrictor – and you'll be the next Donald Trump . . . Yeah, right! I wonder if 'spells that really work' are really tax deductible.

When you go from the fake New Orleans of Disneyland to the real one, where the captain of the paddle-wheel steamer says it is possible to see alligators on the banks of the river, and then you don't see any, you risk feeling homesick for Disneyland.

Umberto Eco, 'City of Robots', 1986

5 p.m.

It's bright and sunny outside, but thundering constantly anyway. Very weird weather. Could it be my less-than-respectful voodoo thoughts? Is old Marie pissed at me? From beyond the grave? C'mon Bonus Un-Hexer, work your funky stuff!!

We're having our first drinks of the night and waiting for Gwyneth and Brad and that crazy musical prankster Beck to arrive. They should've been here by now.

9.50 p.m.

A few drinks later, and quite oiled and disappointed by our

non-friends' non-arrival, we walked for about two hundred steaming blocks trying to find somewhere to eat that was 'not too restauranty' (David's request, by which I knew he meant 'cheap'). Eventually we stopped at Felix's Seafood and ate Po' Boys – baguettes with stuff in them. Fried shrimp for Sean and a shrimp/oyster combo for David. They were very nice and when we asked if we could congratulate Felix, we were told he was out having dinner with the Paltrow-Pitts and some 'funny little guy with two turntables and a microphone'.

We have to become drunk and depressed now because we're going to the House of Blues and we don't want to seem out of place. It's our last night in New Orleans, our last night in America's south.

House of Blues

Inside the men's can at the House of Blues is a little 'men's store' run by a short black man called Melvin Stoval, who has a mouth full of gold teeth. He sells a huge array of cigars, cigarettes, gum (by the pack and by the stick), hair gel, hair spray, hair wax, aspirin, Mylanta, eye drops, mints, toothpicks, mouthwash, deodorant, moisturisers, earplugs and twelve different sorts of cologne at 'two squirts foah a dollah'. It's fantastic – and very convenient if you find that you've gone out for the night and forgotten to bring . . . everything.

Tito Puente looks like my grandmother in a man's silver wig, but he sure can hit them timbalés. The legendary House of Blues (at least this particular member of the legendary franchise) is full of short, fat, sleazy drug dealers wearing shirts with coloured buttons. They have dark, lazy eyes that stare at women with a cash-funded lasciviousness that you can almost breathe when you stand too close. (My hatred for them leads to an imaginary death scenario where I try to save one of the female innocents and am hunted down by the dealers' hit men, who send me to 'sleep with the alligators'.)

Back at the Soniat House we watched a chilling episode of 'The Twilight Zone' about an old lady in Maine who was receiving telephone calls from her dead fiancé, Brian. See, a violent storm had brought down a telephone pole onto Brian's grave, allowing him to make the creepy calls. It was very good. And quite scary. Directed by Jacques Tourneur.

Hours later, I am still awake, covered in a sweat that feels alive and sick on my skin. This is a city of long heat – heat which stays and follows and waits around corners for you, not leaving when it's night and sitting heavily until you wake. A slow heat which meddles with your thoughts until they are mush and turns the next day into a dream.

David wanders into the room in which I am not sleeping. 'You still awake?' he asks.
'Yeah,' I say through the mosquito netting. 'This weather is amazing.'
'It's not so much the heat, it's the . . . no, it's the heat.'
'Still, it's a nice place to visit. And I'd like to live here.'
'New Orleans doesn't belong in America. It's too foreign.'
'Is it like the old Orleans, the one in France?'
He wanders over to the balcony and opens a door. 'It's exactly the same, but here there's more heat. And humidity.'

The
Southwest

*I opened the door and faced the semi-nude army, waving a
large pair of white underpants in my right hand . . .*

The Tonight Live Show. **With David as Letterman and Sean as Leno. Features an impressive prosthetic chin and dental gap. Rated CBS/NBC.**

12.42 p.m.

Heading out of N'awlins on 10 West, a freeway passing by stilled carnivals, empty houses clapping in the hot wind, sidewalks full of rubbish and weedy growth covering everything like a brown-green cancer. Au revoir, New Orleans. Goodbye South. Hello West.

THE CAJUN KITCHEN. MULATES – CREOLE AND SEAFOOD. THE CRAW-FISH KITCHEN. MISS HELEN'S CAJUN SEAFOOD. KETTLE KITCHIN – HUGE PORTIONS! GOODY'S GUMBO. JAMBALAYA PALACE. CHEF ROY'S ACADIE CAFE. CAJUN HAVEN. CAJUN CONNECTION. CAJUN DRAGON – SEAFOOD, STEAK, GRILL. CAJUN TALES SEAFOOD RESTAURANT.

3.30 p.m.

The highway has big irritating bumps every .8 of a second that cause weird humps in our conversation and give us mild stomach aches. Or maybe that's from the cajun smoked cajun chicken cajun sandwiches we had for lunch. It's pretty misty and kind of scary in western Louisiana, like the strange, wet brightness before a hurricane. The wind bends the weak, old trees and birds tumble out of the sky like little feathered cripples. I peer into the bayou country that frames the highway and wonder if, just a few miles away, there are lots of cajun guys, talking patois, playing zydeco, eating 'gator and shooting people they think are from Maine. Or would they be more likely charging tourists five bucks a throw for a look at their lousy teeth?

We've just cut out of a town called Sulphur. On the radio a preacher is reading rather disinterestedly from Matthew: 'We are all but ghasts in the house ahf Gahd.' Following the liturgy is an awful song; the only words I can make out are 'Jesus', 'love' and 'come and die'.

'What do you know about Texas, David?'
He accelerates as we begin to overtake a car with a 'Purple Heart Veteran' tag on it. 'Apparently it's big,' he says.
'The second biggest state, I think.'
'Which is the biggest?'
The driver of the Purple Heart car is wearing a military beret. As we flank him, he turns and snaps off a quick salute. I nod and smile politely. 'Either Rhode Island or Alaska. How long will it take us to drive across it?'
'I'm not quite sure. But long.'
'Texas Rangers, Texas Longhorns, Texas T, Tex-Mex, Tex Avery, *Texasville*, "Texas Flood".'
'What are you doing?'
Behind us, the veteran slows to turn into a cemetery driveway.
'Acclimatising.'
'You forgot one: Don't Mess with Texas.' I can hear the stern capitals in the words.

4.38 p.m. Texas

The highway improves as soon as we cross the border. A sign says 'Drive friendly – the Texas way'. Awrighton! We pull over to take a look around and I survey the scene by standing on the roof of the Neon. They're right, it really *is* bigger than Texas.

'Where will we stay?'
'Galveston, probably.'

157

'Sorry, where?'
'Galveston.'
'Oh, Galveston.'

5.26 p.m. Gas and Food (No Lodging)

Because we've stopped at a gas station in Nowhere, Texas, and because I cannot think of anything better to do I've bought a packet of Hostess Twinkies®. They are, after all, an American institution and the favourite food of Zippy the Pinhead. And if they're good enough for him, they're good enough for me. They are, however, so sickly sweet that there should be a warning printed on them: 'See your dentist after every bite'.

Snapshot

The Gulf of Mexico is a hundred yards to our left. The landscape is flat and cheerlessly etiolated, marked only by an infinite line of telegraph poles disappearing into the dusk that is our destination. White birds stand on the backs of cows, hitching a slow ride to nowhere in particular. David is taking photographs; holding the camera in his left hand outside the car, steadying the wheel with his right. A police car flies past in the opposite direction, its red and white lights dulled in the dingy sea air, its siren silenced by the wind. There are no houses or stores, just bleak flatness all around and an oil tanker up ahead. I suggest to David that we stop and let off some firecrackers. He shakes his head, still searching for the perfect firecracker place, which I suspect exists only in his mind. The Twinkie taste won't go away.

6.45 p.m.

A ferry is taking us to sandy Galveston Island; its deck of black tar creates the effect of a floating road. A no-longer-young blonde in a red convertible is being ogled by a group of Hispanic teenagers leaning out of a minivan on the upper deck. They are too far away to see that she's old enough to be their mother's best friend. All they can see is her hair colour and her sporty car. It's enough.

8.07 p.m. Galveston Island

Galveston ain't very nice. There's a hopeless, thin beach here, lots of cheap hotels and a Wal-Mart for every man, woman and child in the city. As a 'resort town', I have to say that it fails. Except compared to Surfer's Paradise. And Pigeon Forge.

We briefly discussed the idea of crossing the border into Mexico. But why should we? We haven't done anything wrong.

Westward Ho . . . tel! Rated ★.

Checked into an Econo Lodge with a view of a car park and a drugstore. The room is tiny and smells of putrid mould. There is one towel between the two of us, the toilet flushes itself constantly and the complimentary Econo-pencil is a stumpy little number that you couldn't finish a laundry list with. But there's cable TV, so I'm fairly happy.

The teenage receptionist who checked us in asked, 'You guys Aussies?'

'No,' David said, pointing to our car. 'We're from Maine.'

The Host with the Most

Back from a glutinous Chinese meal, we're now fatted out on our beds, rubbing our distended guts and watching a telemovie about Letterman, Leno and the coveted 11.30 p.m. spot on NBC. It's good. I always enjoy catching a glimpse of the lives of the wealthy. But if they truly think that they work 'really, really hard', as these TV billionaires keep insisting, they're kidding themselves.

'I dismantled and erected scaffolding for a day and a half in 1985. *That* was hard work, baby,' I tell David, indignant with him because he has the same first name as Letterman.

'I cleaned house bricks one summer,' he says, not to be outdone. 'That was shitful work.'

'I think I'd make an excellent tonight show host,' I say, examining my chewed fingernails and realising I'd have to get a manicure first.

'Everyone thinks that. You'd want to lose some weight or the networks wouldn't even look at you.'

'I know. Jay Leno's kind of fat though. And he's got that ridiculous chin. Look at that chin, it's straight off of Mount Rushmore.'

'Stop talking American,' he says disdainfully. '*Off of.*'

'I'm practising.'

'And you'd have to learn to be interested in people other than yourself.'

'I could learn. I really could. Besides you wouldn't *actually* have to be interested in them. You'd just have to pretend. "Hi, Dickbrain, it's great to have you on the show! It's been so long since we've seen you. Don't be such a stranger, okay? I really mean that! You're fantastic! Come back real soon!!" Then the idiot guest sits on the couch and tells some stupid, made-up, three-minute anecdote from the film set or recording studio to promote their latest movie or album or whatever, then they fuck off back to the green room, drink some free booze and bitch about what an asshole I am.'

'Come to think of it, maybe you'd be perfect for the job.'

'Maybe I'd be better as the host's sidekick. They're usually a little portly. Who do you think is the sidekick out of you and me?'

'The one with less charisma, charm, looks, personality and teeth – you.'

'Ha ha ha ha ha ha ha ha ha ha ha ha ha ha. Good one Dave!'

'Say goodnight, Seanie.'

'Goodnight Seanic.'

Zabriskie Pointless. **A lot of staring and desert. Directed by Michelangelo Antonionionionio.**

11 a.m. Heading out of Galveston

There are lots of large, fat, black insects buzzing around the car. They just hang around out there, staring in at us. It's quite unsettling. What do they want? Have we captured their leader or something? Whenever we hit one of them, it makes a really loud crack on the windscreen but doesn't die – merely bounces off and continues on its fat, black, buzzing way. My they're tough.

Chewing the Fat of the Land

David is eating his third stick of the most disgusting chewing gum known to human kind – Big Red. It has a sharp, sickly cinnamon flavour that was first used to keep astronauts awake. Oh my God, he's shoving a *fourth* piece in there.

'It's not food, y'know,' I tell him.

'You've got to get a good wad going.'

'You're disgusting.'

'Hey, *you've* chewed tobacco.'

He has me there. Nonetheless, I open the car window and let in all that big Texas heat to clear out the Big Red air.

We're in the popular heart of the American West. If you're a moron, all that the West means to you is cowboys and indians. But in many ways the idea of the West is the essence of America: land wars, the double-crossing and murder of the Native Americans, the birth of true nationhood through the railway, Gold Rush fever and the crazed courage of the settlers, who acted like so many Northern franchisers of Union and Democracy. It's a fascinating place.

'I wish there were some cowboys around,' says David.

'And indians,' I add. We're both morons.

SIGN: JESUS IS COMING SOON. ARE YOU READY TO MEET HIM?

SEAN: Yes, but I think I should change out of these shorts into something a little more formal.

DAVID: Will He call first to make sure I'm in?

Washing

Rolled into San Antone in a spludgy haze of butterflies splattering themselves gooey yellow on the windscreen. From what I could see through the ooze, it's a pretty nice looking city, lots of old buildings (like the Alamo) and plenty of Mexican/Spanish-influenced architecture (like the Alamo). And the Alamo.

We're on our way to do some more laundry, which is a great thrill and one of the main reasons we came to America in the first place. We couldn't see any laundromats downtown so we asked the concierge at the Fairmount Hotel for directions. He was so nervous and thorough in his eagerness to please that I tipped him

$5 for his trouble. The poor guy was on the phone to laundry chains, asking if they were safe for out of towners, writing down instructions, drawing maps, the whole works. It was touching. And kind of pathetic.

Turns out the little prick sent us to a barrio. This laundromat is full of Mexicans eyeing David and me with unabashed suspicion. It seems to double as a daycare centre for children – they're everywhere. One little curly-haired girl in sandals keeps running around the bank of washing machines shouting 'Come and get me!' over and over again. 'Come and get me! Come and get me!' But nobody's chasing her. The other kids are just sitting on the bench, half nude 'cause it's wash day, watching her run around and around.

Today we're using Tide Ultra, a 'grease releasing' detergent that is harmful if swallowed. We've got two loads going, which means we'll be here for a little over an hour. It's too long – we could be caught in a drive-by. There's a shirtless guy on the telephone outside, his whole upper body covered in old-style tattoos of Jesus and the Virgin Mary. All the signs in here are in Spanish. Why do all the Mexicans keep pointing at me and saying Ringo? Yes, I play the drums but my nose isn't that big. Nobody likes us, they don't understand why we're here. *We're here to do our washing, folks, that's all. Just the laundry.*

Alamo-Go-Go

There weren't any dryers available so we grabbed the stuff from our three washing machines and went back to the hotel to drape the bathroom with wet clothing. It was then that I discovered I'd made some sort of machine-setting error – many of my clothes had become worn, discoloured and much, much larger. Great pairs of big-ass jeans, droopy muscle t-shirts and green bikini-style men's underwear. What the . . . ?

There was a knock at the door, and David peered through the window.

'There's about forty armed Mexicans out there,' he said. 'Including a guy on a horse. With a sword. What do you think they want?'

I pushed a large couch against the door and turned off the lights. 'I think they want what's rightfully theirs. But that's just a guess. D'you have a Bowie knife, by any chance?'

'No.'

'I'd get down if I were you,' I warned him from beneath a table.

'I don't think so,' said David from the bathroom. 'What's with all the fat guy denim? You joining Los Lobos?'

'I accidentally stole it from the Mexicans in the laundromat.'

'Well give it back.' He threw a pair of damp white y-fronts at me.

'I can't,' I told him, removing them from my head.

'Why not?'

'Remember the Alamo?'

'Vaguely. What happened?'

There was a pounding on the door. 'The Mexicans killed everybody,' I whimpered.

'They were fighting for Texas, not weekend wear. Go and give them back their clothes,' he ordered.

'But what about our honour?'

'There's no honour in lime thong-style briefs.'

He had a point. I got out from under the table, shoved all the foreign clothing into a bag and approached the front door, pushing aside the couch. 'Cover me,' I shouted, glancing at

David. He was mixing a drink. Taking a deep breath, I opened the door and faced the semi-nude army, waving a large pair of white underpants in my right hand.

Ouch

David had some specific ideas about dinner. 'I feel like a bit of surf and turf, some beef and reef, a little prawn and lawn, some . . . haddock and paddock.'

'What did you have for lunch?' I asked. 'A rhyming dictionary?'

On our way to find some food that rhymed, I got a killer of a headache. A real skull-fucker. I could barely walk and couldn't speak, staggering along in the heat clutching my head like Mr Hyde.

I decided that first thing the next day I'd face the American Health Care System, no matter what.

Rancho Notorious. **A western-style thriller culminating in a knife-fight near an okay motel. (Director's cut)**

Before

I'm sitting in the empty waiting (and waiting) room of the Alamo City Medical Group. So far I've spent forty-five minutes alone in here. It's my punishment for being Australian and not having a social security number. 'As the World Turns' is on TV. I wish *this* little world would start turning. *And* they're gonna touch me for at least forty bucks. I'm thinking about telling the doctor that I'm suffering from white line fever. What would he prescribe for that?

165

Fifty-seven minutes later, and I've had my vitals checked by a nurse. They're all there.

After

In fact it was *sixty* dollars for Dr X. Garcia Marco to tell me what I already knew (that I was getting headaches) and then offer the brilliant solution of travelling the country with an oxygen unit strapped to my face at the cost of only $500. We compromised on a prescription for painkillers and some stuff called Sumatripan which costs $123.18 for a box of nine pills! I told the pharmacist to go to hell and ordered just the painkillers, which I'm sure will be utterly useless. The lesson here is do not get sick in America: it'll fuck you up.

These are American Headaches. They are the coagulated absorption of every poison in the country – the Texas dust, the tainted steam of the Louisiana bayous, the great carbon clouds of New York City and the cold stench of the poverty and racism that is everywhere – all clouded into my swelling, aching head. Maybe it *is* white line fever.

1.25 p.m. Heading out of San Antonio

I didn't even get to see the Alamo. However, Davy 'Crockett' O'Brien checked it out and reported that it wasn't much chop and that you'd probably have more fun in a clinic watching 'As the World Turns'. I think he might have been lying to make me feel better, because when he came back he was whistling 'The Yellow Rose of Texas' and wearing a coonskin cap. 'Yeah, I am lying,' he said. 'Actually, I'll never forget the Alamo.'

As with most other cities, there are lots of malls on the way out of town. David says, 'Big business has swallowed up little business and now all the big businesses are in competition to shout the loudest.'

I agree. 'And all the visual noise they're making is truly awful.'

'It makes my eyes water,' he sobs.

I wonder if we're both just a bit too sensitive for America.

THIS IS GOD'S COUNTRY – PLEASE DON'T DRIVE THROUGH IT LIKE HELL

There are lots of signs for highway crossovers lining the road. This leads to a conversation about a woman David knew in college who became a man called Andrew. 'She just showed up at college one day and was a man.'

'I'd love to do that,' I thought aloud. 'Transform myself into my opposite.'

'You'd be thin and happy and handsome and fun to be with and witty and –'

'Yeah, I see your point.'

'And smart and conscientious and fit and h–'

'I understand what you're saying, David. You can stop now.'

What he's failed to realise is that if I could transform myself, *I'd* be the host and *he'd* be the sidekick. I'd get all the best lines.

'What are you smirking about?' he enquires.

'Nothing,' I lie, with a glittering smile at camera three.

Passed through a town called Dunlay that didn't have a single chain store in it. Impressive. Hondo, a few miles later, was the same. Maybe all is not lost. Which is all very well for me to say, speeding through at 50 mph, but would I like to live somewhere without a McDonald's? I don't think so.

We're eating these things made by the good people of Frito Lay called Baken-ets Traditional Fried Pork Skins (ingredients: fried pork skins, salt). They're absolutely disgusting. And there's only a few left.

The radio says: *If you don't trust the driver, don't get in the car. Also, try to avoid wearing velvet clothing in cars with velour interiors or you'll have immense trouble getting out of the seat.*

Dozens of suicidal black butterflies are throwing themselves in swarms against the windscreen. Clearly, Texas is not a good place to grow up as an insect. It's still flat (and still green) but all the signs of 'civilisation' are long gone. The towns are all but abandoned; weedy, dusty places where the bone-bleaching light is dry and over-exposed like faded film from a 1970s road movie. Most of the gas stations, stores, hotels and bars ('Eduardo's Place' – a shack with a wire door and a Coke sign out front) are closed for good. The only thing keeping the towns on the map is a concrete factory or some small mining interest employing maybe a dozen sorry bastards who call these hot, forgotten places home.

Inside Eduardo's Place (circa 1972)

'Hey, Eduardo.'

'Hey, Frank. What'll it be?'

'Gimme a tequila. Beer back. I'm as thirsty as a Sunday snake.'

'Comin' up. How's business anyway?'

'Goin' real good. Every town needs a pool hall, don't it?'

'Sure does. The movie people finished there?'

'Oh yeah, long gone. Kinda miss 'em too. Me and that Cloris had a sort of a thing goin'. She was nice. Funny lookin', but a real sweetheart. And she had great breath.'

'That last picture show might put us on the map. That'd be something, wouldn't it?'

'Sure would . . . How about that Nixon, huh?'

'Yeah, what an asshole.'

OSCAR GONZALEZ FOR SHERIFF – VAL VERDE COUNTY. JIM METZLER FOR SHERIFF. RE-ELECT JOE BOB BRIGGS SHERIFF. HERTZBERGER FOR SHERIFF. BILLY BOB THORNTON FOR SHERIFF: HE'LL MAKE THINGS RIGHT.

4.36 p.m.

Have just recovered from a powerful bad headache. The 'painkillers' Dr Marco prescribed had the effect of adding new dimensions of brain-scraping agony to the experience, and as a result I was clutching my skull and covering my eyes with my hands when all the interesting stuff happened. When I looked up ninety minutes later, everything had changed, like a clumsy edit.

The Interesting Stuff

I remember glancing through a crack between my fingers as we were cutting through a huge ravine. Just as I was reaching a sharp peak of pain, nausea and body sweats, we were pulled over by the Texas Department of Public Safety (police). I lay convulsing in the passenger seat, hiding my face like a criminal or a wetback, while David was hauled out of the car and made to stand on the spot.

'That spot there, Sir,' said the Officer of Public Safety (policeman).

'Here?'

'Right there.'

'Just next to that brownish rock?'

'Stand on that spot right now, Sir!' shouted the officer, his right hand wavering next to his holster. 'Now the reason I've stopped you is because you were clocked at seventy-one miles per hour. Is there any reason you were travelling that fast?'

'I thought the speed limit was seventy.'

'It is.'

David was issued a written warning advising him that if he was caught speeding again, there would be real trouble.

'What's up with your buddy?' the officer asked, waving a pen in my direction.

'He's Australian.'

Now that the pain has subsided, I can face America again. Everything's much more Texan now – little canyons, gorges, gulches, boulders and huge expanses of dirt-brown nothingness. A row of shade-tinted Mexican hills over the border to our left and a dry gulch with an abandoned yellow school bus in the middle on our right. *This* is Texas.

7.50 p.m.

We're at the Rancho Deluxo Motelo in an untouched highway strip town called Sanderson, flanked by mountains which change colour as the sun sets. I've bought a pair of brilliantly evil 'black fly' sunglasses, along with a six pack of Coors Banquet Beer and some corn nuts. It's lovely here – the only chains are Texaco and Exxon, both with regular height poles – and the late-evening light is beautiful and sharp. A sign on the way in says, 'Sanderson – Good Folk, Funny Cactus'. You have to like that.

Still, we may have the crap beaten out of us later. Or get hit by a pick-up truck. You never know in a place like this. Indeed, on a bedside table there's a crusty, ring-stained pamphlet entitled *A Brief History of Murders in Your Room.*

'July 7 1949', the first passage reads. 'Robert Lee Haggert, dishonourably discharged from the US Navy six months earlier, checked into Room 8 at the Rancho Deluxo with his girlfriend Faye Clements Hall and a friend, J. D. Newcombe Jr, a state boiler inspector. Some time before midnight, an argument began when Haggert accused Newcombe of sleeping with Hall. Haggert shot Newcombe in the face and beat his girlfriend to death with his fists. He then dragged both bodies into a ravine and covered them with rocks. He was caught three days later outside Eagle Pass and returned to the scene with police, where he identified his girlfriend's body. "That there's the tooth that used to hurt me when I kissed her," he said. Haggert was executed on 10 January 1950.'

I had to read more.

'Room 8, Rancho Deluxo, 21 October 1972. Marian Zetkoff, a 34-year-old divorcee from Chicago's Little Poland section, checks in. She is accompanied by her two children, six-year-old Jacqueline and four-year-old Bobby. Just before dark Miss Zetkoff runs into the car park screaming for help. When police and ambulance arrive, she claims that her children have eaten rat poison. Both are found dead in the motel room; however, an autopsy reveals that they have been fed macaroni laced with ground glass. The children's mother confesses to the crime and is sentenced to life imprisonment.'

' "I'm fit as a fiddle and a-ready to hang," crooned Eli Kirkbride as the executioner's noose was slipped around his neck. Like many unemployed young men during the Depression, Kirkbride dreamed of making it big in entertainment. On 2 September 1933, while passing through Sanderson on his way to New Orleans in search of nightclub work, Kirkbride shared Room 8 with a middle-aged business man, Lawrence Shead of Paterson, NJ. When Shead made advances to him, Kirkbride hit him over the head with an iron and then strangled him. Afterward he cleaned himself up in the shower, put on the dead man's suit and fled with $300 he had discovered in Shead's wallet. He stole a car but then made a fatal mistake. He removed the licence plates from the vehicle and pasted a hand-written sign on the back that read "New Car in Transit". Texas police pulled him over and immediately became suspicious. Taken to the police station, he was grilled at length and confessed: "Sure I killed him. This is his suit I'm wearing now." He was convicted of first-degree murder and sentenced to die on the gallows. As he was led out of the courtroom, he sang "Sweet Rosie O'Grady".'

'I'm hungry as a horse and a-ready to eat,' I sing to David, who is climbing all over the furniture swatting flies with a rolled-up magazine. 'Let's blow.' As we leave I notice that a white van with tinted windows has pulled up at a nearby room. The driver is unloading something large and heavy rolled up in a dusty floral curtain.

8.30 p.m.

The Kountry Kitchen restaurant is in 'central' Sanderson, a two-minute walk from 'greater' Sanderson. It is a bright, large place with a great many trinkets and mobiles hanging from the ceiling, tinkling in the breeze. Everybody is drinking some sort of cloudy substance with fruit in it out of pickling jars with handles. By ordering beer, which comes in a frosted plastic glass with no handles, I fear we've made a terrible mistake and offended someone, the head pickler maybe. Tacked to the wall is an old 'medical emergency' poster, curling and stained, which explains the Heimlich manoeuvre (which is, I believe, the routine my father pulled on my mother to first capture her attention – it was a popular courtship ritual amongst post-war youngsters).

Ended up in the only bar in town. Wooden-floored, ceiling-fanned and C & W-spewing – Randy Travis, Travis Tritt, Taylor Tyler Tripp, Titt Ravis, Andy Bundy, Randy Bland and Sandy 'Sugar Boy' Tandy. And me and David drinking a few beers, playing some pool and minding our own business. All the while this twitchy guy was watching us, a thin, hipless dude about forty with a low-slung butt and a dopey face that turned mean on close inspection. Every time we'd catch him staring at us, he'd shudder, flick his eyes away and brush at his face like there was a fly on it. He had a grey moustache dripping down the sides of his mouth and a tattoo of a yacht on his right forearm. He also had a large knife strapped to his belt. But most horrifyingly of all, from time to time he'd smile at me, slowly unbuttoning his shirt as he leered, while I furtively took notes on a pad about how insane he was.

David began a game of darts with the locals, leaving me standing alone at the bar. The madman immediately came over to me, shook my hand limply and said, 'Name's Lionel.' Then he laughed at something over my shoulder, saying that he liked beer and women 'in that order, but sometimes you just gotta take what you ken get.' He winked at me and my legs almost buckled.

'Where are you from, Lionel?' I asked, meaning, 'Which mental institution?'

'I's born in Minnesota, bu' I lived in New Mexico, Arizona . . . all aroun' these parts, bro. Where you from?'

'Er . . . Australia,' I answered, as I edged along the bar towards David, who was winning at darts and loudly proclaiming that he was the Bar Sports Champion of Terrell County. Lionel slid right along with me.

'Whassat you been writin' there, bro? Gimme a look.'

'No,' I stammered, terrified. 'It's just some crap.'

'Lemme see.'

'It's nothing. You wouldn't be interested.'

'Lissen you dirty kangaroo fucker, show me that goddamned paper!' All of a sudden the knife was in his hand and pointed at my stomach.

'You'd better show him,' said David, scoring a bull's-eye.

I handed the pad to Lionel. His eyes slitted and travelled slowly across the page, his right hand lazily gripping the knife. After a moment his moustache shivered, his shoulders shuddered and he started to laugh. 'Twitchy Lionel!' he spluttered. 'You callin' me Twitchy Lionel?'

'Yes,' I said. 'But in a *good* way.'

He threw his head back and laughed up at the roof. 'Hey y'all,' he called over to the men at the bar. 'This feller's made me a nickname. Twitchy Lionel! That's me!' He turned back to me. 'I been searchin' fer a nickname my whole goddamned life. And y'all come in here and find it fer me! Lemme buy ya a beer.'

'No thanks,' I said. 'We've really gotta get going.'

He showed me the knife again.

'Okay,' I said, weakly. 'That'd be great . . . Twitchy.'

So Lionel and Dave and I sat at the bar, three cold Michelobs in front of us. 'What's yer nickname, bro?' Lionel asked me. 'Is it Fatso?'

David guffawed. I kicked him in the shin and told Lionel that no, my nickname wasn't Fatso. His hand drifted down to the knife.

'Well, a *few* people call me Fatso,' I said.

'What do they call your buddy? Do they call him Curly Sue with Eyes of Blue?'

'Just Curly Sue,' David said, following the remark with a deep burp.

Lionel said, 'Twitchy, Fatso and Curly Sue. We like some sorta gang, ain't we?' Then he whispered, 'Hey, bros . . . wanna go rob some graves?'

I couldn't help feeling that it wouldn't be long before an updated edition of the motel murder booklet would be required, covering Lionel's recent work.

***Non-Incident at Roswell.* Sean and David join the long list of people who have seen 'saucer men'. Rated UFO.**

Shopping

There's no doctor in Sanderson, but there is a gun store. Given the town's history of homicide in just *one room* of *one motel*, this comes as no surprise. I decided to enquire about a purchase (I figured a gun might come in handy if I met any more Twitchys or nude Mexicans). David refused point blank to accompany me.

'Hi,' I said to a John Huston-faced guy around fifty.

'Same back to ya. How can I help you today?' he asked, with a dopey little inflection on 'you'.

'Well . . . I'd like to buy a gun,' I said, with a dopey little inflection on 'gun'.

'Well git yer hands outa yer pockets an' look me in the square eye, Son. It ain't nuthin' to be shamed of. It's not condoms, y'know. Or Tampax.'

'Right. Sure.' I blushed anyway.

'So whaddaya want?'

'Well, y'know, a gun please,' I said.

He wobbled his head as he spoke. 'Lemme ask you a question, Son. If you're in a supermarket and somebody offers you some help, do you tell 'em, "Why yes, I'd like to buy some food"? Or do you go to the hardware and tell the guy, all sweet and sunny, that yer after a tool? Or would you be more specifick, say . . . macaroni and a hammer, for instance? I think you would. Some carrots and a chisel, mebbe. Whatever. The details don't matter, but you see what I'm getting at?'

'You'd like me to be more specific?' I offered.

'Yes. That's exackly right. Specificks. They're very important – in all things, mind, not just yer armaments, y' hear me?'

'Yep. Absolutely. It's like this, see . . .' I hesitated, trying to think of a plausible story. 'I'm . . . I'm a private detective, just starting out, and I need a gun.' He lowered his puffy eyelids at me. 'A handgun,' I added quickly.

'And what calibre do you think you'd like?'

'What's calibre exactly?' I asked, clearing my throat.

'Calibre is how big a hole you want to make. You ever fired a gun before, Sonny?'

'Well, actually no, I haven't. But I think I'll have some lessons if you'd recommend it.'

'Oh, I'd recommend it. I'd definitely recommend it. Just so as you know which way to point the damned thing, pardon me Lord.' He quickly genuflected and crossed himself. I bowed my head – his piety was viral.

'So you're a detective are you?' he said after a time.

'Uh, yeah. Returning lost bibles is my specialty. It's darn hard –'

He slammed his huge palms onto the counter with a thunderous clap and bellowed, 'Don't you dare blaspheme in here, Boy!'

'Sorry. The fact is, Sir, I don't rightly know fer sure exackly as what sorta weapon I require,' I said, accidentally slipping into his crazy lexicon, like a long-lost son or something.

'Well, what yer gonna shoot, Boy?' he asked.

'I don't know . . . other people, I guess. But I'm not really sure. Fackt is, I'd rather scare 'em than shoot 'em.'

'Softie. Well, what you want is something big and mean looking – get their pants wet a-quick. How about a .36 Baretta Parabellum with the fearsome slide? Or a nice juicy Magnum?'

'What's that teeny job there?' I asked, pointing to a small black pistol lying on a piece of cloth. Compared to the shocking and serious-looking guns I'd seen so far, it looked like a tin toy.

'It's almost a hunnerd years old, Son. I got ten rounds. And that's prob'ly all there is left in the entire world. You'd be very foolish to purchase that weapon if you're serious about firearms.'

A few minutes later I walked out of the store, the proud new owner of a 1908 Belgian Bayard pistol. David refused to look at it or talk to me until I threw the bullets away.

11.19 a.m.

We've been on the road for about an hour – Sean and David, and David's best friend, Neil Young. We're driving through south-

177

west Texas, over dead snakes and porcupines, under an open sky and pairs of circling vultures. It's hot and still. The land is dish-flat and scrubby, old green and older brown, broken only by the odd windmill or butte far off in the distance. There are almost no cars on the road – just our little white shell, air-conditioned and soundproofed, travelling at Mach speed in the surrounding stillness.

As we cut north toward New Mexico, the land becomes even flatter (I'm not sure exactly how, but it does) and the dirt is now that desert red I've been so looking forward to. A roadrunner just ran across the road (to my eternal disappointment, it wasn't followed by a wily coyote strapped to some ACME product). The funny thing is, I'd pretty much forgotten that roadrunners are *actual* birds rather than smarmy cartoon characters with rubbery tongues. America is just full of surprises.

The radio says nothing. We're in the middle of nowhere.

Ballistics Report

Even though I am the registered owner of a registered firearm, I do not feel compelled to shoot anything.

For lunch I had a homemade burrito from a stand outside a shopping mall in Pecos, and in so doing contributed $1.50 to the Earl Bell Scholarship Fund. I don't know who the hell Earl Bell is, but I sure hope he gets a good education, because the burrito was delicious. As I was leaving, I heard a woman in an orange frightwig and matching pantsuit say to the ladies running the stall, 'Doing well today?'
'Yes we are, Pamela-May.'

'Well praise the Lord.'

'Praise the Lord,' they responded.

'Praise the Lord,' I said. 'Did He make these? No wonder they're so good.'

1.49 p.m.

We've veered left toward the Guadalupe mountains. There's a high-yellow dog sitting by the side of the road. Being a fool for canines, David insists we pull over and check it out. Sitting on its hindquarters, the dog turns its fine, sharp head toward us as we crouch toward it along the dusty highway.

'Hey fella, how's it going?' says David, rubbing his long-fingered hands together.

'It's going well today for me,' says the dog. 'The sun is high and shining. The animals are happy in themselves.'

Obviously I'm having some sort of whacked-out 'holy-burrito' vision. I turn to David, who is staring drop-mouthed at the dog. Neither of us can speak.

'And how are things with you?' asks the dog. 'Is your adventure going well?'

'Is that dog speaking?' I ask David. David says nothing. His mouth is opening and closing, but producing no sound.

'Don't be afraid. I am from the time when dogs could speak,' the dog says. It has a very pleasant voice. Kind of furry. 'You are in the ancient, sacred territory of the Anasazi.'

'Uh huh. And they are who, exactly?' I ask. Specificks.

'A long-vanished tribe that once lived in this world. When it was a world of good things.'

'What happened to them?'

'Other tribes. Spaniards,' the dog says dolefully. 'The conquistadors believed there was gold in seven mythical cities.'

'Gee, I'd've thought they'd gotten enough from the Aztecs.'

'Who are the Aztecs?' asks the dog, cocking its head.

'Another tribe, way further south. They're gone too,' I explained. 'We will all one day be gone. You, your mute friend . . . all of us. Only the desert is eternal.'

'Lucky desert. Lemme ask ya something. Which do you recommend – burial followed by rotting or a nice, quick cremation?'

'Either way you will return to the earth.'

'Is it possible to return to a hotel suite?'

'You are a foolish man. You should be more careful with what you say.'

'I know it Fido.' The dog bites me on the leg then disappears into the desert. I lead David back to the car, put him behind the wheel and tell him to drive. After a second, he shakes his head, mutt-like, and says, 'I just had the weirdest daydream.'

3.09 p.m. New Mexico

We are on the outskirts of a town called Artesia, which looks like it was built in the late 1950s and abandoned in the early 60s – probably because there was no McDonald's. I passed out for an hour from a headache, but then I got the hour back because we crossed into a new time zone.

1600 hours

Just drove past the turn-off to Roswell, site of the notorious alien landing and subsequent military/government cover-up of 1947. Apparently, a silver cigar-shaped spacecraft crashed in the desert, an event witnessed by numerous New Mexicans, a notoriously honest, reliable people. But the military swooped in, took

180

the aliens away to do experiments on them and told the New Mexicans that the crash never happened.

'Which poses an interesting question: if the alien visitors made it back to their own planet after their surgical ordeal, would anybody believe them if they said they'd been kidnapped and experimented on by aliens? I just bet they wouldn't.'

'That's a very interesting thought, Shane. Very interesting.'

'D'you really think so?'

'No, not really.'

Somewhere outside Alamogordo

We're cruising into what looks like the hills surrounding the 4077th M*A*S*H. Really. We're in the mid-70s TV Hollywood version of 1950s Korea.

'Lucky we came this way,' says David, becoming dangerously sarcastic. 'Or there wouldn't be nothing to see!!'

Then we saw a UFO, but I'm not going into that because people are just too damned sceptical.

Palookaville

We ate early at Shoney's Classic American Food. There was *nowhere* else except Dunkin' Donuts, Dairy Queen, Burger King, Taco Bell, Wendy's, KFC and Arby's. Shoney's offers 'homey' stuff like fresh spring shad, wild pigeon pie and Mom's Classic Meatloaf®. All of which adds up to the Classic American Heart Attack. The featured dessert was Oreo Cookie Pie. Mr Restraint didn't have that.

Once you've eaten there is *nothing* to do in Alamogordo – the town has one bar, which looks too scary to even drive past let alone sit in, and one 'country niteclub', which was full of counts. Besides that, we are beat from eight hours' driving – especially David, who actually did it. So here we lie, a TV remote bolted to the table between us, waiting for *Raging Bull* to come on cable and illuminate our lives with its meanness, violence and rage. It comes on, but is cut like **** for TV.

A few 'fuck'-less hours later, we go to sleep – sad, tired, bored and fat. A real pair of Jake La Mottas.

And what do I get? A one-way ticket to Palookaville. I was never no good after that night, Charlie. It was like a peak you reach and then it's downhill. It was you Charlie. You was my brother. You shoulda looked out for me a little bit. You shoulda looked out for me just a little bit. You shoulda taken care of me just a little bit. Instead of making me take them dives for the short-end money. You don't understand. I coulda had class, I coulda been a contender. I coulda been somebody, instead of a bum, which is what I am. Let's face it, it was you Charlie. It was you . . .'

Robert De Niro pretending to be Jake La Motta,
who is pretending to be Marlon Brando pretending
to be a fictional character named Terry Malloy

Home on the Range. Or are they? Rated Silver K.

The smelling salts of our own desperate effluvia – a sharp concoction of fatigue and ennui – bring us round at 9 a.m. and we set about our morning ritual. David showers; I shower. We choose some ridiculously wrinkled fresh clothes to wear, put the 'maxi bar' booze back in the cooler, zip our packs, carry all the stuff out to Leon the Neon, check out of the motel and leave town, never to return. But just before we depart, I jump out of the car.

'Sorry, David,' I say, running back to our room. 'Left something behind.' He looks kind of bitter, but I have to do it. I'm only gone a few minutes.

YOU CANT HAVE GOD'S BEST WITHOUT GOD

10.30 a.m.

We just drove into the White Sands National Monument/Missile Testing Range and decided that we would not pay five dollars to see some white sand dunes and possibly be hit by an unscheduled Tomahawk. Besides, the white sand we've seen so far looks just like the back beach at Gunnamatta, according to Surfer Dave. The expansive silence of the desert seeps into the car. David tells me to turn on the radio, that the quiet is too loud for him. I press the button and hear the disc jockey saying, '. . . that was the brand-new number two spot on the country hit parade, "Them Ole Nashville Blues" by Fat Bob and the Heavy Experience. I just lerve it!'
Fat Bob, you bastard!

11.14 a.m.

Crossed the San Andreas mountains and shot through a tiny town of Catholic and Baptist churches called Organ. Now we're heading into Las Cruces: lots of auto-parts stores, the Post 6917 American Legion Bingo Hall, a big water tank with a garish painting of the *Challenger* crew on its side, a flea market and several churches. Behind the town, the sharp peaks and ridges of the San Andreas mountains look quite lovely. The reason I know this is because we've turned around and are headed back toward the flea market.

12.16 p.m.

Big Daddy's flea market was full of crap, and therefore pretty good. We both bought plenty of spearmint-coloured shirt-shaped polyester for only a few bucks apiece. There were lots of Mexicans in cowboy hats from whom I was careful not to steal any clothing. I ate a chorizo sausage and egg burrito. It was called 'the breakfast burrito'. And it was 'not very nice'.

'Why do you keep eating that crap?' David asks, peeling an orange.

'I can't help myself with American food,' I tell him, well aware that burritos are Mexican, but that around here the difference is negligible. 'It's so . . . me.'

'You keep on eating like that and there's gonna be *two* of you by the time we leave.'

4.11 p.m.

My feeling is that while it is extraordinarily beautiful, New Mexico is pretty much just a desert full of canyons and mountain ranges. And you get bored with that after a couple of days, so it's just as well there are plenty of missile testing grounds to liven things up – including the daddy of 'em all, good old Trinity, where they tested the first nuclear bomb. Day One, Ground Zero, 'My God, what have we done?' and all that. The fact that they chose this area for those kinds of stunts says more about New Mexico than I can.

Raging Bull-session

'David, I want to ask you something.'

'Feel free.'

'Do you look out for me a little bit? Just a little bit?'

'What?'

'Like a brother, do you take care of me just a little bit?'

'Not particularly, no.'

'Would you if I called you Charlie?'

'No.'

'What I mean is, if you saw me heading for trouble, a real bad situation, would you try and help me? Look out for me?'

'Well, I feel that you're adult enough to be responsible for your own actions, Seanette. But if I thought that you were being especially stupid or crazy, I'd do something about it. I'd look out for you.'

'Would you make me take dives for the short-end money?'

'You don't understand, you got no class. You ain't a contender.'

'But if I was?'

'You ain't.'

'Well, it's your fault, Charlie. You was my brother.'

'Don't call me Charlie.'

Ballistics Report

I still don't have the urge to let off a few rounds of Belgian gunfire at any small animals or unmoving cacti. I tell David this good news, but he still doesn't want to talk about the gun. Some brother.

Highway 60. A straight black stripe running along the basin below the Manzano mountains. Scattered on either side are caravans surrounded by four or five rusted cars or school buses. I saw a kid with a bow and arrow sitting forlornly outside a caravan. The sight was depressing as hell. There are some nice purple and yellow wildflowers around here, though; and maybe, as he gets older, they'll cheer the little feller up. Yeah, and maybe he'll open a florist in nearby Bernardo (population: 65).

We're heading for a place called Mountainair, which, if nothing else, at least sounds nice. But that could be a bad thing. I mean, Truth or Consequences was named after a TV quiz show, so Mountainair could be named in honour of a long-distance running shoe. There could be no mountain there at all. Maybe not even any air.

Somewhere in Between

I feel strangely happy despite the desolation that surrounds us. I feel that way because I'm listening to the Undisputed Truth and it reminds me of being at MoMA. I didn't particularly enjoy the experience at the time, but I now look back on it with great fondness. We have stopped to look at the ruins of an eighteenth-century pueblo mission somewhere in between Bernardo and Mountainair. It is warm and bright, and apart from the music in my head, quiet. We are alone. It's not particularly exciting, but I realise that soon, somewhere in the future, I will look back on this warm, bright and silent moment with pleasure.

Having abandoned our plans to stay in any small towns because of their lack of motels (Mountainair) or their sheer dumpiness (Mountainair) or both (Mountainair), we're about a half-hour outside Santa Fe. The sun is setting over an endless sea of brown grass that seems to stretch as far as Lincoln County – a large, barren area in which Billy the Kid spent a great deal of time dispensing his unique brand of left-handed mayhem.

A Short History of Billy the Kid

17 September 1859 – born Henry McCarty in New York. 1873 – moves to Santa Fe. Changes name to Henry Antrim. 1876 – arrested. Escapes jail and flees to Mexico. Changes name to Kid Antrim. 1877 – returns to New Mexico. Shoots and kills a blacksmith. Changes name to Billy Antrim. Joins posse called 'The Regulators'. Shoots three more people. 1878 – changes name to William Bonney. Gets shot in leg. Steals some horses. Shoots corrupt Sheriff Brady. Moves to Fort Sumner, New Mexico. Changes name to Billy Bonney. 1880 – steals some cows. Kills a guy in a bar. Changes name to Billy the Kid. 1881 – shoots another blacksmith. Pursued, captured and jailed in Lincoln, New Mexico, by friend Sheriff Pat Garrett. Shoots two deputies and escapes to Fort Sumner. 14 July 1881 – is shot and killed by ex-friend Pat Garrett. Unable to change name again, is forever known as Billy the Kid.

7.15 p.m. Santa Fe

Our motel room is sad and dumpy, yet quite expensive ($87.50); it stinks a bit and has the usual micro-tolerance shower tap deal (pull out delicately and nudge slightly to the left using a gentle tapping motion) and beautiful fire-retardant carpet. The TV remote control is bolted to a metal swiveller between the beds.

'Why would anyone want to steal a remote control?' asks David, modelling one of his flea-market shirts, a caramel and orange three-button job with an enormous, stiff collar.

'Beats me,' I say in the same shirt, only green.

On a Balcony Downtown

We're watching the local 'errant youth' being rounded up by

some cops in a patrol car straight out of 'Policewoman'. We're also talking about marriage (who's doing it, who's undoing it) and related subjects (having children, mowing the lawn, beer, etc).

'Do you think you'll ever get married, David?'

'Hard to say. Probably, but I'm not in any hurry.'

'The thing I'm most reluctant about is the invitations. Exactly who do you invite to the great event?'

'Yeah, it's like the ultimate band set list.'

'And your relatives are the hits from twenty years ago.'

. . .

A waiter appears on the balcony and asks, in the distinctive Santa Fe drawl, 'You . . . guys . . . want . . . a . . . nother . . . drink . . . ?'

This is our first exposure to the Santa Fe accent . . . a hot and dopey hybrid . . . of slow Mexican siesta . . . and California surfer/doper . . . Everybody around . . . here talks like . . . that . . . It's incredible . . . like they're all . . . doing comic . . . impressions . . . of each other . . . except it's like . . . real, bro . . . Really . . . real . . . y'know?

Back at the motel, David switches on Letterman and takes notes. With some alarm, I realise that Letterman has no sidekick.

The Air Up There. **A miracle in Santa Fe. Guest appearance by Robert Stack. Rated O$_2$.**

Just before we leave the motel, I jump out of the car. 'Sorry, Dave, I left something in the room.' He looks kind of pissed off, but it has to be done. I whip back a few seconds later. 'Let's go already.'

We've moved to a new place – the legendary lost Hotel Eldorado. I am already in love with it because it supplies oxygen to its air-depleted guests – for free! – as there's lots of headaches and fainting and nausea going on up here because of the thin air. It's a barrel of laughs, I can tell you. I'm *almost* looking forward to today's instalment of headache agony so I can see whether that quack in San Antone was right about the benefits of snorting oxygen.

Art/History

Santa Fe was founded in 1609 by Pedro de Peralta (Spanish explorer/skateboarder), which makes it one of the oldest cities in the US. Like most old cities, Santa Fe has a great many museums devoted to its history. And since much of Santa Fe's history centres around art, there are a great many museum/galleries here. And since everybody's gotta make a buck or two, most of them are really museum/gallery/gift shops.

We hit a few of these joints. At the American Indian Art Gallery there was some digital photo art by Buffy Sainte-Marie. She wrote 'Up Where We Belong' (indeed she won an Oscar® for it) so it was hard for me to like her stuff, but I tried to be an officer and a gentleman about it. The thing about places of great natural beauty is that they always seem to attract artists of great natural lack of talent.

'What do you know about the so-called Santa Fe style of design?' I asked David, keen for an aesthete's penetrating insight.

'Well, it's pretty rude – a lot of pinks and pastels and Aztec shapes. Basically a cross between Memphis and Native American, with a bit of 80s LA thrown in. Very popular with creative

189

directors of advertising agencies a few years ago. So quite dated and tasteless.'

'Any thoughts on Georgia O'Keeffe?'

'Her early stuff reminds me of the doodlings that teenage girls do with coloured pencils while they're on the telephone discussing horoscopes and pop stars.'

'I'd quite like to see that.'

'No you wouldn't.'

We did anyway and he was right – I didn't.

After that we visited something I definitely *did* want to see: the Loretto Chapel, which has been featured in one of my very favourite TV shows, 'Unsolved Mysteries', hosted by the great, if barely alive, Robert Stack. The chapel is home to the famous Miraculous Staircase, completed in 1878 after the nuns had spent a week praying to the patron saint of stairs. A mysterious stranger built the engineering marvel – it has no central or side supports, so it really should collapse (or at least faint from the thin air) – and then disappeared without asking for payment or health benefits. Some think the stranger may even have been Jesus C. Himself. Well, Robert Stack does. I'm agnostic when it comes to miraculous carpentry. It's a nice staircase, but you're not allowed on it in case it crumbles and becomes non-miraculous.

There was an anti-nuclear demonstration in Santa Fe's plaza park, which we watched for a while. It would've been more significant if they'd demonstrated at Los Alamos, half an hour away. When I told them, they cried as one, 'My . . . God . . . what . . . have . . . we . . . done?'

But . . . this . . . is a . . . very . . . small cup.
I know it's . . . a . . . small . . . cup. I don't want her . . . to drink . . . so
much. I'm . . . trying . . . to get her down to . . . three . . . pees . . . a . . . day.
White male and female demonstrators, approx. 40, with child,
approx. 2 (silent)

The Santa Fe skyline is beautiful – because there isn't one. The building code won't allow anything higher than five storeys, which is very smart. Looking out over the hotel balcony toward the hills in the east, I can see dozens and dozens of low adobe houses nestled amongst the trees on the mountainside, the setting sun lighting the terracotta walls. Oh yes, it's very beautiful. Lots of Hollywood types have houses here, so it has to be.

After the sunset we wandered around downtown looking for laughs. It was Monday night so there were barely sniggers. Most of the bars were either closed or populated by a few 'sports fans' drinking Buds and telling the NFL players on TV what to do. 'Arm out, Reichenbacher, you fucking pansy!! Put your arm *out*!!'

Eventually (well, it was only 8 p.m., but it *felt* like eventually), we found a scummy, subterranean bar/pool hall with a jukebox screaming out late Stones and the late Hendrix at the fearsome collection of skinheads and wife-beaters hunched around the felt. We'd shot only four games, David whipping me soundly every time, when I felt a headache coming on. I ran back to the hotel and asked for some oxygen to be sent up to our room. It was immediately delivered by an absurdly fat man called Leo, who warned me that fire and oxygen are not friends before looping a tube over my ears and up my nose. Being careful not to light a cigarette, I sat on the bed and breathed deeply for a couple of minutes. And then, Holy Miracle, the pain faded. I felt like bawling with joy and relief, but merely hugged the tank to my chest, stroked it and called it sweet names ('Oxy', 'O. T.', 'Wonderdrug', etc) before falling asleep still plugged in.

White Lightning. **A good cast makes this drive-in stock entertaining but like most of Burt Reynolds' car films it is gimmicky and predictable. Rated V8.**

11.20 a.m.

We're back on the road, with a 400-mile trip ahead of us, and have just discovered that the brakes don't work properly. This is extremely alarming, as my feeling is that effective brakes are a near-essential part of the driving process. There's a strange puffing noise whenever David plants his foot on the brake pedal, as though his sneaker is panting. It's not a good sound.

SMOKING DEATHS THIS YEAR: 307,396 AND COUNTING

Well, I hate to rain on your scary statistical parade, Mr Sign, but in a country of 255 million people (and counting), that's a pretty small percentage.

The spectacular, awesome and breathtaking buttes around here look raw and exposed, like the inside of an open-cut mine. The odd thing is there are dozens of boulders suspended midway down the cliffsides, and yet at the foot of these cliffs are caravans, huts and adobe abodes. What if the boulders start to tumble? Squash-a-rama, that's what.

Impossibly long, thick and puffy vapour trails from air force jets intersect the clouds – a rigid and unnatural design element in an otherwise random sky. Perhaps a metaphor for David and me traversing the flat, straight highways down here on the ground. 'Oh *please* . . .' says David.

'Do you think I need another haircut yet?' I ask him, trying to quickly put the metaphor behind us.

Twenty-six miles later he has given the question its due weight and answers, 'No.'

This is how conversation in the desert goes.

Just passed a truck with a realistic rubber foot poking out of the driver's door. A truly ripe gag. David is getting into some sort of *Duel* situation with another big truck. This is not good. Especially without brakes and neither of us being Dennis Weaver.

DAIRY QUEEN BRAZIER – WE SELL FIREWORKS!

How can they sell fireworks at a takeaway food store? And what *is* that Brazier thing? We still haven't lit so much as a teeny little penny banger from our Tennessee haul, because David wants to find the mythical 'perfect spot'. We're in the desert, for God's sake. Who's gonna see? But, as usual, he's right – even though this is an official desert, there's still plenty of traffic and people and water and stuff. When, oh when, will we have some big laughs with small explosives?

The clouds are too low. They're making me hunch with claustrophobia. When will all this natural spectacularity end? We recently saw a huge, full-colour billboard for Sizzler – I always find that a forty-foot picture of a big pink steak breaks up the environment nicely.

Ballistics Report

Just had my first twinge of desire to shoot something (see above).

2.48 p.m. Arizona

We've crossed another border. Where New Mexico was brown, orange and earthy, the 'Zona seems to be grey, green and dirty. We passed a dead coyote, too. It was quite sad – the sight, I mean, not the coyote. The coyote was dead. Yeah, that's right, you heard me, *dead!*

'When do you think I *will* be ready for another haircut?' I ask.

3.48 p.m.

A few moments ago, we left the Painted Desert. It was pink and sandy and went quite well with my pastel orange shirt. Now we're driving through the Petrified Forest which doesn't co-ordinate with anything I'm wearing. I enjoyed experiencing the petrification up close. From a distance the 'forest' looks like chunks of wood, but when you touch them you realise they've turned to a kind of marbled stone. It's amazing! What's more amazing is that just about everybody in the world already knew about it except me.

'In about three weeks,' he answers.

Holy Fork!

I'd been worrying that the mud on the floor of the car might lose us our deposit, but I'm not too concerned about that any more. Because only seconds ago the car got hit by lightning: an enormous bang and brightness which stabbed out of the heavens

194

to strike us. There's a smoking black hole the size of a record in the roof; it stinks, and tons of rain and spray from other cars is getting in.

'D'you think it's a sign?' I ask David, my voice quavering.

'If it is, it's not a good one.'

'I'm impressed that you didn't lose control of the car.'

'I'm a professional, Sean.' He pulls over to the side of the road and we get out to have a look. The roof is slightly buckled and the paint around the hole has turned the colour of burned butter.

6.06 p.m.

David revived me and somehow dragged me back into the car after I fainted. There's gravel in my forehead.

I can't believe I actually fainted. I feel like a Beatles fan.

Up ahead, Flagstaff sits at the base of a grey-blue mountain whose peak is covered by a cloud, like some corny picture on a bottle of cheap wine. Boy, will we be tired, cold and wet by the time we get there.

Closer now, and there's another big mountain – mostly smooth, brownish rock with tufts and clumps of trees here and there. It looks like it's having chemotherapy. Poor mountain.

10.10 p.m. Flagstaff

We ate in a beer-barn called Bun Huggers, a name I found most unappetising, indeed slightly repellent. Nevertheless, they served fabulous hamburgers which were perfect for our faded hangovers. David drank a Coors Lite while I had a root beer. He's tough; I'm weak. That's our story. While we ate, David read out a news item from the *Arizona Republic* about a sixteen-year-old

195

schoolboy who'd been seduced by his female teacher. Now the boy is suing her.

'So the ungrateful little bastard is ruining the chances of every other kid in the country,' he editorialised scornfully.

'Do you think we've been spared?' I asked.

'Spared what? Sex with schoolteachers?'

'Our lives. We could've been killed by that lightning today, but we're still here. Maybe we've been spared for a special purpose. A sacred mission or something.'

'The only mission we have is to get to the other side of this country in one piece. And that's going to be hard enough.'

Back at the hotel we watched a documentary on all-American killer Charles Whitman, the Austin university shooter. This is what he took up with him on that day in 1966 when he shot thirteen people dead from the top of a tower: a knife, a machete, a hatchet, three rifles, two pistols, a sawn-off shotgun, 700 rounds of ammunition, an alarm clock, some deodorant, a roll of pink toilet paper, a family-sized can of Spam and a jar of fruit cocktail.

The devil is in the details.

Grand Central Canyon. **Cameos from the Brady Bunch, Ernest Hemingway, Bill Haley and the Comets, and Clu Gallagher. Rated G.**

12.05 p.m.

In Albertson's Pharmacy and Food Barn I saw a woman buying a quarter ton of mince and some hair curlers. A big barbecue and she wanted to look pretty. The pharmacy wouldn't sell me any products containing codeine without a prescription. In America, you can buy a machine gun but not decent headache relief.

'This country wants to inflict pain, not cure it,' says David.

I pat the gun in my pocket and consider inflicting a permanent cure on myself.

A small strip of the legendary, literary, musical, historical, numerical Route 66 runs through Flagstaff. And boy, they sure don't let you forget it: the Route 66 Hotel, the Route 66 Motel, the Route 66 Hotel/Motel, the Route 66 diner, bar, restaurant, bowling alley, auto-repair shop, hardware store, bakery. There's even a Route 66 Record Store which only sells records that mention Route 66! Strangely, though, I'm not getting my kicks off it.

'Did you know,' David asks, and I'm already sure I do not, 'that "Route 66" was written by Bobby Troup?'

'The same Bobby Troup who showed up on the TV show "Emergency" in the 1970s?' I ask.

'That's the one.'

'Me and my sisters once saw Randolph Mantooth from "Emergency" in a hotel in San Francisco. He was the first famous person we'd ever met. The bastard wouldn't give us an autograph.'

'He'd give you one now, though.'

'Now that nobody knows who the hell he is.'

'That anecdote needs work, by the way,' David advises me. 'There's no closure or punchline.'

'How's this?' I ask. 'Get fucked.'

On Our Way In

We've patched up the lightning hole with industrial packing tape, and now I'm busy looking through the car-hire insurance policy to see if there's an Acts of God (or gods – it could've been Thor) clause that might cover the damage. The brakes are still busted and the car smells of cigarettes and abandoned medicinal products. We're on our way to the Grand Canyon – one of America's biggest and best national icons. I hope I like it.

We're in gorge and canyon country. They're all over the place – rocks, red dirt and gaping holes. I'm trying not to look at anything because I don't want to gorge on gorges until we get to the Big One. There are also lots of Indian roadside 'trading posts' selling crafts, pottery, rugs, etc. As part of their strange sales pitch, these depressing little joints fly the flags of other countries, presumably in the hope that Joe (or Joachim) Tourist will be so overcome by the sight of his country's colours, he'll make up for being away from it by spending lots of money somewhere else. Flapping urgently in the brisk desert wind are Germany, Italy, France, Belgium, Ireland, England, Canada and New Zealand. That's right, *New Zealand!* But nowhere have we seen the Australian flag. And we're not buying a bloody thing until we do. Strewth!

Q: What's white, pink, yellow, red and bright green?
A: The hot dog I just ate. (Bun, dog, mustard, catsup and relish.) It was delicious, and quite frankly I enjoyed it rather more than my first glimpse of the Grand Canyon which immediately preceded it. Will I be allowed back in America after saying that?

We pulled over for a look at a different angle of the GC. Despite our being surrounded by noisy German tourists, the view was spectacular, awesome, breathtaking, etc. We wondered if the canyon had ever been a river. Probably, we figured.

'And I reckon they could get other stuff easily as good as this if they drained a couple of seas,' says Dave 'Natural Wonders' O'Brien.

'Who is "they"?' I ask.

'The people in charge.'

'Of what?'

'Everything.'

We've been goofing around the Grand Canyon National Park for a while now – a couple of nature walks, more rim-viewing of the depths and weaving through the hundreds of open-mouthed tourists, little oral canyons in every face. It's quite good and there's a real sense of history about the place too. I keep thinking I'm in 1950s America – the pine forests, the neat little trails, the rangers in their cornball ranger hats. It's straight out of Frontierland in the Wonderful World of Disney.

On Our Way Out

I wish it had been just me and David and some mules, nobody else. Well, except for the hot dog people who do such a wonderful job. And the Bradys. I liked it when the Bradys went to the GC in that legendary three-parter, even though they took that mugging bonehead Alice with them.

'Hey, David,' I say as we pass the Coconino Plateau, heading south toward Red Lake. 'Did you ever notice that in the credit sequence of "The Brady Bunch" they're not just looking at each other at random? They look at one another and then away from each other at choreographed points. All except Jan, who continues staring at Carol long after her mom's moved on down to

199

Cindy. That's typical Jan, if you ask me.'

'Who's asking? What is this, one of those meaningless Tarantino conversations?'

'Don't give me Tarantino, David. This is not mere maundering. This is very pertinent. *The Bradys* went to the Grand Canyon. *We* went to the Grand Canyon. If anything, it's *too* real.'

'It's just television.'

'Just television! How can you say something like that? Where did you first *see* the Grand Canyon? Real life or television? Television, that's where. And which gave you the better view? Television. It's how we understand the world. So quit knocking it.'

'I'm not knocking it. I just prefer the real world. For example, last year I was at a cocktail party mixing up something disgusting with eggs and tequila and tomato juice when in walked the lead singer of the Hoodoo Gurus. We chatted about how horrible the drink was and then he made a really nice one with cranberry juice and vodka . . .'

We drive past a motel whose rooms are individual concrete tepees. TELL YOUR FRIENDS YOU SLEPT IN A TEPEE, a sign urges. 'No,' I say under my breath. Further down the road is a brightly coloured concrete motel representation of Bedrock from 'The Flintstones'. Happily, TV's influence is everywhere. Even when it's not on.

'Anyway,' David continues after photographing the motels, 'it occurred to me halfway through our cocktail chat that I should shake this guy's hand.'

'Why?'

'Because I realised that he knew the band's guitarist, Brad Shepherd. And Brad used to go out with Susan Olsen, the person Cindy Brady grew up to be. So there's my real-life Brady Bunch adventure.'

It's a fine story, but I think 'adventure' might be a little strong.

5.23 p.m.

I'm talking to Sally from a public phone next to a pawn shop in a small Route 66 town called Williams (bypassed by the Interstate in 1987). There's a drink-vending machine by the phone and while I'm asking her whether our apartment has been burgled or flooded, I put in 50¢ for a root beer. The can won't drop, so I jiggle the coin return lever and press a few buttons, which yield nothing more than noise. Then this guy emerges from the pawn shop, threading a path between all the crap he's got for sale on his porch. Sally's telling me about the terrific hangover she's got and I'm just staring at this grey-bearded guy wearing jeans and a jacket and boots. He's a reedy fella around fifty. He nods at me and my eyes drop to his hips: he's also wearing a holster with a Colt .45 in it.

'What didja want?'

'Um, a root beer please,' I say very politely, but he pulls out the gun anyway. Back in Australia, Sally is still talking. I begin to quiver.

Dead on target, he smacks the root beer light with the butt of the gun, the can drops, he hands it to me, reholsters his gun and walks away.

'A cowboy just gave me a beer,' I tell Sally shakily.

WILLIAMS TRADING POST – BEER, WINE, HAY

The I-40. Between Williams and Seligman

It's very mountainous around here. Sharp, rocky peaks and dips everywhere. No cactus. No big red rocks balanced on top of other big red rocks. No mesas or buttes. None of the Arizona clichés: just rocks and dirt. The desert traffic is trucks, pick-ups and motor homes. The occasional old vehicle loaded with tools and spare tyres and water bags and washtubs and chickens and mattresses, a bunch of children and grandparents hanging off the side, Hank Fonda at the wheel looking grim, gaunt and determined. There are no cars except for our busted little Neon. And nobody seems to care any more that we're from Maine.

'We're *not* from Maine,' David reminds me.

Completely Routed

We're sitting on our beds describing our room at the Historic Motel 66 in Seligman (bypassed by the Interstate in 1978). 'Dark, and yet strangely dismal,' I say.

'Yes, it's horrible, and yet charmless,' suggests David.

'I find it revolting, but nonetheless somehow disgusting. Rude, and yet foul.'

'It stinks, but retains a certain malodorousness. Small, and yet tiny.'

Sixty-seven dollars a night, and yet way over-priced.

According to the plaques on various doors, famous people who have slept at the Historic Motel 66 ('On historically historic Route 66') include the Comets (as in Bill Haley and the; presumably Bill himself was at the Seligman Hilton), Clu Gallagher and the guy who played Timmy in the last series of 'Lassie'. There was as yet no name on our door.

Diner for Two

Pasted to a window outside the diner is a hand-written sign spattered with random capitals and bizarre punctuation: 'What was the Last Miracle Jesus, performed before He was crucified! If you can, quote the scripture; you will get a free taco$$!' Religion and food: America's favourite convergence. I know the answer, but don't want to let on in case anybody gets the wrong impression about me. I'm not in the mood for a taco anyway. I have bigger plans for dinner.

The waitresses are beehive-haired twins, Delia (blonde) and Ada (brunette). Each lets out a short gasp whenever they catch a glimpse of the other – as though she were surprised to see herself. David has fricasseed jackrabbit ears with a side order of rattle-snake hips while I realise a life-long culinary dream – eating a chicken fried steak in a roadside diner, Hemingway style. CFS is a piece of thin steak coated in chicken-style batter, then deep fried for a couple of hours. It comes out crunchy as hell and is almost inedible except to the most committed diner diner or Hemingway fan. It's surrounded by mashed potato and coated in a disquietingly white 'country' gravy and black beans. It'd be ideal for a hangover, but unfortunately I don't have one; perhaps I'll mail it to Sally. I follow the CFS with a Tootsie Roll. A classic American dinner and dessert: unhealthy, yet fattening and dangerous.

Well I'll be Goddamned

Back at the motel, I paid a visit to the manageress to tell her that David and I were pretty big television stars back in Australia, and that she should put our names on our door. That other Australians would be thrilled.

'Well, I guess you'd better come in fer a minnit,' she said wearily, evidently having been through this routine many times before.

Even her stringy yellow hair looked tired, right down to the dark roots. The place smelled like dinner time at an old people's home.

'D'you mind if I smoke?' I asked, taking out a pack of Virginia Slims.

'Yes, I goddam well do. Why do you want to burn my sorry-assed house down for anyway?'

I put the pack away, red-faced.

She sighed. 'Name's Violet, what's yours?'

I swallowed dryly and croaked, 'Sean.'

'I'm in the process of becoming a divorcee. I get a little crazy when I remember that goddamned fucking dried-up come stain I was married to. Bastard took off with the third sister of those two dopey bitches at the diner. Her and her goddam big hair and double D cup. Jesus, I want a drink. You want a drink? Whadja say yer name was?'

Before I could answer, she'd poured a couple of greenish-black drinks. I took a sip and nearly fell off the chair. I winced and thought I heard her mutter 'Pussy' bitterly under her breath.

'Well, here's to you,' she said. 'You dumb asshole, stopping in this fucking dump on the way to fuck knows where. Cheers!' She drank half her drink in a single gulp. 'Whadja say your name was again?'

'Sean.'

'Right, whatever. What's yer TV show about?'

I forced myself to take another sip of warm hemlock. 'Ummm. It's . . . it's about these two guys who . . . get into all sorts of crazy . . . scrapes. Sometimes they . . . errr . . . solve mysteries.'

Violet finished the rest of her drink. 'Sounds fucking wonderful,' she said. 'What's it called?'

'The . . . aahhh . . . "Sean and David's Crazy . . . ness". It's very popular with the younger audience. Anyway, I thought I'd just let you know who we were so if you wanted to put our names up . . . I guess I'll get going now. Thanks for the drink and . . . I hope the divorce goes all right.'

She stared at me long and hard, a deadening look that made me feel uncomfortable, strangely watery. 'You ain't off TV at all, are you? I can tell by your dull teeth.'

'Well . . . no.'

'So what's with you coming in here and runnin' this line at me, you little shitheel? You a professional smartass, or what? Lemme tell you somethin', Shane. If I had a gun I'd blow one of your little balls off, you know that? Your left one probably. How would you like that? That'd be a story you could tell people, and at least it'd be true. How'd you like to have only one nut?'

I took a deep breath. 'Well, as a matter of fact, I *do* have only one testicle. I was in an industrial accident when I was seventeen, and it got caught in a leather stamping press. We manufactured . . . umm . . . briefcases. I've got one real one and one aluminium job.'

'Well, I'll be goddamned. Pull down them pants and lemme see.'
I was in real trouble now . . .

Back in our room David was sitting in front of the TV, his bearded mouth agape, a slender finger pointed at the screen. 'This woman thinks that her daughter is an alien sent here to kill her,' he said. 'She really believes it. What is up with people in this whacked-out country?'

What could I say?

***Viva Las Vegas*.** **Sean and David try to weasel in on what's left of the Rat Pack. Co-starring Gabe Kaplan as Frank Sinatra. Rated ◯◯◯ .**

<u>12.23 p.m.</u>

Minutes before we stop at the Hoover Dam on the Arizona/ Nevada border, a rock thrown up by a sudden dust storm cracks my side of the windscreen. This car is finished.

The dam is amazingly large and impressive and has some brilliant sculptures outside the administration buildings. Apparently, it's traditional for the recently divorced to come here and toss their wedding rings into the water. I wish I'd brought some scuba gear.

The region is altogether valueless. After entering it, there is nothing to do but leave.

Lt Edward Beale, Congress report on Arizona, 1858

<u>2.30 p.m. Nevada</u>

We're in Las Vegas. Here's how I know – the cashier who relieved me of $15 for a sandwich and fries is named Katherine String. You couldn't get a job doing *anything, anywhere* in the world except Las Vegas with a name like that. City codes just wouldn't allow it.

I pretty much hate the place already. It's as I expected it to be, only much, much worse. We're staying at one of the new 'family-oriented' hotels called Treasure Island. It has 2400 rooms and no cable because you're not supposed to want to sit in your room watching TV while there's all that fun and money to be had down in the guts of the casino. Thirty-one storeys below me is a gargantuan lake with a pirate ship on it. Several hundred people are crowded along the deck that leads from the sidewalk, over the lake and, surprisingly, straight into the casino. Several hundred money-widened eyes staring at the ship, waiting for it to do something. Like sink.

The worst thing about all this is I'd only have to win about twenty bucks for me to be absolutely in love with Las Vegas. *That's* the kind of absurd hypocrite I am.

4.10 p.m.

The pirate panto in the pool is over now and I must say it looked quite spectacular, awesome, breathtaking, etc, even from up here in the Condescension Suite. The pirates beat the hell out of the navy, which is probably some none-too-subtle metaphor for Joe Gambler striking it rich in the shark-infested waters of Vegas and sticking it to the government by quitting his job. Maybe. I could be reading too much into it.

Thanks for calling the MGM Grand and you have a wonderfully lucky day. How may I help you?
                              Female telephone operator, age unknown

I ask David if the window in our room opens. 'Not in a town like Vegas, Seanie.'
'Don't start that "Seanie" business again, I'm depressed enough as it is.'
He points out a newsreader on network TV called Rikki Cheese. That cheers me up a little. Katherine String and Rikki Cheese, proud daughters of Sin City.

Later on tonight we're having drinks with Sammy, Dean, Peter, Frank and someone called Joey Bishop – they seem like guys who know how to have fun. And the dolls they hang out with – hubba hubba! *They are built!*

GAMBLING PROBLEM? CALL 1-800 LOSER

GAMBLING PROBLEM? CALL 1-800 LOAN YES

A Night on the Town on the Make

We joined the mass of neon-stunned punters snaking in and out of the dopey, low-rent joints on the 'wrong side of the street', and settled on a particularly pathetic place called Casino Royale. While drinking ten-cent beers and waiting for an opening at a low-stakes table, I looked in vain for smooth types in tuxedos clutching highballs and cracking wise with the waitresses or glamorous dames with low-cut dresses and lower morals. But the Royale was not about style, good times and the spirit of sophisticated libertinism. It was about one thing only: losing your money.

Our chance came at last. Blackjack, dollar minimum, five hundred maximum. Keeping a fifty in reserve, I cashed a C-note and sat next to Donny the ex-navy torpedo operator and his girlfriend the denture maker with the crystal meth problem. They were very helpful when it came to advising me on my many blunders. ('You always double down on eleven.' 'Always?' '*Always.*') A real couple of swingers.

We were joined by Trisha, Tracey and Trudy from Oklahoma City, who were here on a girls' weekend. They couldn't abide foul language so I started swearing my head off until a pit boss came over and told me to 'Cool it, Sonny.'

Trisha said, 'We're staying at the Shamrock. They have a spinning tam o'shanter out front. Don't you think it should be called the Tam O'Shanter? What's a shamrock, anyway?'

I suggested that maybe it *was* called the Tam O'Shanter and it was a spinning shamrock out front. She shrugged her shoulders and flicked a chip onto the table. 'I could care less anyway.'

Trudy said, 'They bombed my city, you know that? I *knew* some people who worked in that building.' She was sniffling and teary. 'Have they ever bombed where you live?'

'As a matter of fact they have. Mostly in the 80s. The police headquarters, an embassy and an apartment block. I was within a couple of blocks every time.' I really was.

'Were people killed?'

'Yes. And a woman lost her feet in the apartment explosion.' She really did.

David was shaking his head at Tracey who kept asking, 'Do you want to come disco dancing with me?'

'I don't dance,' he said. He was lying; I've seen him dance, and now that he's learnt the macarena he's quite a show-off.

Tracey turned to Donny's girlfriend. 'Will you come disco dancing with me?' *Disco dancing.* The kid was crazy.

David asked Donny what it was like to operate a torpedo.

'Serious, man,' he replied, clenching and unclenching his fist as he waited for his second card.

'Let's get married while we're here, huh Don? It's a tradition,' Donny's girlfriend said, sitting on seventeen. 'You guys can all come.' She smiled at us all and looked like she was going to cry. 'Can we Donny?'

Donny said 'Maybe' in a way that meant 'No'. Then he bust. Twenty-four.

'Any of you girls wanna get married tomorrow?' David asked Trudy, Trisha and Tracey.

'We *are* married,' they all said quickly, in a tone which suggested they were both angry and proud. They held up three ring fingers and waggled them at David. 'See?'

'To Trevor, Troy and Tristram,' I said, doubling down on eleven.

'To Larry, Harry and Garry,' David said. Sixteen. His third card was a four of hearts.

'To CJ, DJ and PJ,' Donny's girlfriend giggled.

'No. To two Franks and a Freddy,' the Ts said snootily. All three of them had blackjack.

By 1 a.m. everybody was drunk. Especially David, whose eyes were slitted and red. He was placing very large bets and producing a strange hissing noise whenever he got a bad card. Or a good card. The Drunken Snake Boy seemed to be enjoying himself. I like that about David, he has a vice streak a mile wide. Donny kept saying, 'For the love of everything that is holy,' or moaning 'Oh, the humanity,' every time he got bad cards. I found it quite amusing. The first ten times. It paled around two-thirty in the morning. Trudishey giggled every time. Boy, were those girls married.

By about 3 a.m. the pointlessness of it all, the humanity and the eight hours of free booze on an empty stomach hit me like a wall to the forehead. This was going precisely nowhere: Trisha, Tracey and Trudy looked and sounded like one person in three pastel blouses; Donny's girlfriend kept falling asleep in her chair; Donny kept nudging her and saying it was 'against house regulations'; Snake Boy was hissing and focused; and I was wheezing and felt blurry. 'Everythin' I has yours,' I dribbled to the dealer, as I slid her my last two quarters. She rapped them sharply on the table rim twice by way of unspoken thanks and I walked out of the Casino Royale a free man – free of all the money I'd come in with.

Late as it was when I began the long lurch back to Fantasy Treasure Love Boat Island, there were still hundreds and hundreds of people on the streets and inside the casinos, all of them hoping to win a new Lexus or a new life. And drunk as I was, I knew that all of them were losing. I hated to think of myself as one of them, but one of them I was: a stupid shitkicker heading back to the only place where winning is real – dreams.

The Last Straw

At 6.40 a.m., the room fully lit by the awful flashing blue of a digital clock, I was sharply woken by the full-pitched grip of another headache. I sat up holding my head together, David's wheezy snore floating in and out of my panting. Every few seconds a sharp spasm shot from my head down through my entire body, jarring my legs and twisting my toes. Minutes passed with aching slowness. By the time dawn broke into room 31066 of the Treasure Island Hotel and Casino, Las Vegas, Nevada, USA, my goal for the morning was clear: fill Dr X. Garcia Marco's pricey prescription for potential pain relief. Then win a Lexus.

West Coast

Some saint or other winking at you from beneath a low-buttoned shirt; the ace of spades dripping out of a sleeve . . .

California Here We Come! **Sean and David head for Palm Springs. Song by Ethel Merman. NC-117.**

America loves food, but it worships breakfast. Our hotel's all-you-can-shovel buffet is one of the most magnificent things I have ever seen: a great, steaming, sizzling, grease-glistening display of literally heart-stopping indulgence. As we walk the quarter-mile line of food that takes us from breakfast to brunch, through elevenses and then on to lunch, Snake Boy tells me that he's learned how to count cards. 'It's highly illegal, but piss-easy. And anyway they can't stop you,' he explains. 'About an hour after you left, I got up to about seven hundred bucks at the Royale, and then I went to Caesar's Palace and it just started happening again.'

I'm listening, but I can't take my eyes off the food. It's both heaven and a shortcut thereto: pork sausage, gipsy ham, Canadian bacon, scrambled eggs, fried eggs, boiled eggs, poached eggs, eggs Benedict, eggs Hollandaise, omelettes, liver, steak, kidney, tongue, kippers, flapjacks, muffins, hash browns, baked beans . . .

'I was betting small at first, then bigger and bigger until I had about two grand. Then I thought it was definitely time to go. I was on my way out when this big Italian bloke in a tux stopped me and said, 'Would you care to come this way?' I thought they were onto me, that they were gonna take me somewhere and put a glass rod down my dick and break it, and I'd be pissing blood for a month.'

. . . Cheerios, Coco-Pops, Applejacks, Post Toasties, Cornflakes, Frostie Flakes, Fruit Loops, Honey Smacks, Rice Krispies,

Sugarinos, Special K, Puffed Wheat, Weetbix, sweet Crunchy Granola, oatmeal, yoghurt, pies, cakes, French toast, British toast, American toast, international toast, plain toast . . .

'But he took me upstairs to a private room with a huge roulette wheel and only five players sitting around it. The guy made me put a tie on my blue polyester number from Big Daddy's and I sat down. And it just went crazy all over again, but this time it was pure luck. A hundred down on black; black comes in. A hundred on evens; thirty-two comes up. A waiter offered me a drink; I asked for a whisky and he brought me a bottle of Glenlivet. A whole bottle. D'you know what that's worth?'

. . . milk, orange juice, apple juice, tomato juice, grapefruit juice, mango and banana juice, strawberry juice, carrot juice, every imaginable tea, instant coffee, brewed coffee, decaf, espresso, cappuccino, champagne, Bloody Marys . . .

'I lost maybe two or three times out of every ten spins. Then I started going for individual numbers – thirty-five to one shots. And when you win, there's no whooping or clapping or anything, just a shovel full of chips pushed toward you. I kept thinking I was going to leave after the next spin but I ended up staying until the bottle was empty. Then I fell off my chair and decided I absolutely had to go. I got up, cashed my chips – and guess how much?'

'I don't know. Half a million bucks?'

'Twelve thousand seven hundred and eighty *US* dollars.'

'In-fucking-credible!'

'I know. I keep thinking it's a dream like that one I had about the talking dog in New Mexico.' He pulls out a huge wad of greenbacks. 'But I know better.'

I sigh, my breath rank with envy.

'Breakfast is on me, by the way,' he says, burping.

But I've lost my appetite.

Leaving Las Vegas

We drove through the city's wide suburban sprawl looking for a drugstore. It was like a huge retirement village out there – identical tract housing that went on for miles and miles, a plaza or mini-mall every few hundred feet so you didn't have to walk much, or ever. Inside the drugstore were a dozen or so slot machines being played by all the freaks and desperadoes who'd been banned from the casinos. I waited in the din of electronic bells and whistles while the pharmacist took my details, typed up the labels, got excited about how much commission she'd make off this one deal, and finally called me over to the counter. 'There's a problem,' she said, holding the box of pills a few inches from my face. I looked up at her. 'Your doctor didn't sign the prescription. He wrote it out but he didn't sign it. I can't give you the pills.'

Back in the car I called Dr X every name in the Hispanic swear book, ruined what was left of the Neon's upholstery and almost broke my hand by punctuating my truculence with a fisted bash on the inside of the door.

There was only one thing to do: spend another ninety minutes waiting to see some incompetent bastard masquerading as a health professional; pay him $60 for simply *copying* the details of the unsigned prescription onto his own pad, then – and here's where the years of medical training come into play – signing it!!;

216

then go back to the pharmacasino and shell out $120 for nine pills that probably wouldn't work.

All of which I did.

3.30 p.m. California

Satan, from one of his elevations, showed mankind the kingdom of California, and they entered into a compact with him at once.
Henry David Thoreau, February 1852

It's hot as hell out here on the traffic-heavy I-15, the Cady mountains on one side of us, the Soda mountains on the other. The Prince of Darkness somewhere above us, and nothing in between.

4.52 p.m.

We're cutting through the desert from Barstow, heading south toward Palm Springs. There aren't any towns on the map (or out here in reality, either), but every couple of miles we see a squat concrete dwelling – a compound, a bunker, a domestic command centre – set back from the road and completely surrounded by twelve feet of cyclone fencing and ribbon wire. One house even has white vertical bars covering every facade – not just the doors and windows, but each and every wall. This is real nut-job survivalist territory, where the true patriots live. It's absolutely the middle of nowhere – but the air is clean. Me and my pistol feel right at home.

'Those maniacs'd kill you for having a tiny little gun like that,' says David.

'They'd have to kill me first.'

217

5 p.m. Palm Springs

Douglas Coupland's fine mcnovel *Generation X* is set in and around Palm Springs. That's the main reason I wanted to come here, to see first-hand the city of best-selling, phrase-making disenchantment. And because Bob Hope lives here – although, sadly, not on Bob Hope Drive, which seems a bit of a waste. I'd live on my own street if I had one, but I can't even get my name on a motel room door so I guess it'll be some time before they start naming tar after me. I'd prefer a museum, anyway. The Sean R. Wiesenheim Museum of Contemporary Stupidity. It's got a ring to it.

'Not so much a ring as a clunk,' says David.

I poke my head through the lightning hole to get a better look at the place as we cruise through. I can certainly see how a book about despair and hopelessness would spring from these Palms – it's little more than a resort in the middle of nowhere. In Native American society, old, sick people used to wander off into the desert to die, and it's pretty much the same thing here: lots of doddering ancients waiting in the desert to kick off, surrounded by five-star hotels, restaurants and over eighty golf courses. There is a soft quality to this city, something whispery and dim like the quiet, sterile hallways of a hospice. Everything seems geared toward making the inhabitants' last moments on earth as comfortable as possible: no litter or ragged grass to offend their failing eyes; ice-cream for sale almost everywhere, cooling and sweetening their final days. Along the main restaurant strip, a fine mist of water sprays onto the sidewalk – a light, refreshing rain, courtesy not of the heavens but of the corporeal city council. And, indeed, perhaps that's the essence of Palm Springs – a kind of earthly introduction to the enchanted climate of heaven.

It is, however, a very expensive place so it's probably much easier for a rich man to enter the Kingdom of Springs than any subsequent stop on his journey.

Touching David

Checked out *Casino* on hotel TV and my second viewing only confirmed that I much prefer the Vegas of Ace Rothstein and Nicky Santoro to that of Ted Turner and Kirk Kerkorian. Sure, back then if you screwed up you got put in a hole in the desert, but there was a certain integrity in that. These days they just put a hole in your credit rating and it takes longer to die. At the end of the movie, Ace Rothstein (Robert De Niro) laments that the town will never be the same. That it looks like Disneyland. Until I went there, I never really understood what he meant. I thought, 'Oh c'mon, it's just a mob-controlled money-laundering strip.' But now I get it, and it really is sad. These days the only people you can have cocktails with are a couple of Harveys from Somewhere You Never Heard Of in the mid-west. And the broads they hang out with. Boy are they built – for comfort.

The movie credits roll. 'So, David,' I say, trying to sound lightly conversational. 'About that money. I can't help but feel, in a crazy but very *real* sort of way, that it's kind of –'
'I'm not giving you any,' he says bluntly. 'It'd be too much like charity and you wouldn't want that.'
'Oh no, no I definitely wouldn't want that. No way . . . But on the other hand –'
'What I think we'll do is stay in some decent hotels in LA.'
'And when you say "decent", you mean?'

'More stars than there are in any studio.'

'All right!' I feel like hugging the guy, but it'd be dangerous – he hates to be touched.

Thyme is on Our Side. **The search for the meaning of lifestyle takes Sean and David to a San Diego restaurant. Rated MSG-free.**

Had the scheduled headache at around 5 a.m., popped a $15 pill, and waited. And waited. It didn't work so I had another – and it didn't work twice. I guess I'll see another 'doctor' in San Diego. It will be good to give more money to medical America.

I ordered a coffee at a place called LaLaJava this morning. 'And an ashtray too please, Ma'am.'

'I'm sorry, you can't smoke here, Sir.'

'You can't smoke in a coffee bar?' I coughed, outraged.

'In California.'

Oh my God . . .

Just before we check out of the hotel I tell David I've left something behind in the room and rush off to the elevator. He looks kind of irritated but it has to be done.

We're on our way out of Retirement City, USA, and the sun's as hot as a melonfricker on my right arm. Not only do they have Big and Tall Casual Menswear here, there's also Small and Frail as well as Old and Senile. The gear's not very nice though, too many checks and plaids. I'll wait until we get to LA and buy something at Young and Foolish.

LIFE, WHAT A BEAUTIFUL CHOICE. CALL 1-800 BIRTH

MICROSURGICAL UNVASECTOMY. CALL 1-800 REVERSE

We're driving along a treacherous, twisting, falling-rock-infested, car-accident memorial-crucifix-laden highway from Palm Springs to Temecula through the San Bernadino National Forest – a barren wasteland of death. The road is potentially fatal in a number of horrible ways: you could have a head-on smash, be crushed by a falling boulder, get whipped over a cliffside by high winds, have a heart attack from being scared, etc. Plus we're listening to David's bootleg of Neil Young at Jones Beach, and although I like it well enough, there's a heavy, morbid quality to it that makes it sound like it *wants* to accompany a death. Not so much 'Tonight's the Night' as 'Today's the Day'. I'll be glad when we're on the other side (of the mountains, not the Other Side).

2.39 p.m. The Other Side

We've made it and now find ourselves whipping through California crop country. It's very beautiful and could almost be heaven – if you're a farmer. As we pass through the sea of oranges and apples and grapefruit (so *this* is where breakfast comes from), we have a competition to see who can name the most Californian clichés.

'Health-consciousness, spiritual-consciousness, unconsciousness, est, crystals, cults, therapy, New Age-ness, the 80s, the sun, the beach, beach parties, surfing, the 60s, hippies, yuppies, yippies, Charles Manson, OJ, Rodney King, cops, guns, gangs, gangsters, gangstas, convertibles, Death Valley, Silicon Valley, silicon implants, valley girls, SoCal, Tang and earthquakes,' I pant.

'Not bad,' says David, shifting down to take a sharp gravel corner. 'Not smoking, not drinking, not eating, not taking drugs, taking drugs, taking meetings, taking control, jogging, the Hell's Angels, hot rods, Santa Everything except Fe, lifestyles – rich, famous and otherwise – the 70s, the Eagles, the Bangles, the Doobie Brothers, doobies, brothers, AOR, skateboards, rollerblades, saying "I'm okay with that", calling LA "Tinsel Town", trying to make it as an actor, director or screenwriter, getting discovered, signing a deal, buying a deal, selling a deal, saying "No deal!" and livin' it up at the hotel you-know-where.'

I'm impressed by the vivid impression we share of California – the quintessentially American State; the state of the 21st century.

4.07 p.m. San Diego

We're doing our washing at a place called Fluff and Fold, on the busy corner of Grape and Columbia, next to Miguel's Tacos. (He makes tacos, and his name's Miguel.) Today we're using Biz Ultra with Color Fastener, even though most of our stuff is black or white or grey. It's 75¢ for powder, $1 per wash and as much as you want to spend on drying, which won't need to be a great deal because it's already extremely hot in here. There aren't many people in the 'mat, but as usual the few there are look at us with patent wonder and fear. There's a little kid playing with one of those tops you spin with a rope. He's pretty good at it too, flicking it onto the worn concrete floor, then looping the string to pick it up and set it spinning on his hand. I'd like to have a shot at it but we don't speak each other's language – him being about eight and me being about thirty-one.

What a Gish!

San Diego is a very pleasant city – and that's its main problem. It suffers from what I call the 'beautiful sister syndrome', a condition where a place (or person) is quite lovely in a mild, understated way but nobody notices because its sister city (or sister) is an absolute knockout. Think of Mariel and Margaux Hemingway; Juliet and Hayley Mills; Miss Dorothy and Miss Lillian; Adelaide and anywhere else in the world. SD is smaller, prettier, friendlier, safer, sunnier and about a thousand times more 'livable' than LA, but nobody wants to live here. Why? Because it's smaller, prettier, safer and about a thousand times more boring than any other major Californian city. It's not so much a second or even third city as a *fifth* one. That's why they have a very impressive zoo.

In a strange way, I think San Diego's loneliness and sense of sullen disappointment is reflected in its rather torpid traffic management system. All the desolate one-way streets go the wrong way and the faded red lights never turn green. Never. They just can't be bothered. At dozens of intersections there are strange little street scenes of cars that haven't moved since 1989. Because they can't be bothered. Because they've already been to the zoo and there's just nowhere else to go.

Perhaps things are more lively when the city has the America's Cup trophy, which from time to time, when it can be bothered, it does. It would, however, make no difference to me as I think yachting is a 'sport' for rich, badly dressed idiots.

'But you're generally anti-sport, aren't you, Seanopolous?' says David, leafing through the hotel literature for the gym details.

California's pervasive health-consciousness has its hooks in him already.

'Why do you say that?' I ask.

'You didn't do any sports at school, you don't play any now and you don't watch any. You're just not interested in sport.'

It was quite a comprehensive answer. And even though there was some truth in it (when I was a teenager my parents sent me to a sports psychologist to find out why I didn't like football), it made me sound like a real milquetoaste. 'I used to play hockey and I still watch soccer on TV,' I say, hunting for my arm muscles.

'Why did you give up hockey?'

'I hated getting changed in front of everybody. I was a . . . a late developer.'

'Pubeless?'

'Not completely, just kind of . . . downy.'

View One – The Target

I look out the window of our twentieth-floor hotel room, way, way down to the great glass roof of Seaport Village and the Embarcadero Marina Park, a lovely square of still blue. There's a commotion around the marina park – dozens of people, flashes of light, trucks, stretch limousines. Out on the balcony with some room service binoculars, I take a closer look. It's some sort of film shoot deal featuring dolphins, fire, smoke machines, long-haired people in baseball caps and security types keeping the rubbernecking public at bay; the security people outnumber the human and dolphin population five to one. The whole scene is especially unlikely because, in keeping with San Diego's beautiful sister syndrome, I can't think of a single film set here.

1.22 a.m. Hotel room (twin share)

We're back from a night drinking at a place called Croce's, owned and run by dead Jim's widow, who has her own cookbook/autobiography called *If I Could Put Thyme in a Bottle*. If I was ever tempted to read the life story of a woman who was once married to a dead folk singer who had one hit in the 70s, that title would sure make me think twice. Even worse, the only food Croce's seems to serve is full of vitamins and minerals and roughage and other stuff which my body can't stand. We have to get out of here before I die of 'the good life'.

California Dip
Dried onion soup mix. Sour cream. Combine. Serve.

Trailer. A trashy combination of live action and animation which examines life behind closed screen-doors. Funky soundtrack by the Ohio Players.

Got up late and returned what was left of Leon the Chrysler Neon to Charles Limburger Field aka San Diego Airport. It was sad to say goodbye to the sleek white steed that from DC to Diego had served us so faithfully (except for the wipers, brakes, windscreen and its attractiveness to lightning).

'What's this?' asked the rental attendant, pointing to the hole in the top.

'It's a sun-roof,' David told him. 'The guy in Washington said we could put one in if we got too hot.'

'We're Australian,' I added, helpfully.

'So fucking what?' he said.

The saddest part of giving up the car came when we had to remove the twelve tons of junk we'd accumulated and stored in it. The two Reader's Digest boxed sets of easy-listening vinyl I'd bought in Nashville weighed fifty pounds each. Plus there were several bags of shoes; a camera; forty-seven unread paperbacks; various maps, guide books and tour books; my medicine cabinet containing Anacin, aspirin, Tylenol, laxatives, anti-nausea syrup, Alka Seltzer, Mylanta, Band-Aids, cold tablets, throat spray, sinus tablets and those useless $120 headache pills (which I might sell to some primary school kids); hundreds of half-empty food and drink containers; postcards; matches; my gun; batteries; pens; pencils; cassettes; CDs; fireworks; film; and a possum. To say nothing of our emotional baggage, which everybody in California must carry.

We were just about to leave when David said, 'Wait, I think I might have left something behind.' I looked kind of annoyed, but he was determined to do it. That was when he discovered the pile of unbolted hotel TV remote controls hidden under the passenger seat.

'What the hell are these doing here?' he demanded angrily.

'Oh yeah, I forgot about them,' I said, trying my hardest to sound sheepish. But really I was glad, proud even. It had to be done.

'Why?' he asked, waving a big Phillips in my face.

'Because they were bolted in the first place. It seemed so stupid and pointless. I mean, who would bother *stealing* them?'

'You.'

'Exactly. Now there's a reason for them to be bolted down. Don't you *see*?'

'Yes. Unfortunately, I think I do.'

Came back to the hotel to ceremonially dump all our garbage into an industrial waste container and watch Mel Gibson's *Bravehair* on HBO. *They may take our lives, but they'll never take our blue face-paint!!*

View Two – The Shoot

'Hey, David,' I said. 'I'm going to investigate that film thing down there. Come with me, I might need backup.'

'All right,' he said. '*Braveaccent*'s got me in the mood for a fight.'

As we were waiting for the lift, I told him I'd forgotten something and ran back to our room. The elevator car arrived as I returned and we stepped in, listening to Ludwig van piped through the small speakers.

'I thought all this saying "I've forgotten something" and then running off to steal a remote control was finished,' David rebuked me.

'It is,' I told him truthfully. I was cured all right.

Naturally, we weren't allowed anywhere near the set – a beefy row of muscle t-shirts kept us out. Behind the testosterone curtain we could hear a great deal of shouting and carrying-on. The loudest and most belligerent noise was a squawky whine that contained equal measures of self-importance, hysteria and crackling nastiness. I could have sworn I knew that precise tone from somewhere. We *had* to get in and see.

'It's impossible,' said David. 'This is one very warm security blanket.'

'There's a cold spot that's our way in. Follow me.'

I almost drowned several times while we swam the fifty yards from the sea wall back to the marina park, where we climbed out, shrunken, cold and exhausted. On the set, all heads were turned toward the Star's trailer. A moment later the door opened and out stepped Troy McClure – in the flesh. David and I seized the opportunity to run semi-naked across a stretch of concrete and hide behind a catering truck, where we hurriedly dressed. I felt a small, reassuring lump in the pocket of my pants as I pulled them on. Then we joined the throng which was hanging on Mr McClure's every movement as he took his place before the camera.

'Hi, I'm Troy McClure – you may remember me from previous product endorsements like the Pet Rock, the no-fuss, ingenious pet. Or DentScumGo, industrial-strength toothpaste. Well, today I'm here to tell you about Peeple's Video, the video people who rent videos – to people! Go there now and rent something, or you're a loser baby, so why don't I kill you?' McClure shook his head and leaped out of character. 'Who wrote this shit?' he cried.

'*I* did!' I shouted. 'And you're losing the irony. You're supposed to say igneous pet. *Igneous!* It's a rock thing.'

Then things started to go very, very wrong.

'Who the hell are you?' a guy in a 'Top Gun – Top Crew' baseball cap shouted, as David ran away.

'Uh, nobody,' I murmured, coming to my senses. 'I was just leaving.'

'Hold on a minute!' ordered a guy in a 'Days of Thunder – Crew of Wonder' cap holding on to me.

David had been captured and was being marched toward me by a guy in a 'Pretty Woman – Ugly Crew' t-shirt. A tall, angry-looking guy with a 'Bad Boys – Good Crew' belt buckle strode over to us. 'Who the fuck are you?'

I trotted out the usual reply. 'We're Australian.'

His face opened up. 'Oh,' he said with a mixture of disappointment and pleasure. 'I'll go get the others then.'

I didn't know exactly what he meant, but since the gang of teamsterish lugs surrounding us fell away, things seemed to be looking up. McClure lit a cigar and puffed away in celebration of not being whacked by a pair of damp assassins. The tall guy escorted us to a trailer and told us to wait inside, as our 'friends' would be there shortly.

'What's going on?' asked David, helping himself to a Perrier and settling into a couch.

'We're Australian,' I told him.

'So fucking what?'

There was a knock at the door and in walked the last person I expected to see. The last person I *wanted* to see.

'Jesus Christ!' he spluttered. 'What the hell are *you* doing here?'

'Oh my God,' I splattered. 'You . . .'

'Who the hell is this?' David asked, pointing the bottle at the pudgy newcomer, whose pocked red face glistened with sweat and shock. He hadn't changed a bit – still wearing a white dress shirt tucked into a pair of bursting blue jeans and tasselled loafers on his feet. Mr Style. Still wearing the same old blank expression, too. 'Who *is* it?' David repeated insistently.

'David,' I said, finally recovering some composure, 'this is Richard Milhaus, my former agency boss.'

'Condon,' said Milhaus, a smug grin pulling at his face, 'I hope you and your hippy mate have enjoyed your "little trip". I'm glad you're here. I really am, because I'm gonna drop you in so much shit for this you'll wish you were back in your office in Melbourne.'

'Oh, I wouldn't be too sure about that, Milhaus,' I said wryly, wishing like hell I had a martini to go with my attitude.

'Why?' he said.

'Yeah, why?' David asked me. Then he looked at Milhaus. 'And don't call me a hippy, mate.'

'Because,' I said, standing up and reaching into my pocket, 'if you make one wrong move, or one stupid, idiotic, insulting, patronising remark, there will be trouble.' I pulled out my gun and cocked it; coupled with Milhaus's feeble whimper, it was a very satisfying sound.

'I want you to apologise for being such a prick,' I said to my ex-boss.

'Sorry,' he said.

'Oh no, that won't do. That won't do *at all*. I want something a little more sincere and . . . lasting.'

Following the instructions I had given him, Milhaus approached the director and told him that he wished to deliver a short address to camera. He took his mark and the ritual began: 'Camera?' 'Rolling.' Milhaus cleared his throat. 'Sound?' 'Speed.' Milhaus sighed. 'Action!' Milhaus spoke.

'My name is Richard Milhaus. I am an advertising copywriter. I earn far too much money for this unutterably trivial work, which I am barely competent to perform. I therefore insist that my salary be halved. I hope that others will follow my example so we can put an end to the egregious folly that is the advertising salary. I say this of my own free will and in full possession of my limited faculties. Also, I wear lifts, have poor taste in every-thing and a very . . . small . . . penis.'

He struggled with 'egregious' and 'own free will', and there was real trouble with 'small penis', but he made it eventually. Once it was done, I asked the camera assistant for the film and a DAT of the soundtrack. I thanked him politely as Milhaus led David and me off the set, my gun in his back all the way.

On the way back to the hotel I tossed my gun into the sea, saddened at having to let it go but pleased that, at least once in its long life, it had been put to good use.

California Doctrine
Balance between appropriative and riparian rights to water. (1886)

Spit 'n Polish

I'm not permitted to smoke in the Japanese restaurant where David and I are having dinner, so I'm smokin' it up outside on the street when I see a shoeshine guy and ask him how much.

'Two dollar for the genneman an' a dollar for the ladies.'

I sit down on the bench and we get to talking. His name is Allan Thornhill, 'Shoe shine Al', from Dayton, Ohio.

'That's where the Ohio Players are from,' I say, and he starts singing 'Fire'. Then we both hum the spiralling guitar riff from 'Love Rollercoaster'. He tells me about his ex-wife cutting the strings off his Fender and wrapping his Gibson around a telephone pole. I tell him that the trumpet player from the Ohio Players, Marvin Pierce, ended up working at the same ad agency as me in Melbourne. A little later I hem and haw about something that's bothering me.

'Talk to me, Sean, talk to me,' he says, his harelip stretching sideways as he says my name, a little spit landing on my shoe as he speaks.

And so I lay the whole 'white guilt about a black man shining

231

my shoes' trip on him. He just says, 'C'mon man, I'm makin' money and that's it.'

And then I give him ten dollars to prove it. Fact is, he did a terrific job and I had a great time.

LA Story. More of an anecdote really. Rated EH (Elizabeth Hurley references).

'California or Bust'
Popular declaration among dust-bowlers during the Depression.

11.55 a.m.

We have to leave town in semi-disguise, in case there's any fallout from yesterday's 'incident', so we're wearing each other's clothes. It feels sartorially schizophrenic. There's still a couple of minutes to wait before this crowded, hot and stinking Greyhound bus expresses its way to the City of Angels. It will take about two and a half hours to get to LA – too long with a crying child and its mother right behind me, and the child's small, quiet, teenage Spanish father next to me. We're all sitting right next to the toilet, the most evil spot on any bus.

The population of the bus is all black and Hispanic, plus two white homeless guys – me and David. The Spanish dad makes the sign of the cross, kisses the crucifix hanging around his neck and we're off to Los Angeles.

1.40 p.m. Still on the Bus

Read about E. Hurley's fabulous, but heart-breakingly difficult, life as an actress/model/film producer. She and Hugh have a 'tiny flat' in London. I am on a Greyhound bus heading to LA and she has a 'tiny flat' in London.

I want to be a film producer. I want a tiny flat. I have an idea for a screenplay . . .

You Have the Right to Remain

We pull over to the side of the highway and are all ordered off the bus by three fat men with automatic weapons. I am not scared; somehow I've expected this all along from LA. Besides, I am not Mexican, Cuban or Puerto Rican; it's the darker skinned amongst us who are sweating and nervous, whispering with worry. We are all asked to produce identification – licences, passports, visas – and one of the fat men stares at them hard, almost willing them to be false, out of date, inadequate. Sadly for the officials, we all have a right to be here and are allowed back on the bus to resume our seats and continue our journey. But I wonder, has all this been about keeping undesirables out of the United States or Los Angeles?

STONE CONTAINER CORP. ALLOY TOOL STEEL. FRIGID COIL (A DIVISION OF THE HART CORPORATION). ARCO. HUGHES TOOL CO. HEMTECH. FRAZEE PAINT & WALL COVERING. HAITAI INC. PALLETS AND JACKS-R-US. EMERGENCY INC – MANUFACTURERS OF LADIES APPAREL. LANGENDORF BREAD. MARX BROS FIRE EXTINGUISHER CO.

2.15 p.m. Los Angeles

LA does indeed seem to be a great big freeway. If only we could put a hundred down and buy a car. Then we could find our way to San José. 'Or just walk on by,' sings 'Hal' David O'Brien.

Cabbed through an industrial wasteland/slum that appeared to be home to the homeless. Right next door was the 'fashion district', home to the brainless. Checked into the Biltmore Hotel, which is home to the rich, the Japanese, and lucky gamblers (David) and their free-loading friends (self). It's utterly beautiful, weepingly ornate, stylish and lovely. They used to hold the Academy Award ceremonies here. I want to be buried in the former lobby turned lounge and have people drink and dance on my grave.

What's your last name? I need a last name to go with my first name. It's Arapanee. Arapanee something. My name needs an ending. I'm an actress.

White female, approx. 22, in Biltmore lobby

It feels great to be in Los Angeles; it seems like a whole different country to the rest of America, it's almost as though we're 'back in the world'. My world anyway. The stupid, obvious, easy, normal, regular, predictable, happier, western world where there's coffee, sandwiches, office buildings and office workers, short streets with traffic lights instead of highways and Humvees, cars instead of pick-up trucks, handguns instead of rifles, earthquakes instead of tornadoes, McDonald's everywhere but not a Shoncy's or a Waffle House in sight, lots of voice-mail but no happy messages . . .

6.30 p.m. The News

Richard 'The Night Stalker' Ramirez is getting married. Besides the fact that the guy is evil and fiendish, he is so freakin' ugly. What could she be thinking? One year after the verdict, OJ Simpson jurors are tired of people harassing them about their decision. (OJ's obviously evil and fiendish too, but at least he's handsome, so you can understand why they let him go.) Jewellery once belonging to Gloria Swanson, Gene Tierney and some other dames is being auctioned at Christies. Four kids were hit at two separate crosswalks today. *Four.* The guy accused of murdering a blonde model is insisting they had consensual sex and that he didn't accidentally run over her in a car, as he'd earlier claimed, and that although her legs were forced open with rope and she had rectal damage, he knows nothing about it. It's going to be 84° tomorrow, 86° on Saturday and 84° again on Sunday.

David knocks on the door of my room. 'Here,' he says, holding a plastic bag as far away from himself as he can. The bag seems almost alive with a bloated smell. 'I've been feeling really weird all day. Sort of foolish and irresponsible, ill and jaded. There's a cynical misery inside me, an indefinable despair.'

'That's terrible, David. What's wrong?'

'I forgot to change out of your clothes.' He drops the bag at my feet and shakes his head. 'I don't know how you stand it, I really don't.'

Seconds later I call him on the phone and tell him it's not easy.

La Luz de Jesus

A little after eight and quite a lot to drink, we catch a cab driven by a very talkative Irish gardener/cab driver who is full of advice about where to go in 'Poly-nee-sia' and giving up smoking (even though I'm not planning on visiting either of those destinations). He also tells us to watch our wallets as we alight in Silver Lake, in front of a bookstore with a bright neon sign on the roof that reads 'Wacko'. 'It's unseemly around here,' he says.

Behind the bookstore is a gallery called La Luz de Jesus, and that's where we're headed – to the light of the Lord. David, me and the entire LA Hot Rod Art Scene are all crowded into the small room. There's a tiny band playing surf tunes squashed in a corner. Lots of men and women wearing super-hip gear and tattoos. Whole arms, backs, necks and chests covered in ink: some saint or other winking at you from beneath a low-buttoned shirt; the ace of spades dripping out of a sleeve. Sizzling blue cheongsams or tight leopard-skin dresses on the busty broads and Hawaiian originals on the slick-haired fellows. Packs of Latino brothers mill about in the heat, wearing singlets, crucifixes and wraparound shades. Most of the guys who aren't Latino are pretending to be by adopting the Los Lobos facial hair: a long jet of goatee shooting down the chin; a six-inch wedge of manliness. The broads at the bar are wearing bikini tops, grass skirts and plastic devil horns, sexily dispensing bright blue punch or beer with free red licorice. It occurs to me that what they have created tonight in La Luz de Jesus is Hell, as rendered in an old Warner Bros cartoon.

While I'm smoking in the car park outside, a girl with fire-coloured hair says, 'Excuse me, Sir. If you're going out with somebody, do you dump them if they "turn ugly"?' 'Of course not,' I say. 'My first girlfriend was a hunchback with halitosis and only one eye. And *she* dumped *me*.' The redhead is a charming 25-year-old twelve-stepper called Spring Cooper. 'Yeah, Spring,' she repeats to my raised eyebrows. 'Not Frank. Not String. Not Swing – Spring. My parents were Jewish hippies. It's really Cooperman. On my library card, it looks like the name of an unpopular car. The Cooperman Spring.' She tells me that she's recently moved to Hollywood, 'the suburb, not the idea'.

She's an open and engaging conversationalist. I'm beginning to realise that the West Coast is a much friendlier place than the East.

She's very ditzy. She's very . . . art. *She's* very *art.*
                    White female at La Luz, approx. 23, talking to same

To Coop's Coop in a Coupe

Back inside David has finally made contact with the friend of a friend who invited us to the gallery and whom he only knows by telephone. Chris Cooper (no relation to String), a graphic designer popularly known as 'Coop', described himself as 'a guy with a goatee hanging around with a woman called Ruth with big huge tits'. This description fits about two hundred guys here, so David had wasted a lot of time going up to lucky mock-Latinos saying 'Chris?' and being glowered at.

David discovered the real Coop and Ruth just as they were leaving in his purple primer-coated 1950 Ford two-door with chemical green hubcaps. 'C'mon back to our place,' says Coop. His vehicle has no door handles and from the outside can only be opened with an electronic remote device. Ruth, Chris and I squeeze into the front while David crouches on a cushion in the hollowed-out rear shell. When customising a car, anything deemed extraneous is removed – like handles, seats and, my favourite things, seatbelts. As Von Dutch or Ed Roth or one of those hot rod legends once quipped, 'If it doesn't make it go, it's gone.'
'Besides, seatbelts are for fairies,' says Ruth, when I accidentally comment on the lack of.

Coop turns the engine over and, all around us, other rods start up. The weight of thunderous noise is incredible: a demon roar as we leave Hell in a chopped and cropped chariot, burning black rubber into the night.

Coop and Ruth's house turns out to be a shrine to 50s/60s/70s kitsch. There are display cases of toys, models, robots, horror figures, cars and everything ever available in a cereal box (except cereal), racks of mint-condition hot rod mags from 52-56, tacky paperbacks, a million tikis, three beautifully restored 50s pinball machines, a collection of shriner fezes, books about everything, original art pieces by Jack Davis and Daniel 'Fuckin' Clowes and loads of other stuff I couldn't notice because of all the other stuff. David being a collector himself, his eyes are almost falling out of his head.

Ruth and Chris are a great couple, saying the same words at the same time and finishing off each other's sentences and food. And they're quite a contrast: he is kind of small and Oklahoman, while she is as big and brash as her home town of Chicago; she looks like a bondage madam (because she was one) and used to work for Larry Flynt.

They share each other's enthusiasms – his for toys and robots and hers for leather and whips. Which is nice. But their shared joys don't stop with that comparatively drab stuff, oh no. Both of them are ordained ministers of the Church of Satan and good friends with its founder, Dr Anton LaVey. They show us a photo of LaVey's son, a cute little kid by the name of Xerxes, whose eyes follow me around the room in a very creepy fashion. It also transpires that they're both card-carrying members of the

National Rifle Association ('The Church and the NRA are the only two organisations we belong to,' drawls Chris). Before we know it, they're unloading Magnums, Colts and a pink, pearl-handled Lady Derringer (Chris's birthday gift to Ruth) and laying them out on the kitchen table for us to admire.

'Is this all of it?' I ask, gingerly pawing the Colt.

'Oh no,' says Ruth. 'Honey, where's the shotgun?'

'Under the bed,' answers Chris, clearly amused by our fascinated horror.

'Oh God, this is so embarrassing,' calls Ruth from the bedroom.

'Why? Is it all dusty?' asks Chris.

'Yeah, d'you mind giving it a clean before we show it to the guys?'

It's a beautiful domestic moment. And very . . . *LA. Very* LA.

The West promises to beat in the game of brag even the stout champions I have been quoting. Those belong to the old Eastern States; and the other day there was sent to me a Californian newspaper which calls the Easterners 'the unhappy denizens of a forbidding clime', and adds: 'The time will surely come when all roads will lead to California. Here will be the home of art, science, literature and profound knowledge.'
Matthew Arnold, *Civilisation in the United States*, 1888

The Defiant One. Lying in bed, Sean reviews a day in LA. Cameo by James Woods. Rated R.

12.40 p.m. The Biltmore

I'm hung over and I smell of engine fumes. It's hot outside, and Californian. I wish I was in Australia, where the bacon and egg sandwiches grow on trees.

12.40 a.m. The Regent Beverly Wilshire

The twelve hours in between being hung over and then drunk again were spent doing the following:

- Catching a cab a long way down Wilshire Boulevard to the Beverly Wilshire and beginning to realise that LA is a hell of a lot bigger than I thought. Shelling out forty-seven bucks for a cab ride helped me realise this. Beverly Hills really is the way it looks in '90210' and *Pretty Woman*. There's those tall but sickly looking palm trees lining the streets full of expensive, exclusive stores and smart but faintly sickly looking women shoppers. Rich, but with cancer. You can't see more than about a mile in any direction because of the haze of smog. It's as though the whole city, except right where you are, has been airbrushed out. And I'm sure that most people around Beverly Hills like to think of it exactly that way.

- Seeing Britt Ekland or Elke Sommer or one of those 70s blondes from some European mountain region walking through the hotel lobby toward me and not holding the door open for her because I just didn't damn well feel like it.

- Eating an enormous pastrami sandwich at Johnie's Fatboy on the corner of Wilshire and Fairfax. Also on the menu was pork chops and eggs with mash, toast and jelly. Neither of us had that – we were hung over, but not insane.

- Visiting the Peterson Car Museum (diagonally opposite Johnie's Fatboy) and ogling the rods. I like kustom kar kulture. It's kool. David could tell the makes, models and years of all the hot rods with just a glance. All I could say was, 'Look at the blue car.' Or, 'Gee, I like that red one. I bet it goes fast.'

- Catching a bus down Fairfax to Melrose Avenue. We weren't real sure where to get off so I asked this fifty-year-old dame hugging some sunflowers where Melrose was. 'Umm . . . umm . . . I'm only going to Fairfax,' she stammered. 'We're *on* Fairfax, Ma'am. Do you know how far Melrose is?' 'I'm only going three blocks,' she whimpered. What she was really saying was, 'Please don't talk to me. Please don't hurt me.' It was sad. And fucking annoying.

- Wearing out shoe leather all the way down Melrose Avenue, weaving in and out of every overpriced, undersized vintage clothing store between Fairfax and La Brea. In the three hundred stores we went into we saw some pretty cool stuff but it was all priced and sized to fit the Japanese tourist – they're crazy about all that wacky, polyester shit. Saw a pair of Nike 'collectables' from 1972. They were locked in a glass cabinet and cost $795. I was quite tempted to buy them – in the same way that I'm tempted to cut off my penis and eat it.

- Missing a bus back down Fairfax by four seconds and sitting with the crazy people at the bus stop for half an hour watching the arrogance and stupidity of LA drivers and wondering why more of them aren't dead. (Which brought to mind some interesting statistics I'd seen earlier at the Peterson Car Museum: number of deaths per hour on US roads – 5; number of disabling accidents per hour on US roads – 500. That's 12,000 disabled Americans created every day!)

- Passing a store called Sidney's Fine Shoes for Wide Feet. I laughed – to myself, not out loud like a nut job.

- Having more ideas for my screenplay. It's kind of autobiographical, but it's really coming together.

- Harassing cold-blooded actor James Woods who was standing on Sunset Boulevard (waiting to be rediscovered, probably). Here's how it went.

SC: Mr Woods, I'd just like to shake your hand because, well, I'd kick myself if I didn't. Y'know, when you pulled that gun out of your guts in *Videodrome*, it was cool.

JW [LAUGHS AND POINTS TO TWO BONEHEADS STANDING NEARBY]: These guys like *Best Seller*.

SC [THINKING, '*BEST SELLER* IS A TERRIBLE MOVIE. WHAT'LL I SAY?']: *Best Seller* is brilliant, Sir. I watched *Casino* last Sunday. You were great in that.

JW: Thank you. I was only on that movie for three days.

SC: Well, it was certainly an impactful three days.

JW: Where are you from?

SC: Australia.

JW: Just visiting LA?

SC: Yeah. I like it a lot.

JW: Well, have a safe trip home and it's really been a pleasure meeting you. [SMILES AND LOOKS SINCERE BUT MEAN]

SC: Say, Jimmy, that Sean Young is a pretty hot babe. Is she a good kisser?

JW: You'd better step away from me now.

- Stepping all the way back to the hotel to mix it up with the beautiful people. Getting drunk so I can stand to watch them looking at me with uninterest.

• Watching *The Defiant Ones* on cable. It's a great movie. In a way, David and I are like the defiant ones, except we're not chained together and we're both white. Except for that, we're them.

Hotel. Sean and David enjoy the good life using Arthur Hailey's best seller as a guide. Rated $.

Moved from the Regent Beverly Wilshire to the Beverly Hills Hotel (David wants to try out all the best joints in LA), where we hope to catch up with Howard Hughes. This is what we saw from the cab going down Rodeo Drive: Tiffany, Cartier, Christian Dior, Valentino, Bally, Salvatore Ferragamo, Chanel, Bang & Olufsen, Ralph Lauren and Little Richard in a green lamé suit bashing the eighty-eight keys for a video shoot. The houses around here are all mansions, but only small ones; Elizabeth Hurley probably has three.

California Suite
Enjoyable 1978 film adaptation of Neil Simon play involving various inhabitants of a Beverly Hills hotel. Stars Jane Fonda, Alan Alda, Walter Matthau & Herb Edelman.

The Beverly Hills Hotel is large, mostly pink and completely fabulous. Howard Hughes used to keep his star-lookalike playthings in the bungalows out back. And they called him *crazy*.

I'm sitting by the hotel pool, working on the second draft of my first screenplay and drinking a third coffee purchased from the trés casual coffee shop. They're $4.60 each, so it's definitely my last. Dyan Cannon just walked past. I wasn't that thrilled at first, but then I remembered that she was once married to Cary Grant and became latently thrilled.

Screenplay-ground

'You're missing one very large point about popular Hollywood success, Seany-Sean,' David tells me, stretched out beside me soaking up the smog-filtered rays.

'What's that?'

'You're not beautiful. You have to be beautiful or nobody'll even look at you. Literally.'

'So what you're saying is that even if I wanted to make it as a screenwriter, I'd have to have plastic surgery?'

'Couldn't hurt.'

When I make a few calls to small-time agents and producers, trying to set up a meeting to discuss my screenplay, I tell them that both the work and myself are 'very, very attractive. Practically gorgeous, if you want to know the truth.'

It's mostly the over-45 dental/psychiatry crowd down here poolside. They're chubby, brown and loud. You can rent a private poolside cabana with own phone, fax, TV and toilet for $125 a day. The only people doing that are younger than me. Presumably, they're paying for it with drug money; maybe they sell Sumatripan. There's a Japanese woman eating alone and shaking her head sadly at her food. I think she might also be talking to it every now and then. Considering the fine weather and extreme indulgence of it all, the atmosphere is strangely bleak. I guess it's because anybody who's here, doing this on a weekday, *must* be some kind of asshole. Except me and David.

'Hey, Seaniewicz,' David murmurs from the towel. 'This screenplay of yours, am I in it?'

'Yes, you are.'

'How do I come across? Likeable, wise, sexy?'

'I'm not comfortable portraying you as a sexual person, David. There's no-one for you to work off except me, and I'd really rather steer clear of that.'

'Yeah, you'd better. What about the other things?' He's propped up on his elbows now.

'You're super cool and a real stunt-driver. But I've shortened your hair and shaved off the goatee.'

'But my hair is a big part of me.'

'The *real* you. Not this you,' I tell him, tapping the wad of paper with a pen.

'Let me have a scene with a beautiful woman. Just one. I'll make it worth your while. And hers.'

'Maybe.'

'And give me back my hair. I feel naked without it.'

Harry? Harry, pass me my pina colada. If I move I won't get an even tan.

Dentist's wife, approx. 19 – 70

After Three Martinis at the Chateau Marmont

'You guys are Australian?' she asked, showing perfect teeth and skin. Her name was Barbara. 'How come you're not wearing those hats?'

'We're in disguise,' said David. 'As normal people.'

'Oh, I get it,' she said, winking a long-lashed left eye. She was beautiful. 'But normal won't get you far in this town. This town

245

doesn't *understand* normal.'

'What do you do, normally?' I asked.

'Singer, actress, model, whatever. Mostly whatever, but y'know
. . . whatever.' She was twenty-two. There was a tattoo reading
'I am' on her bare shoulder. She was.

'Do you know Heidi Fleiss?' I wondered aloud.

'My boyfriend knows her, but only as a friend. She's planning
to make a comeback with a line of lingerie.'

'Butt Fleiss,' I said. David guffawed. Barbara said, 'Huh?' I told
her it was an Australian thing which wouldn't translate.

'Oh, I get it. Like in German or something, right?'

'Ja.'

'What's your boyfriend do?' asked David.

'Chauffeur, pool cleaner, gym instructor. But he's gonna be
somebody quite soon.'

'Isn't he already somebody?' I said.

'More,' Barbara told me. Turning away, she said to David,
'You're all right, you know, but your buddy, I'm sorry to have
to say th.s, he gets on my nerves. You should lose him if you're
serious about yourself.' She blew a jet of smoke from her
panatella. 'My boyfriend would've already hit him over that
Heidi Fleiss remark.'

'I wouldn't blame him,' I said, mournfully rubbing my jaw where
the punch would have landed.

'See, there you go again with that mouth.'

'He didn't mean anything bad by it,' said David. 'Americans just
don't understand him. Especially in California.'

Barbara said, 'Well I'm sorry, but if California doesn't get it,
what's the point?'

Horribly disconcerting as this observation was, I understood
exactly what she meant.

'I know exactly what you mean,' I said.

'Oh, just stop it will you!?' she cried, and I left, giving up the chatty sidekick business once and for all.

I stood outside on Sunset Boulevard, a warm Santa Ana wind tickling my tri-martini sensitised skin. High above me loomed the famous Marlboro Man billboard, a tough, leathered cowboy enjoying a quiet smoke after a roundup. In a few months he would be gone, a victim of the culture of litigious complaint that has overrun this country as it wheezes and screams toward the millennium. A landmark sued into oblivion.

I headed down to the Viper Room to see if I could scare up some trouble there. 'Who are you?' asked the bouncer.

'I'm the son of the guy who played Timmy in the last series of "Lassie",' I told him, reaching for my SAGMS (Screen Actors Guild Member's Son) card.

'We don't look too kindly on television here,' he told me brusquely. 'We feel it's an inferior medium to that of the motion picture.'

'That attitude appals me.'

'So be appalled. You still can't come in.'

I decided to try a new angle – the truth. 'Listen, I'm not really that guy's son. I'm Australian.'

'SFW? Last Aussie we had in here pulled a mock-Phoenix. We didn't like him one bit. He lacked originality.'

I had to agree. 'So what you're telling me is there's really no way anybody who's a nobody can get in here?'

'S'right.'

'So how do you prove that you're somebody?'

'You either are or you aren't. All these questions prove you're not.' He started rolling his shoulders like a boxer between rounds. 'I have work to do, Mac.'

'You're doing it. You're keeping me out of in there,' I told him. He wiped his face with a soaking sponge and made an 'ooohhh-aaahhh' sound.

'So what's it like in there?'

'You'll never know.'

Snot

Back at the hotel I feel a tremendous pressure in my right nostril and my nose begins expelling very thick and viscous, cancer-brown lavas of old blood and snot. I think it is dead blood from way back in my infected sinus. There is several pounds of it. It strikes me as profoundly ironic that my clogged and rotting sinuses should find relief in a city renowned for its concentration of filth and smog. Considering the fact that we no longer drive a couple of hundred miles a day, maybe it really *was* white line fever.

Who Is?

David staggers into the room around 4 a.m. 'I've had the most amazing night,' he slurs.

'What happened?'

'Me and Barbara went to some clubs. It was brilliant.'

'Like where?'

'The Roxbury. Brilliant. St James. Fabulous. The Viper Room. Absolutely superb.'

'How did you get in?'

'She just showed that tattoo on her shoulder and all doors opened. Lotta free booze too. She didn't like you, y'know.'

'I know.'

'Sh' liked me.'

'I know.'

I am. I wanted to be, too.

'What about her boyfriend?'

'She made him up. He didn't exist.'

Well, at least I had *him* beat.

***Night and the Naked City.* Starring Gloria Grahame as 'Gracie' and John Garfield as 'Walt'. Rated RKO.**

California Gold Rush
1848 – 53.

10.20 a.m.

We've checked into the Overdose Suite at the De Franco Hotel on Sunset. The Scene of the Crime: a white stucco ceiling, strange stains on the carpet, peeling wallpaper, a dead fish tank set into the wall, a crushed can of soda spilling thick residue in the bottom of the fridge, huge mirrors so you can watch yourself suck or blow or get sucked or blowed, a suicide balcony that plummets straight down to where your chalk outline will be drawn opposite the House of Blues, next door to the Comedy Store, just down the road from the Marlboro Man. Roy Rogers used to live here – with Trigger.

11.50 a.m. Laundromat

The Sunny Super Wash Coin Laundry on Sunset Boulevard is about twelve thousand footsteps from the Police Bust Hotel. We're using Tide for the whites and Clorox 2 for the greys and up, because it's tough on stains and easy on colours (I like to think of *myself* as tough on stains: tough, but fair). On the pinboard in the 'mat is a business card that advertises 'Ritchie Bitch, LA's only nude drummer'. No fooling. As I have no firm employment prospects back in Australia, I'm toying with the idea of becoming Melbourne's only nude drummer – although I bet there's some health regulation that will stop me. And would I have to be naked while I was setting up the kit? That could be kinda dangerous . . .

3.10 p.m.

After being in residence for just a few hours we're checking out of Sex Crime Central. We both felt there was too great a possibility of our being murdered in our sleep if we stayed overnight. In the lobby a demented fat guy wearing a towelling hat and an MC Hammer t-shirt is telling everybody that he just got on 'The Price is Right'.

'I just got on "The Price is Right",' he pants red-faced and wild-eyed to the desk clerk.

'Good for you, Leonard,' she says. I grin at her and she rolls her eyes for just a moment.

Leonard staggers off on fat, sweating legs, shouting at a porter, 'I just got on "The Price is Right"! So now you know somebody famous! My aunt's gonna went crazy when I tell her about it. She got on in 88, so now we're even more bonded.'

SAV-ON DRUGS. ALBERTSONS DRUGSTORE. THRIFTY DRUGSTORE. VALU-APE PHARMACIES. UNITED DRUGSTORES. STEVE REXALL'S DRUGS. DRUGTOWN PHARMACY.

5.40 p.m. Loew's Hotel, Santa Monica

Late in the afternoon the fog lifts from the beach and reveals the

LA seaside we've seen so many times in movies. It's very appealing, especially after the urban concrete and heat of the rest of the city. A huge Ferris wheel at the end of Santa Monica Pier dominates the beachfront; it looks like a whole lot of fun. Nevertheless I have spent most of the afternoon in the hotel room working on my screenplay while David combed the beach on his beard. His beard on the beach. It has been hard work but I care not, because at last I can see the sea.

We are in view of the ocean. This great Pacific Ocean which we have been so long anxious to see. Oh, the joy.
William Clark, explorer, November 1805

V/O:

There is a cinematic sheen over much of Los Angeles – everything you see, you've seen somewhere before on film. The colour-drained, LA heat-haze of *Chinatown*; the deserted streets and grim shadows of *Double Indemnity*; the deadpool in *Sunset Boulevard*. The familiar unreality gets under the city's skin. Willingly or unwillingly, knowingly or obliviously, its people walk the streets of a huge set, taking direction from far beyond or somewhere deep within. There is no shortage of bit players in Los Angeles, all reading from an old B-movie script written on the faded pages of their dark souls.

FADE IN. EXT. SANTA MONICA BOULEVARD. NIGHT.

It is long after midnight and the fog has settled, diffusing the quiet buildings, the deserted streets, the rolling ocean. Two figures walk along opposite sides of a wide street through the dense mist. As they approach the camera, we see that they are SEAN and DAVID. They're wearing hats and trenchcoats, and they walk with the easy confidence that comes with packing .45 calibre heat. DAVID starts throwing coins across the street to SEAN. We cannot see the coins but they make a light, tinkling sound as they skitter across the road. Pennies, nickels and dimes spin and splash over the asphalt like shining drops of manna from heaven, as the opening CREDIT SEQUENCE rolls: *Sean and David's Crazy . . . ness. Episode 27: The Case of the Suitcase-Sniffing Shark.*

CUT TO:

A faded, peeling sign advertising 'Oysters & Seafood'. The camera pulls back and we see a run-down bar called Chez Jay's – a small concrete building, both wan and lurid, sickening but somehow irresistible. SEAN and DAVID go inside.

INT. CHEZ JAY'S BAR. NIGHT.

A row of weakly coloured lights strung above the bar tints the dim faces a touch more blue, red and green. The place is full of shadows and rough, whispered conversation. SEAN and DAVID take a seat at the bar near WALT. He looks like he might once have been a boxer; his face, cut and roughened by years of beatings, has now finally been beaten by the years. He's forsaken the sweet science for sweet liquor. Next to him is GRACIE, tired and toothless, heavy earrings of scimitar and crescent moon hanging at her neck. Ella Fitzgerald plays softly on the jukebox. GRACIE silently mouths the words, and in the dark shadows, if you don't look too hard, she begins to look like her.

WALT (TO GRACIE)

I guess you're trying not to remember me, huh?

GRACIE

I try not to remember a lot of things.

WALT

You want another belt, honey? It might bring somethin' back.

GRACIE

The only thing it'll bring back is lunch. And you should ease up, you've been drinking straight since four. That's kinda early.

WALT

Honey, when you drink as much as I do, you gotta start early.

WALT swiftly downs the rest of his bourbon and nods to THE BARMAN for another. The movement is so slight it's almost imperceptible, but this routine has been playing forever. Everybody knows exactly what's needed, and when.

WALT

Do you believe in love at first sight?

GRACIE

I did once. It saved a lot of time.

WALT

Time to do what?

GRACIE

Develop some sort of second sight.

WALT

Do you miss the good old days?

GRACIE

How old?

WALT

When we were old enough to be good.

GRACIE

We were never that old, Wally. Or that young.

Watching WALT and GRACIE in the mirror behind the bar, DAVID dips a finger into his vodka and squeezes the lemon slice against the glass – a prearranged signal that means 'wait'. SEAN glances at GRACIE – he too is mesmerised by her raw weariness. He takes a slug of Pernod and lights a cigarette. THE BARMAN calls time by striking three loud tongs on an old ship's bell. SEAN offers GRACIE a cigarette. She takes one and raises her forefinger – a quick thank you – only half listening to WALT who is winding up his pitch of 2 a.m. woo.

WALT

Your head's sayin' one thing, but your body's saying another. Let your body win, Gracie. It's used to it.

GRACIE

You gave it a lot of training. Remember our marriage?

WALT

Yeah, I'm sorry honey . . . I guess my ship is sinking and the sharks are sniffing at my suitcase.

GRACIE

And I'm your life-raft? Your desert island stopover?

WALT

Save me tonight, Gracie. It won't kill you.

Through the door the Santa Monica fog is rolling into Chez Jay's. SEAN takes a last look around the bar, and in the half light everybody seems frozen. Everybody except WALT and THE BARMAN, who are singing loudly along with Frank Sinatra:

WALT and THE BARMAN (SINGING)

I'm gonna roll myself up . . . and die.

DAVID picks the lemon wedge out of his glass and twists it – the 'go' signal. SEAN draws his revolver and shoves it into WALT'S ribs, as DAVID does the same to GRACIE.

WALT

What the!?

SEAN

You and the dame are coming with us.

WALT

Where to?

DAVID

Somewhere the two of you should've gone a long time ago – Acting School!

SEAN

Not only that, Wally boy. You and the floozy are gonna be entirely rewritten – modernised and beautified. We're axing the clichés and replacing them with pop culture references. Total character makeover, understand?

GRACIE

I'd rather die.

DAVID (DRINKING FROM A CAN OF PEPSI MAX)

Sister, what's gonna happen to you is *beyond* death.

GRACIE

I loved you, Walt.

WALT

You too.

GRACIE

The way we were, I mean.

WALT

Yeah, baby, the way we were . . .

The camera follows SEAN and DAVID, guns on WALT and GRACIE, as they all head outside. It is misty and dark, but small flashes of light dance off the coins scattered on the asphalt. And if you look hard enough, it does indeed seem that these mean streets are sometimes paved with gold.

FADE OUT

The Third Act Man. How low can you go? Starring William Conrad as 'the Agent'. Rated 25% of the gross.

Unnatural Acts
In the interest of keeping our travel marriage a happy one, David and I agreed to a trial separation for the morning. Which suited me fine, because I had an appointment with a real live Hollywood agent, Herman Rothstein of Herman Rothstein Inc.

I was ushered into a large, sweltering office and seated opposite a mass of oiled sweat in an expensive suit and cream tie. 'Talk to me,' ordered Herman.
I spent a half-hour taking him through what I thought was an exciting, inspired screen creation called *Drive Through America.*
'. . . but it turns out that Sean is really the host and David's just the sidekick. But you don't find out until the end.'
He looked at me from across his desk. 'Then what happens?'
'Nothing,' I said.
'That's *it*?'
'Yeah.'
'There's no third act. And I *hate* everybody in it. Especially the Arizona lady with the foul mouth. What is she so pissed about?

The only thing it's got going for it is scenery – what is it, a freakin' *nature movie*!?' Herman shouted. 'Listen, kid. I don't know you too well, but I have to ask, are you meshuggah? Tell me the truth – are you freakin' *crazy*?'

I assured him that I wasn't freakin' crazy.

'But two guys who drive around talking crap all day long? What's going on here? Surely you don't expect me to sell that idea. There's no third act. There's too much desert. C'mon, kid, really . . . Hey, does he really only have one ball?'

'Well, I'm sure the idea could do with a little development, but it's not that bad.'

'Not that bad? *Not that bad?* It's terrible! Come on, tell me you're kidding around here. Please. Tell me you've got the next *British Patient* in your pocket.'

I wasn't kidding around. I thought that my screenplay had some merit – not a lot, I was beginning to appreciate, but some. And I wasn't being unrealistic about it – I couldn't see Tom Cruise as the young hero (me), but John Cusack maybe. 'What about if there's a scene where the two guys drive down the wrong side of the road screaming with joy? And they pick up some lady hitchhikers and get married the next day,' I offered. 'One of them has white line fever. One of the guys, I mean.'

'Sean,' said Herman, leaning pleadingly on the vowels. 'Why do you write this sort of crud? You have such beautiful hands, why waste them? This is not entertainment. This is not popular cinema! Such a beautiful right hand. Here, give me.' He looked at my hand as though it was something he'd spied through the glass of a delicatessen counter. 'C'mon, give me!' he demanded, almost salivating. I placed my hand on the desk. 'Find your voice, Sean. Find your voice and use it to tell a wonderful, wonderful story.' His eyes misted up rheumily. 'Give me a man who whispers sweet nothings into the ears of his equine friends. Give me a wise little alien sausage creature who teaches lessons to children on bicycles. Give me an earthquake, a volcano, a *flood*, for Christ's sake. Give me sex, a beautiful woman and a little gun play, and I'll be happy. That's all I ask, Sean. That's not so much, is it? Am I being *unreasonable* here? Just one lousy sex scene.'

I told Herman that he wasn't being unreasonable, but the sort of stuff he wanted just didn't occur to me. It appealed to me like hell, but it didn't *occur* to me. 'But I'll try to change my mindset and think along those lines, I really will. Sex and guns, sex and guns.'

Herman slowly nodded his huge head. 'Hard-ons and hardware.' He nodded some more, then his eyes drew mine down to my open hand, which still lay on the desk. 'Go on, take it away!' he spluttered. 'I'm not gonna touch it. What do you think I am – a pervert? It's probably not even kosher!'

Catching Up

Over a couple of burgers in a Santa Monica mall, David asks, 'So how did it go? Are you rich yet?'

'No. I think I'm in either development or turnaround.'

'Did he suggest plastic surgery?'

'No. Herman thinks I've got beautiful hands, but I need confirmation from a leading manicurist. Most of all, I need a beautiful mind.'

'Even that probably wouldn't do. A beautiful body would get you further in LA.'

'Or a nice car. A nice car'd get you places – from B to A-list. God, what a town . . .'

'Yeah, it's pretty bad isn't it.'
'Fuck no, I love it!'

California Über Alles
California üüüüüüber alles!

What Goes Up

The Ferris wheel at the end of the pier is spinning; a bright, neon whirr the colour of happiness. I find myself tracing a zombie-like path toward it.

'Where are you going?' asks David.

'Must . . . ride . . . coloured . . . wheel . . .' I mutter.

'I'll see you back at the hotel. I vomit on those things.'

Tired as I am, I wander to the end of the pier and take the last ride of the night. As I rise slowly into the air, the lights of Santa Monica and Venice Beach present themselves to me, a dark carpet scattered with jewels. Higher still, the carpet unfurls to reveal the diamonds of Beverly Hills and the snaking pearl of headlights on Sunset Boulevard. I think about how I've walked over much of Los Angeles, how I know its shape and currents. What was once only a faint impression, a myth almost, is now texture and memory. It is real. The lights blur as my eyelids droop. High above the black Pacific the wheel descends, easing me into sleep.

I wake up stiff-backed and yawn. It takes me a moment to realise where I am, and when I do, I almost scream. I'm still on the Ferris wheel, in a car that's stopped at the very top. Way down below me, the pier is totally dark. 'Hey!' I shout into the dizzy void. 'Hey, Ferris wheel guy!! Up here! Help!!' It's like some lost scene from *The Third Man*. Lucky I'm not as fat as Orson Welles, or I'd be finished for sure. I think I can hear a zither playing somewhere nearby.

Shortly after 5 a.m., I'm still up here and completely swaddled in fog – it's like being caught in God's chilly beard. The seat lurches horrifically. I'm being lowered slowly through the fog; my bones ache with cold. I wonder if there'll be police and a news crew down there, waiting to thrust microphones into my face and question me about my ordeal. I rub the sleep from my eyes and pat down my hair. What will I say? A tough and pithy remark, something *Apollo 13*-ish. The seat pulls into the exit area. 'Morning,' I say to the operator, a teen who just stares open-mouthed at me. He probably cannot believe that I survived the trauma.
He finally speaks. 'D'jou pay for this ride?'

In silence I hand over another two bucks and slowly walk back down the pier. No police, no news crew and no purse-clutching, hand-wringing astronaut's wife in a sexy blue twin-set.

***Death in Venice*. Sean and David get very drunk. Rated 4.6 (blood alcohol).**

Morning

We've moved to yet another hotel, the ritzy Ritz-Carlton in Marina Del Rey. 'Where were you this morning?' asks David at last, as he unpacks his suitcase. 'I got up for a leak at six-thirty and you weren't there.'
'I was stuck on the Ferris wheel all night.'
'Oh.'

Afternoon

We hire a couple of bikes and take a ride along Venice Beach – us and about 14,000 other cyclists, bladers, boarders and roller-skaters. Hanging around a place like Venice Beach is no good for my flimsy self-esteem – it's teeming with tanned, healthy, vibrant, happy, attractive, well-built babes and bohunks. If they're not tandem-blading in some mini flesh train, they're diving into the sand in a spectacular volleyball leap or doing deep push-ups on the parallel bars or just about anything to make normal people feel inferior.

David and I cycle past the scattered palmists, tarot readers and spiritual advisers pushing Hare Krishna, Islam, Whole Earth Person philosophies and Christianity (the Christians all wear sandals with white socks and carry banners condemning marijuana. 'For all you dope smokers, hell is gonna be one LONG BURN!!!'). Past street performers by the million – breakdancers, limbo dancers, line dancers, two guys spray-painted silver doing the old 'robot' act, a spaced-out chick playing bad electric guitar to a life-sized doll called Ruffy, miserable comedians, singers, cartoonists, pot-smokers, nut jobs, crackheads and vagrants weaving in and out of the tourist mass.

A bunch of loud and menacing African-American militants calling themselves the Nation of Israel have cordoned off a large grassy area with rope and posted guards holding enormous swords at each corner. They're wearing battle fatigues, black berets and huge leather armbands and belts. Most are around thirty but there's a twelve-year-old boy in there looking meaner than he should be able to. As one member holds up pictures of

261

lynchings and other horrors, another shouts through a loud-hailer about paying the White Man back double what he put the Black Man through. 'Double?' David muses quietly. 'The same amount would be fair enough, but double seems a bit much.' I pull him away before they kick off the payback with two extremely innocent Australians.

I will execute on them sore retribution by acts of furious chastisement, and they shall know that I am the Lord, when I carry out my punishment upon them.

Ezekiel 25:17 / Samuel L. Jackson

Night

We drank two bottles of white wine. Each. It was the beginning of my Great American Drunkenness. As far as I want to remember, we ate expensively at a restaurant called James Beach, before crossing the street to a bar called Rebecca's which was full of drug dealers, high-class hookers called Tiffany and Mahogany ('No splinters on her, man'), pimps, porno actors and models.

I asked one extraordinarily tall and beautiful woman about the drug she was on.

'It's called Fame,' she said, with a notorious smile.

'What happens?' I asked.

'You get a sudden rush of delusional grandeur. The world is yours.'

'Cool. How long does it last?'

'Fifteen minutes,' she replied. 'Gotta go – I'm peaking.'

California Girls
(I wish they all could be.)

Somehow I got talking to a bald guy named Jim or Jack and his muscly friend named Matt or Mike. Hoping to have my head beaten in, I opened with, 'So, what are you two clowns doing here?' Unfortunately, they were friendly and just laughed at me. As near as I could understand, Jim or Jack sold TV studio sets (or maybe just TV sets) and Matt or Mike was a music producer, 'a Rick Rubin type guy'.

'But Rick Rubin has a beard,' I told him. 'You don't have a beard.' I was being quite the conversationalist. 'His beard is famous.'

Next thing, David and I were in the back of their car being driven off somewhere to be killed. 'Are you guys gonna violate us before you cut our throats?' I gurgled. 'Yeah,' said Jim/Jack, 'but we have to buy cigarettes first.' As soon as we pulled over at a convenience store, David and I took the opportunity to run – into the store to buy vodka, then straight back to our killers' car and off to another bar/restaurant/bar called Hal's which was full of beautiful young people high on how beautiful and young they were. I was feeling friendly and fashionable, so I slid into a booth next to a guy in a very nice brown suit who was talking to another handsome guy whose clothes I forget.

I led with 'Thassa nice suit and shirt you're wearing.'

'Thanks. Now get lost,' said the guy in brown.

'Hey buddy, I'm on'y tryna say –'

He absolutely exploded. 'DO YOU FUCKING MIND!? WE'RE MOMENTING HERE!'

The whole place stopped and stared. In the frozen silence, there was only one thing I could say. 'Momenting!? What the hell do you mean by that? You Americans just love turning nouns into verbs.'

But our conversationing was over. He smashed his glass on the table top and screamed, 'GET THE FUCK AWAY FROM ME!!'

I was just about to ask my new friend if he had any coke or Fame when I felt a strong hand grab my shoulder and yank me from the booth – just out of reach of the La Motta-like fist that swiped past my face. Shocked, I turned to see who my saviour was.

'Charlie,' I said. 'It was you!'

'Don't call me Charlie,' David shouted through the din. 'What the hell are you trying to do? Get yourself killed?'

'No. I don't know. Maybe. Prob'ly. You know how it is when I'm drunk. I'm very drunk, y'know.'

'Well, try not to carry on like such an idiot. I might not be around next time.'

I was finished in that place – indeed, all of LA was finished with me. Charlie took me back to the hotel and I tried to forget everything that happened. But couldn't.

On the Road Again. **LA to SLO with S & D. Music by Willie Nelson. Lyrics by Jack Kerouac.**

California Split
Poker term.

3.05 p.m.

We're finally on our way out of LA, after many action-packed, booze-fuelled, fun-filled, hot-dogged days. I'm kind of relieved, because although it's a real nice place to visit, I wouldn't want to live there. Unless I had a cool job in TV or the movies. Then

I'd live there. We're in another rented Neon, exactly the same as Leon Mk 1, only red, and therefore even more stupid looking. 'And faster,' adds David. Well, somebody had to.

3.30 p.m.

We're driving through Malibu. They liked to refer to it as 'the colony of Malibu' back in the swinging 50s when people like Paul Newman and Peter Lawford and Adolf Eichmann had mansions (or 'huts') here. It's now called, by me at least, 'the ugly suburb of Malibu' and is the sort of place where Erik and Lyle Menendez would live if they weren't in jail. The people around here drive like complete assholes (wandering all over the road at very high speeds) or complete morons (wandering all over the road slowly). Apart from that, it's beautiful. All those rocks and the crashing blue Pacific.

4.45 p.m.

Still a long way from San Luis Obispo, although we're now referring to it as 'SLO' which should save a little time. We haven't even reached Santa Barbara yet, much less Santa Maria or Santa Claus.

We're talking about novelty songs – 'Shuddupa You Face', 'Eat It', 'The Streak', 'Downunder', etc. The golden age of the idiot tune has sadly passed, but if you could write just one, you'd be set for life.

'How about "Whenever I Look Down, All I See is Down"?' David says, pounding the steering wheel with laughter.

'What about "I Am 32 Years Old and Sleep with My Thumb in My Mouth"?'

He glares at me and swerves hard right, clipping a pole and

releasing the air bag in my face. It's puffy, fluffy and comfy. I rub my face in it for a while, then fall asleep, dreaming of what I might have been.

MO-K-TEL

Reached SLO and the 'world famous' Madonna Inn around six-thirty. Unfortunately, the notorious Rock Rooms were booked out months ago, so we're feeding our desire for hotel cheesedom in the Golfer's Suite, so named because it has green carpet. We're a little disappointed – we were expecting Astro turf and at least nine holes. I *knew* I shouldn't have brought my damn clubs. Oh well, the Swiss Suite probably isn't filled with cuckoo clocks, secret bank accounts and a sense of neutrality either.

Incidentally, the word 'mo-tel' was first dreamed up in 1925 by a SLO innkeeper who wanted to attract people in cars. 'Mo' is for motor, but I'm not sure where the last bit is from.
'Ho-TEL, you boob,' David points out.
And according to an old paperback called *Teen-Age Vice* I'm reading, the original mo-tels were full of '. . . college town prostitutes and professional young hitchhikers out to fulfil their desire to see what is on the other side of the fence'.
We should have booked into the Teen-Age Suite.

8.45 p.m.

Downtown SLO rocks!! We're in a restaurant/sports bar called the Firestone Grill, which like every other licensed joint with a TV is filled to capacity with loud football fans. They're all big and they all love to whoop. Every half-hour (which is how long it is between interesting moments in NFL, give or take forty-five minutes), the whole room erupts with screams, cheers, clapping, whistling and farting. The most recent outburst was so violent and instantaneous, I almost spilled my beer. On the replay, I saw what the spectacular high point was – a wide receiver *actually caught the ball!!*

Didja see that!?
Nah, there was mustard in m'eye.

White female football fans, approx. 27

Barbecue is the staple at the Firestone Grill and I just ate a barbecued sandwich known disgustingly as 'The Pig'. I hated ordering it ('I'll have a The Pig please') almost as much as I hated eating only half of the sauce-smeared flesh fest. It's probably just as well that I stopped – if there had been another sudden, miraculous catching of the ball, I might've choked.

Didja see that!?
Nah, there was a lump of spray cheese on m'face.

White female football fans, approx. 27

'What's your general opinion on drugs?' I asked David.

'I enjoy the occasional smoke,' David replied. 'A joint every now and then.'

'Nothing stronger? You ever had heroin?'

'Of course not. That's madness.'

'You know why it's madness? Because I bet it's really good. I bet I'd love it.'

'I'm sure you would. That's why a person like you should never have it. You have a highly addictive personality.'

'Does that mean you crave me when I'm not around?'

'No, it does not.'

'A bit though. C'mon, admit it.'

'Not a bit.' He seemed very firm about it.

Single Feature

The night was saved from pork and NFL by a marvellous, funny, sweet, smart movie; we laughed into our Milk Duds and Coke all the way through. It was called *Swingers* and was about a bunch of guys called Trent and Mike and Sue looking for love in LA. It was brilliant. I wished I was in it or wrote it or lived it or something. And it made me miss LA. Also, I wouldn't mind being called Sue – it's kind of cool.

'Sue's *my* name,' muttered David, somewhere near sleep.

'You're Curly Sue, I'm *Regular* Sue.'

Citizen Caning. **Anxiety at the Hearst Castle when Charlie Chaplin loses a game of tennis. (Silent)**

3.48 p.m.

Highway 1. Scenic coastline on one side and brown grass with angry cows on the other. We've done the Hearst Castle tour. (My general impression of Hearst was that he was very rich and had a lot of stuff. More opinions later.) Randy's fantastic wealth made us hungry so we stopped by the side of the road near Big Sur to eat an expensive and unhealthy lunch – a kosher chicken hot dog and fries for me and a bowl of spatchcock chilli for David. As we sat at the picnic table, we were gently rained upon by flakes of ash carried by the wind from a coastal bushfire that had been raging for the last week. Some ash got in my dog and it didn't taste too good.

4.38 p.m. Highway 1

We're driving into thick bushfire smoke. There are lots of fire engines and firemen all over the place. Strangely, many of the fire fighters are sitting by the side of the road eating apples. Maybe they cool you down.

I imagine that Cary Grant, who stayed at the Hearst 'ranch' San Simeon more than thirty times ('It was a great place to spend the Depression,' he once remarked insouciantly), must have driven down this very road quite often. I like Cary Grant, even though people often mention that I am nothing like him.

California Dreamin'
On such a winter's day.

10.40 p.m. Carmel-by-the-Sea

Had dinner at Clint Eastwood's Hog's Breath Inn. We had to go there because Clint used to be mayor of the town and I believe he still carries a six-gun. I don't recommend it – I got screwed to the tune of $17.95 for a measly fettucine alfredo! Here in cute little Carmel-by-the-Sea they've banned obscene eyesores like streetlights and street signs, so walking around in broad daylight you don't know where the hell you are. Even indoors in Carmel-by-the-Sea they reject anything stronger than gaslight. They must be afraid of being spotted from the air and bombed or something.

Still, it's quaint as hell, it really is. Even though they screw you for fettucine.

Insolent Pair Ejected from Hearst Tour

The Hearst castle tour is a very worthwhile but very strange experience. First of all, it's not really like just visiting a dead guy's house – it's more like *emigrating* there. Even when booking your ticket you have to give up all sorts of secret information, like your blood type ('Mine's generic,' I said. 'My parents were too cheap to give me a specific type.') and your mother's maiden name ('Guinevere,' David told them). When you pick up the tickets you have to show your passport. 'Where do I pick up the duty free?' I asked the ticket lady.

'On the bus,' she said, but I think it was an order rather than an answer.

The bus took us up the steep hillside to the wild and sprawling opulence that William Hearst (and dozens of freeloaders like Charlie Chaplin and Mary Pickford) called home. It was an incredible place, and it made me very unhappy about living in a three-room apartment in Melbourne, where the only antique I own is my car. Still, a gaff like San Simeon is just one of the benefits of being the media baron son of a mining baron who bought half of California at 15¢ an acre. (As opposed to being the half-wit, drop-out son of a middle-level executive in the flooring biz, who backed the winner of the Melbourne Cup in 1974 and made a cool five quid.)

As we were traipsing across one of the Mesozoic-age floor rugs I put up my hand and asked the tour guide, 'Are we allowed to see where Mr Hearst kept *Rosebud*?'

'You're thinking of Charles Foster Kane, Sir.'

'Where's his place? Is it near here?'

'He was a fictional character. He has no "place".'

Then David put up his hand. 'Whereabouts is the Grotto? Will there be any Bunnies on view later?'

'That's Hugh Hefner,' she said. A few other tourists were staring at us.

'Is it true that he used to have his staff disinfected before they could serve him food?' I asked, genuinely interested.

'That's Howard Hughes.'

'Are we allowed to mention the alleged kidnapping of Patty by the Symbionese Liberation Army?' wondered David.

'Where is Symbia, anyway?' I asked. 'Do you happen to know Ma'am?'

Then, to the delighted applause of the rest of the tour group, we were roughly grabbed by two security humps who escorted us back to the bus.

Some tour – we didn't even get to see Bubbles the Chimp. On the other hand, food-wise it's exceptional: they have a 'breakfast montage' special where you and your wife eat in silence every morning for twenty-seven years.

***The Good, the Bad and the So-so.* Co-starring Clint Eastwood as 'the mayor with no name'. Rated ®.**

I'm tired. All night long the phone kept ringing. 'Hello?' I'd say wearily.

'Play missy fo' me . . .'

'What!?'

'Play missy for me . . .'

'Play mixie's sore knee? Speak up lady, I can't hear a word you're whispering.'

'Play "Misty" for me!'

'What the hell's that s'posed to mean?'

12.12 p.m.

We're getting the Neon out of the sickly sweet hamlet-let of Carmel-by-the-T-Shirt. And we're taking the Seventeen Mile Drive® featuring the Lone Cypress®. (Those registered trademarks are Real-by-the-Way, so if you're thinking of opening your own seventeen-mile-drive scenic strip, forget it. And if you're a lone cypress trying to muscle in on the action, think again fella!!)

We just stopped to look at a rock teeming with seals barking their heads off. It was a beautiful experience and now I feel all touched and warm and spiritual.

'You're supposed to get all that from dolphins,' says David.

'I can feel that way off seals if I want,' I tell him, dabbing patchouli behind my ear and starting work on some batik clothing.

'Yeah, if you're a furrier.'

1.01 p.m.

Drove down Cannery Row in Monterey. It's forgotten its history of labour shame, and is now a tourist joint. Met two guys called Lenny and George who told me to go no further with this idea because they were from *Of Mice and Men*.

3.03 p.m.

We're heading out of Monterey, a much less corny town than Carmel-by-the-By, with the fabulous Fantastic Fifth Dimension blaring 'Black Patch'. We're taking Highway 1, north to San José. And yes, we do know the way.

California Highway Patrol
CHiPS (John & Ponch)

4.04 p.m.

Castroville – the artichoke capital of California, perhaps the world. The Artichoke Inn. The Giant Artichoke. Artichokes three for a dollar. I quite like artichokes, but we're still not staying. 'What's your general opinion on artichokes?' I ask David. 'I have none.' Some host . . .

5.05 p.m.

We've checked into a run-down roach motel in a busted, crime-ridden part of seaside Santa Cruz, right next door to a biker gang HQ and a deadly old rollercoaster park. Everything in our awful room is covered in protective dacron. There are ice cubes from 1972 in the freezer, and there's a weird bubbling sound coming from somewhere in the room – as though we're listening to an invisible fish tank (it's very Zen). On TV, Dick Cavett is interviewing a young Sly Stone who is clearly coked off his crazy head. We're caught in some sort of accommodation time warp. And except for the cockroaches, I'm beginning to like it.

The refrigerator is attempting to resuscitate itself. 'There's a city for every culture, sub-culture, clique, gang, sect and fad in America, isn't there?' I observe, unplugging the beast. 'Oh yeah. You've got your blues thing in Chicago, your Hell's Angels in San Bernadino, the gay culture of San Francisco, a hot Mormon scene in Salt Lake City. Americans love a clearly defined territory.' 'And Santa Cruz is the skate capital of America, isn't it? Probably the world.' 'I once wanted to move here when I was a skateboarding fool.' 'What do you think now you've seen it?'

273

'Not bad. Not bad at all,' he says in his slow, deep, sarcastic voice. The fridge shudders, makes sporadic gurgling sounds, like an old cat with stomach ache swallowing a fish, then sighs gassily.

12.12 a.m.

David just woke up to order me to go to sleep. We have to get up early to return the car because if we're one minute overdue they'll make us pay for another day. I can't sleep though. The polymer bedsheets are making me itchy and nervous and that mysterious bubbling is driving me crazy. Plus I've been re-visiting the New York City of the 1980s by reading *Bright Lights, Big City* – I cannot believe it was a best seller. It's as terrible as the decade to which it belongs. As my hair develops a neat ponytail and a pair of red braces appears over my shirt, I begin barking out orders to my secretary: 'Get me Boesky and Milken on line three, now! Also, I want sushi and cocaine for lunch. And the latest Blondie album.' I'm a real Master of the Universe, merging and acquiring, and right before my eyes the walls seem to be developing pastel hues with touches of salmon.

2.02 a.m.

Still awake. Still gurgling. Still can't believe Jay McInerney is rich. Am no longer a Master of the Universe, but an Anonymous Transient of Santa Cruz.

If You're Going . . . **Where else? Rated R (frequent drug references).**

9.10 a.m.

Downtown Santa Cruz is full of New Age hippies, old age

hippies, crusty hippies and hippy punks – all of them on skateboards. They're simply everywhere, hanging around in filthy haired packs. We ran over a few on our way out of town. It was sad and manslaughterish, but unavoidable. They're in a better world now.

10.10 a.m.

Should I describe freeways? The air force F 1-11s sliding across the sky, the great cliffs tumbling down to the sea? Or should I recount my memories of San Francisco from a boyhood visit in 1977? The thrill of the glass elevators at the St Francis. Spilling root beer all over my sister at Fisherman's Wharf. Asking the Human Jukebox, a trumpeter hiding inside a yellow cardboard box with letters and numbers painted on it, to play a Chuck Mangione tune called 'Maui Waui' that I was keen on at the time. 'You have a very good memory,' David tells me, slowing down because there's traffic ahead.

'Thanks.'

'Very good, but very boring.'

So I describe the freeway.

12.10 p.m. San Francisco Kid

Our introduction to downtown San Fran is not good. The complicated and utterly ridiculous system of one-way streets, no-way streets, no left turns, no right turns and no u-turns makes many areas of the city simply impenetrable. There are several large corporations going out of business here because nobody can get to them. On the other hand, there seem to be more smokers in San Francisco than elsewhere in California, and you can drink coffee through a straw and nobody looks at you funny. On the other hand to that hand, I keep looking out of our

25th-floor hotel room window and thinking about earthquakes. It's very hard not to.

EARTHQUAKE FORECAST – CALL 1-800 USA JOLT

2.10 p.m.

San Francisco must be a rockin' place to live. There's a free street paper here called the *SF Weekly* which is full of all the important stuff like who's playing, what's showing and advice on the gentle art of rimming, provided by a gay man who likes to be addressed as 'Hey Faggot!'

The rules of rimming are:

- Look before you lick.
- Take lots of showers.
- Don't rim on the first date.
- Don't chew gum whilst in the act.
- Use a combination of little licks, darting motions and slow back and forths.
- Bon appetit.

'I want you to forget all that information immediately,' says David, sternly asserting his heterosexuality.

'What would you do if you were gay?' I ask.

'What do you mean what would I *do*? I'd be gay, simple as that. But I never would be anyway, I'm just not a gay type.'

'I think it'd be pretty good. They certainly seem to have a lot more fun than the rest of us: better music and clubs, they get good jobs on arts councils and they definitely have better physiques. On the whole, gay men seem much healthier and happier. I could be gay, I really could. But the thing is they probably wouldn't *want* me to be.'

276

'As opposed to women, who are deeply grateful that you're straight?'
'Yeah . . . I suppose nobody's that thrilled about my sexuality either way. Lord knows I'm not.'

There's also a section in the paper called Missed Connections, which evidently tries to help ships that passed in the night end up in the same port. Here's an example: *You: WF, long-haired brunette, blue sundress, spotlighting for bands. Me: AF, short hair, orange shirt, white pants, smoking outside. We eye-contacted, I wanted to smile but was too shy. Please call 555-Blah Blah Blah.* Or *Dark-haired woman taking the Castle Bar tour 9/29. The blonde woman in chains was thrilled by your attention. The long haired man loved your point of view. Meet us?* And another: *You were a fat, bored, stupid looking guy on a bus. Your drab, ill-fitting clothes and air of self-absorbed misery made me want to slap you. May I abuse you in person?* I wonder if I should call . . .

I'm playing the soundtrack to *Basic Instinct*. It's quite scary. *Me: A large, sweaty policeman – one of three – who stared at you hungrily licking his lips. Later I showed up as Newman in 'Seinfeld'. You: An interrogated blonde in a short skirt. You uncrossed your legs and caused a scandal. Wanna see my truncheon?*

Birthday Party

'Let's get this party started right,' whispered David meekly, conveying irony.
'All right,' I said. 'I'll have a margarita. A small one.'
It was the night before my thirty-first birthday, and we were having a couple of drinks in San Francisco's seedy Mission

District. The Makeout Room. Some advertising awards show was on TV. We looked up at it whilst rimming salty glasses.

'I see lots of sporting heroes advertising stuff, but not OJ Simpson,' said David, pulling a bitter lemon face which made him look like his own grandmother.

'I think it's because of all that murdering and stuff. Cutting people's throats is a poor career move. Still, if they could just find the right product for him,' I replied, salt licks around my lips.

'Pez maybe . . .' We both laughed quietly into our tequilas.

Drugs

As it's California, there's no cigarette machine in the bar. The muscle-shirted doorman directs me to an all-night store a few blocks away. The humidity mixes with my drunkenness, producing agitated sweat that soaks my hair and sticks the shirt to my back. Half a block from the store a scrawny crackhead with a matching dog stops me and asks for a cigarette. 'Sure.' I give him one and ask if he has any cocaine. 'Sure.' Half an hour of screwing around while we avoid imaginary cops and wait for imaginary dealers to show up with imaginary cocaine (a vague idea dusted with icing sugar). The crackhead's name is Wood; the dog's name is Bandit. They're nice guys.

I'm about leave when Wood whips out two plastic-covered rocks from somewhere deep in his gums.

'Crack.' His eyes flit up and down, waiting for me to turn into a narc. 'Twenty dollars a rock.'

'No way. Twenty for both.'

He waits. 'All right, but you gotta smoke some wit' me.'

'Sure.'

We sit on the steps of a brownstone and Wood prestidigitates a crack pipe from nowhere. 'Suck it all the way to the bottom of your lungs,' he tells me as he puts a flame to the pipe. I do so. 'So what do you think?' he asks.

'I feel normal. *Extra* normal, in fact.'

'You think you feel normal,' he says. 'But nothing's ever gonna be the same again. Remember what the dormouse said.' Then he's gone.

'What did the dormouse say?' I whisper into the dark.

Minutes later, hot and wet and panting, I return to the club and find David.

'Jesus, where the hell've you been? What happened to the birthday boy?'

'I don't know. I had some drugs.'

'Real or sugar?'

'Real, I think. What did the dormouse say?'

'What dormouse?'

Before I can answer, I begin coughing and weeping. At first I think I'm dying of some latent drug effect but then I notice that David's gagging and crying too, along with everybody else in the club. There's a crush for the exit, and as we all wheeze and weep outside I overhear the bouncer say, 'Some asshole's sprayed mace into the vents. Again.'

Reefer Madness. **David watches helplessly as his friend's life spirals into an abyss of depravity – the results are hilarious. Rated G.**

It's my birthday today; I am thirty-one. I am also tired and hung over as hell from drinking tequila and smoking crack with a junkie. Now I am an addict.

David and I are in a cafe/laundrette called Brainwash. It certainly is a very pleasant way to get clean – eating and drinking as your stuff whirls through its cycles. We have four machines going, two for whites, one for darks and a whole separate machine for the inaugural wash of my red shirt. Today we're using Wisk Liquid Detergent. There's no need to add any other detergent, powder or liquid: Wisk is all you need. This they tell you in English, French and Español. There are quite a few youth hostels nearby so the place is full of lonely internationals writing post-cards to friends, telling them how much fun it is to do your washing in another country.

David just loaded everything into a couple of dryers. One's set on Hot, for the heavy-duty stuff, and the other's on Warm for our delicates – the sensitive, annoying clothes.

Berkeley in the 90s

To get to Berkeley, on the other side of the bay, we had to cross the Bay Bridge, famous for having collapsed in the 1989 earthquake. It was not a pleasant trip across, and not nearly quick enough.

Berkeley is a very nice, very leafy city absolutely full of coffee shops and second-hand joints selling books, CDs and records. It was, therefore, a very, very bad place for me to be: I spent about $200 in thirty minutes.

After the shopping explosion we took a walk through the famous Berkeley campus. 'This is where it all began,' David said, 'the whole 60s protest movement that has shaped the society in which we live today. They were all here – Abbie Hoffman, Timothy Leary and Unabomber Ted Kaczinsky. Of course, it's not like that now. Today's students only want two things – to produce and consume, produce and consume . . .'

I couldn't help but think that the words were aimed directly at me. Well, the consumption part anyway. And I have to admit, I was pretty surprised and disgusted with myself – I never saw myself as a 'born to shop' kind of guy. I mean, I've been to Singapore and I *hated* it. I really did. But the evidence was right there, in two big bags stuffed so full of consumable product they were almost pulling my arms off. As David Mamet/Elliot Ness/Kevin Costner said in *The Untouchables*, 'I have become what I beheld.'

Of course, when I really thought about it, the only real problem I had with my rampant desire to buy stuff was how the hell would I fit it all in my suitcase?

Sosume

David and I had dinner at a Japanese restaurant where the sushi floated by on little wooden boats. It was nice, but after one too many gyoza I began to feel a little seasick. Suddenly, I vomited into the sushi river, making many diners swoon and causing some of the more adventurous customers to ask the waitress, 'How much is that pink lumpy stuff?'

California Roll
Rice, seaweed, pickled ginger, crab meat

Back at the hotel we watched *Independence Day* – a movie I had long wanted to see. I was glad I'd waited until now, because having travelled the length and breadth of the country, the notion of blowing up portions of America has even greater appeal.

David comments: 'They keep on saying they're going to "kick some alien butt", but how do they know the aliens actually have butts?' It's a good comment.

What *did* the dormouse say?

Luv 'n Haight. **The lads discover that the Summer of Love is well and truly over when a remark about Jerry Garcia's weight incites the rage of a bunch of hippies. Rated ⊗.**

This is how the mornings go: I sleep while David goes to the hotel gym; he comes back an hour later and closes the door loudly or drops something heavy onto my head to wake me; we shower (separately), then go wherever his travel guide research suggests is the best place for a couple of stiffs looking for a good time on the cheap.

My one request is that since we're not going to Cuba, I'd at least like to visit the Castro district. But this bright and sunny morning we're going to Haight-Ashbury, and yes, we're being sure to wear some flowers in our hair (although we will ultimately come to regret this as no-one else is). The bus fare is a dollar, so we've already halved the entertainment budget.

All these gangsters, all this bullshit, they're gonna get it sooner or later. Innocent bystanders are gonna get it too. Unless you ask for His help (pointing through roof of bus to God).
    Puerto Rican woman, approx. 55, wearing Clinton/Gore 96 badge

Haight-Ashbury is a tourist mecca of expensive vintage clothing outlets, second-hand record stores, cafes, restaurants, bong shops and sidewalk-sprawled panhandlers. It's also the 'punk' capital of California – there are skate punks, hippy punks, Rancid punks, deadbeat punks and punk punks. And all of them want your money. I shook my head at one sharp-haired youngster, who began shouting at me, 'There is *so* change in your pocket, man! I can hear it!! I can hear the money in your pocket, don't lie to me!!'

I turned and walked back to him. 'Oh, pardon me. I thought you asked whether I had any change I *wanted* to give you.' That shut him up. Little punk.

So we walked up and down, looked at stuff and didn't buy much. Well, I bought some things – Mexican Day of the Dead knick-knackery, a Hank Mancini album and an Eddie Henderson CD for a buck apiece from a thrift store. David took about two hours to decide whether to buy one measly Hawaiian shirt. Mr Impulsive, they call him around here. 'I have very precise taste in clothing,' he said, 'and the more expensive, the more precise.'

Later we and all our stuff caught a cab about two blocks to the St Francis Hotel. It's old and impressive but the glass elevators that zip up and down the thirty floors are on the *outside* of the building. It frightens the shit out of me. Of all the places not to be in a tremor, this is definitely *the* one. I read in the hotel guide that Paul Newman is the local fire chief and Richard Chamberlain is the slimy architect; the entertainment director is Irwin Allen. These are not good signs. 'We may never love like this again,' David sings quietly as we zoom up.

The Hills are Asleep (with the Sound of Snoring)

David's gone to see Neil Young, David Bowie, Patti Smith, Pearl Jam and the Cowboy Junkies at the Bridge School Benefit concert. I'm frightened of cowboys, junkies and David Bowie, so I'm on my own for the rest of the day. I continue my birthday celebrations by wandering around Macy's in a daze looking for the Designer Crack Pipe Department, searching the streets for the Human Jukebox and spilling root beer on myself, before returning to the evil elevator at the St Frank and falling asleep watching *Mary Poppins* on the Disney channel. It's not very dynamic, but I call it living.

I dreamed that David came back from the concert and told me that he cried during Neil's third song. I knew it had to be a dream because the real-life David is reluctant to speak about emotional matters greater than indigestion. Then he shared the entire three-hour set list with me. It had to be a dream – I remained interested. There was a knock at the door and Sally came in to clean the room and chit-chat with me in a Spanish accent. Speaking with a lisp, she told me she'd been eating peanut butter sandwiches ever since I'd been away. I gave her a big tip when she left, knowing that she would spend it all on 'thandwich thpreadth'.

I woke up in the dark. David was not back from the concert, but the room had definitely been tidied up while I was under. I hated to think of the maid seeing me sprawled in some inelegant sleep position, a tangle of blankets wrapped around my body as I made rude, unconscious sounds. I lay on my back for a while and tried to see myself as others might see me, fat and tragic in the half-light of observation . . .

This is the last thing Sean remembers. David is back, and they're lying in their beds, separated only by a night table and their fierce heterosexuality. The hum of the air conditioner lulls them toward sleep as they talk drowsily, pointlessly.

SEAN: I keep thinking there's gonna be an earthquake. A big one.

DAVID: There won't be.

SEAN: How do you know?

DAVID: There *won't* be.

SEAN [RISING UP ON HIS ELBOWS]: I'm sure everybody back in ought-six and 89 said that too. And they were *wrong*, weren't they?

DAVID: There won't be.

SEAN: Just lying there saying "There won't be," over and over again doesn't mean that there won't be one, you know.

DAVID: There will not be an earthquake.

SEAN: I almost hope there *will* be one just to show you.

Over the next seven hours of near-silence, whenever he snores particularly brutally, Sean wakes and gasps, 'It's the big one!'

The Bad Men of Alcatraz. Rated 25 to Life.

Californ-í-ä
Silly pronunciation.

Sent to Alcatraz

I wonder if they had a snack bar on the ferry that took 'Machine Gun' Kelly, Alvin 'Creepy' Karpis, Leon 'Whitey' Thompson et al to their final four-bar hotel. Sean 'Fatboy' Condon doubts it. It feels quite strange, sneaky and a little bit sick to be visiting

285

this place of abject misery and 'man love' on a pleasant, sunny afternoon. But what can you do?

We get off the ferry and pant up a long hill to a cinema where a short film introduces us to the Alcatraz experience. Here is the history: the rock was formed after the Ice Age, and before it was a tourist attraction it was a prison, and before that it was a prison too – first for the Army, then the FBI. Some Indians nabbed it for a while in the early 70s and now it's 'we the people's' again. (Although for a minute there they almost turned it into a casino, which would have been stupendously ironic. Or coincidental.)

Then it's time to do what we all came for: the award-winning, self-guided, much-hyphenated audio tour covering four decades of degradation and despair. You strap on some headphones and stroll through the cell block house listening to chilling and detailed narrations by ex-cons and ex-guards. It'd be deeply moving if there weren't three hundred other people shuffling around at the same time, producing an unending chorus of 'Ooohhh' and 'Aaahhh' which most people cannot hear because they're all wearing headphones and saying 'Ooohhh' or 'Aaahhh'. Sometimes I really wish I was Michael Jackson and could do anything I like in complete privacy. Well, not *everything*, but stuff like going to department stores and Alcatraz. Still and all, it's an excellent tour, well worth the $10, and a very compelling deterrent for those who, like myself, are considering a life of crime to support their habits and/or families. It also brings the place very much to life – David told me that he lost a double sawbuck in a game of craps with two dead robbers named Gus and Vinny.

Near the dock there was a gift and souvenir shop. I'm not much of a souvenir type guy but because real live ex-con/kidnapper and former Alcatraz inmate Jim 'No Nickname' Quillen was there signing copies of his book, I bought one as a gift and spent a few moments with him. I asked him to write, 'Dear Sally, it looks like crime is finally beginning to pay, but I still wish the kidnapping had've come off good'. He gave me a pitying smile and declined. When he'd finished signing the book I sat in the empty chair by his side, for a photo. As he shook my hand, I said, 'Try to look mean and criminal.' But he just sort of grinned nicely. Like an old man. Sitting next to a young fool.

As we walked off, David and I talked about how great it would be if Quillen the Kidnapper did his book dedications using cut-up newspaper and glue, instead of plain old handwriting. We amused ourselves greatly. Ha ha ha. Then on the ferry I opened the book and read what he'd actually written: 'To Sally. Greetings from Alcatraz. I'm sorry I lost 21 years of my life because I was stupid. Jim Quillen, Prisoner #586.'

And all the way back across the bay I could only think how sorry I was to have said idiotic things to a dignified and redeemed man because I was stupid.

I have no quarrel with society. It ought to have none with me. I've been wrong all my life. Now in this hole, I fight the atmosphere, the silence, the bodies. No one feels the hard misery inside me.
                    Joseph Cretzer, Alcatraz prisoner/rioteer, d. 1946

SIGN OUTSIDE A FULL CAR PARK: SORRY, WE'RE MAXED OUT.
DAVID: And we're like totally bummed about it, dudes.

10 p.m. Clift Hotel

Had a prison chow-line dinner of meatloaf, mash and greens at Lefty O'Doul's, who, judging by the many photos of him in ancient baseball gear posing with ancient baseballer (and Marilyn Monroe baller) Joe Di Maggio, must have been some sort of ball player. He was probably left-handed too.

'And Irish,' adds David.

Now we're watching a sappy episode of 'E.R.', starring a bunch of annoying, good-looking, important young actors pretending to be annoying, good-looking, important young doctors. And even though they're doing a marvellous job, the show lacks authenticity – I've seen a couple of 'em actually *sign* their prescriptions.

EDWIN HOUTKOOPER PODIATRY. CALL 1-800 FOOT

The Mission. **With Robert De Niro as Sean and Willie Aames as David. Subtitled to help explain the religious imagery.**

California Magic
Variety of marijuana.

The Streets of San Francisco

We waded through the Frisco drizzle down to the Mission and checked out a thrift store which was so large we lost each other almost immediately. We'd been together almost twenty-four hours a day, every day, for over two months, so I'm not exactly sure that it was completely accidental on either of our parts. In fact it wouldn't have surprised me if David had headed straight for the airport as soon as he'd gotten rid of me.

In the rain on bleached and treeless Valencia Street, a black man with rotten teeth and a gold tie strangling the crumpled collar of his shirt held up a sign that said, 'Could you spare 50¢ please?' I patted my pockets, shook my head and said, 'Sorry, I've got nothing.' This was, of course, a lie. I had $57 in my wallet. I had plenty. The man looked at me understandingly, and he made rough, tongueless sounds whose tone clearly carried the message, 'That's okay, don't worry about it.' A few steps down the street I realised that he couldn't speak, and my sorry, unfit heart began breaking. 'That's okay, don't worry about it' – as loud and clear as any words I've ever heard. The hollow weakness of 'I've got nothing' swirled around my head. I could have any damn thing I wanted. I had too many CDs and books and clothes and I was still too cheap to give this guy a couple of bucks. The sign, the teeth, the tie, the sounds he made and the rain falling on us both – I could think of nothing else. I walked up and down Valencia, in and out of side streets, all around the Mission blocks in the hot rain, but I couldn't find him anywhere. He was gone, leaving me with an extra couple of bucks to spend on number one.

The Hills are Alive (with the Sound of Mucus)

With two things on my mind – dim sum and luggage – I made my way over to Chinatown. Man, it's steep over there. I'd have caught a cable car but I don't think the city is actually serious about those numbers as public transport: they're the size of toys and always end up so crowded with desperate fools clinging to their outsides, they look like those death trains that streak across

India. So I wheezed and spluttered my way up and down Himalayatown, my knees creaking, my lungs burning. More than a few times, I passed out halfway up a hill and woke to find that I'd rolled back down to the bottom. I was almost dead by the time I found a cafe, but at least I'd saved 80¢.

The food was quite horrible but I discovered a long time ago that you can eat almost anything if you take a sip of Coke in between bites. I read a Hearst paper, the *San Francisco Chronicle*, as I ate and drank – the OJ Simpson civil trial had begun and they'd discovered thousands of deformed frogs up north. The two items were related only in that they both really socked it to my appetite. As I was cramming my mouth with steamed blobs, I suddenly remembered what the dormouse said: 'Feed your head.'
But my head was full.

After the dim (sum total $5.20) I went down to the 'cheap luggage' district, a seedy part of town where I bought a large suitcase for $17. Seventeen dollars is way too inexpensive for a suitcase of any size, and mine was enormous. I bought it anyway, because after this trip I plan to never go anywhere again. About five minutes into ownership, as I was getting on a bus, and while the suitcase contained only *air*, the handle broke off.

That Night

He was obviously blind: there were dim spots behind the smoky glasses and, from lip to bar top and back, his fingers never left his beer glass. He looked like a criminal, hunched with joint-paranoia and arms covered in tattoos. I lit a cigarette and clicked my lighter close.
'Zippo, ain't it?' he said.

'Yes it is.'

'I may be blind, but I know what's what. Name's Dan.'

'Hi, I'm Sean.' I didn't hold my hand out.

He took a long draught of beer, then sighed and shook his head. 'I plucked my own eyes out,' he told me. There was foam on his chin.

'Why?' I asked.

'Sold the corneas to a Chinaman for ten G's. The cornea's 'bout yay long,' – holding his fingers a cigarette length apart – 'pulled a small bit of brain out as well.'

'Oh really?' *That* I believed. 'Ten grand to be blind the rest of your life. That's pretty steep.'

'Money's money, fella. I have glass eyes now. You wanna see?'

'No thanks.'

But it was too late; he whipped off his glasses and held out his palm, a dead brown eye rolling around in it, looking up at me. 'Are you looking at it? Or are you looking in my hole?'

I looked at the hole – a small, dark spot next to another brown glass eye. I could fit my finger in there. I turned away as he replaced the eye, with a noise like the opposite of a pop.

'Not bad, huh?'

'Yeah, they're pretty good. But once you start telling people that you're blind, y'know, it's easier to tell.'

'What are you doing here anyway, fella?' he asked.

'Just visiting.'

'You got plans for the weekend? Saturday afternoon?'

'No, not really.'

'You wanna do me a favour?'

'I doubt it. What?'

'I want you to go to Seattle for me. See somebody. Give 'em something . . .' He took out his wallet and told me to take out

$800, 'for expenses and the rest of it'. I told him that if he thought I was going to deliver drugs to some maniac in Seattle, he'd have to think again. Get some other patsy.

'It's not drugs. It's just a letter. A letter from me.'

'Why don't you mail it?'

'Can't trust the US postal system.'

He had me there. 'All right, I'll go.' He gave me the letter, addressed in wild, spidery handwriting, and recommended a cheap hotel in downtown Seattle. Then he shook my hand and wished me luck.

'Do I *need* luck or are you just being polite?'

'Good luck,' he said again, and I knew our conversation had finished.

'David, you are not going to believe what happened this evening.' He lay on his bed and I told him the story. '. . . so he wishes me luck a second time and that's it. He doesn't speak again. Whaddaya reckon?'

'Are you out of your mind?'

'I guess. But we have to go. I've got the guy's dough. Eight hundred bucks. And the letter.'

'Put your shoes on. We're giving the guy back his stuff. That crack has made you crazy.'

There was a long, heavy silence: Reason versus its more compelling and evil brother, Insanity. David stared at me. My eyes wandered the room and fell to my feet. I put my shoes on and we left.

We pushed open the door beneath a neon sign of a martini glass and stared into the boozy gloom.

'Is he here?' David asked.

I walked the length of the bar, taking a good look at the back of every drinker. 'Nope.'

'Did he give you his name or address or anything?'

'Nope.'

David sighed and pulled at his goatee. 'Oh well, I've always wanted to visit Seattle.'

I wondered whether I'd ever tell David that I'd taken him to the wrong bar.

Sleepless in Seattle. **A sleepless night in Seattle. Rated PNW.**

10.10 a.m.

We're on an Alaska Airlines plane. It's got a huge picture of some big-bearded native American on the tail – the Inuit Jerry Garcia or someone like that. Their safety record must be pretty good because they're not a well-known airline. And I certainly hope they're not about to become one.

We've just taken off and I feel like vomiting, crying and praying all at once – like a Charismatic Catholic. The letter, sealed and intriguing, is in my pocket. I'm pretty sure I'm going to open it later and find out just what the hell we've gotten ourselves into. I'll feel bad about it, but I have to do it.

Here We Are Now

Brown. Every shade, tone, texture and odour of brown. That's our horrible, pokey little room at the Hotel Seattle, in the financial district of downtown Grunge City. On a brown formica desk is a brown TV which receives three channels, all badly. And

293

brownly. The shag carpet is a deep brown that extends up the walls, creating an unlovely 'enclosed' effect in the tiny room. The rest of the walls are covered in brown hessian that secretes a brown/green glue, the colour of the smell of half-cooked cabbage. The brown leaf pattern on the poly/nylon/rayon/dacron/klingon bedspreads encompasses every hue from the most delicate, dirt-influenced beige to an arresting *chocolat à la vomite*. The lamp is brown. The bedside table is brown. The phone is bone brown and the bathroom is faux marble – brown. 'Only a blind guy could recommend a hotel like this,' says David, unpacking some hair shirts from a shopping bag.

The rest of Seattle is beautiful – hills, trees and Puget Sound rolling into a delightful city centre. It's the tree capital of America. It's also the capital of another venerable institution – the shoe-repair store. There's a dozen of them on every block. Why? Do the hills have a damaging effect on shoe leather? Also in abundance are coffee shop chains like Starbucks (that mega success story began here) and Seattle's Best Coffee. Why? Are people depressed by their flimsy shoes? Can only caffeine served by overfriendly, brainwashed youngsters help them?

Difficult to find, however, are hairdressers. I walked all over the city looking for somebody to tame my grey mane, lest I be mistaken for a grunge child. The first guy said, 'No way! I got one more customer then I am outta hair!' The next place, a large, modern 'training salon' full of young boobs wielding scissors and hairdryers, was fully booked 'because we only charge three dollars a head!' Further down the same road (I was cruising the tonsorial district) was a gentleman's barbershop called the Razor's Edge, a small 60s-style one-man operation where I was invited to take a seat and pick up a magazine. Forty minutes later, halfway through an *Esquire* article about why people visit Washington State (grunge, Microsoft, Nike, 'Twin Peaks', Jimi Hendrix, barbershops, apples and rain), the barber told me that he would not in fact be able to 'help' me. 'Because when I'm done with this gentleman here, I gotta get my bus. I'm sorry, Sir, but I'm only tryin' to serve you.' I rounded a few corners and stumbled upon an 80s-style two-woman salon where I sat in front of a mirror, picked up the same issue of *Esquire*, finished the article and then chatted with the hairdresser about grunge, Microsoft, Nike, 'Twin Peaks', Jimi Hendrix, barbershops, apples and rain while my brittle outbursts were shaped and restrained.

'You're very knowledgable,' the hairdresser said, mildly awed.

'Lived here all my life,' I told her.

With hair out of the way and all my shoes in good condition, I was left with nothing to do but come back to the brown room, bash the TV for a while and stare at the walls. My thoughts turned to home and I called Sally on the brown phone.

'I'm a-comin' home, baby!' I told her excitedly.

'Good. If I eat another peanut butter sandwich, I'll die,' she said. It was uncanny. 'By the way, I'm taking next week off so I can hang around with you when you get back, you bastard.'

It was very touching. Then I wrecked the momenting by asking her if our apartment was okay. She hung up on me.

Entertain Us

David and I head to a joint called the Lava Lounge, where we watch people play shuffleboard and sing along to Nirvana on the jukebox.

'Wanna go and check out Kurt Cobain's house tomorrow?' suggests David.

'The mission, we've got the mission, remember?' I remind him.

'Forget about Kurt Cobain.'

'But I want to see his house.'

'Maybe, if there's time. People say Kurt's been seen in hamburger joints around the Pacific North West.'

'*Served* in hamburger joints would be more likely.'

On our way out, a grimy, flannraletted youth grips my arm and pulls me into a shadow. 'Wanna score?' he mutters, looking askance theatrically.

'Wanna score what?' I ask.

He hops from foot to foot as he says, with low eyes, 'Blood. It's a pill.'

'What happens?'

'You become unable to talk about anything other than mortality and physical decay. It lasts from two to four hours; however, trace elements remain in your system. Frequent users build up such a high level that they are eventually completely paralysed by morbidity and die.'

'Sounds like my kind of thing. I'll take two,' I tell him.

Just as I'm reaching for my wallet, David pulls me outside and sharply slaps me twice. 'The mission,' he says. 'Remember the mission.'

'Sorry, can't do it,' I say to my near-dealer.

'Oh well. Whatever. Nevermind.'

With the Lights Out It's Less Dangerous

At night, things at the Hotel Seattle get a lot worse than mere decor. I hit my thin, 45°-sloping single bed at around 3 a.m. I begin to ignore the shuddering pipe sound (a steel rat chasing a tennis ball into the future) at around 4 a.m. and drift off but am roused at 5 a.m. by an urgent squeaking coming from right behind my blood-filled head. We're rooming right next door to Eros Central in downtown Seattle and there are two (or perhaps more) people banging up a storm on their unoiled bed for a good hour until dawn cracks through the brown curtains, bringing the lovers' groaning and my moaning to an end. At around 7 a.m. an industrial jackhammer begins tearing up the road immediately below us. Not just tapping it with a couple hundred pounds of pressurised attack force, but really ripping open the tarmac and smashing into the earth's crust. Jules Verne must be at the controls. After that, I don't sleep.

Mission Time

We catch a bus over to the university district, a nice, verdant sort of place full of students and trees and cheap food joints. It certainly *looks* harmless enough. David is calm and fine, buying us coffee and apples and happily leafing through paperbacks at book stores. I wonder if he's lost sight of why we're here, become oblivious to the mission. Forgetting that my watch is broken, I keep glancing at my wrist. It's always 2.40. Once in a while I wind the hands on to the time I think it might be. But I always end up resetting them at 2.40. It's as good a time as any.

At 2.40 I hail a cab and we drive off in silence. I hope the driver will tell us to stay away from the address I give him, but he seems unconcerned about our destination. And so we head into beautiful suburban Seattle's quiet, tree-lined streets, the crisp and sunny freshness at odds with the fear and darkness in my heart.

The street designated on the envelope is anonymous, the house unremarkable. I ask the cab driver to wait and to pre-dial 911 in case he hears any gunfire. David tells me that from this point I'm on my own and stays in the back of the taxi.

The house is small, with an unkempt garden out front. There's no letterbox but I can see a chute in the middle of the front door, and a printed sign which says 'Deliverys [sic] at rear'. I really don't want to go around to the back of this place, which has suddenly changed from unremarkable to completely terrifying, but I have come this far. However, I decide that I must read the letter before I get to the backyard.

I make my way down a path at the side of the house and stop by a window; I look inside but it is too dark to make out much. I stare at the word 'Private' underlined at the top of the envelope. I slip my thumb into the flap, tear it open and read the photocopied page.

Dear Reader,

I have betrayed you. Half of all that I have told you is the truth. I am not insane, but I sometimes lose my perspective. I am not a drunk, but I take a drink. I am not blind; through one eye, I can see. I can see the truth. *The truth will set you free – or bury you.*

Many years ago, I did sell my cornea, because the person who bought it wished to see the world as I see it. I spend the money by sending people to the place where you are right now. I know what it looks like, but do you see it the same way I do? Will you be honest when you tell others what you saw? Or will you betray them as I have betrayed you? As you are betraying yourself at this very moment by reading these words. You are not the first.

You will not be the last.

Was today like today? Were there birds in the sky? Did it rain? Will anything be the same again?

Milton Paradise, the Disappearer

I feel like I've been standing there forever. When I look down, there are insects running all over my shoes. I lift my feet and walk stiffly around to the back of the house. From a wooden box on the rear porch, hundreds, perhaps thousands, of screwed-up pieces of paper have spilled out over the entire yard like a white sea. Letters and envelopes; most of them rain-soaked, in tatters, eaten, decayed by the elements. All of them say exactly the same thing; all are signed by the Disappearer.

I think about keeping my letter, but in the end I know it has to become part of this strange pale landscape of betrayal and despair. I put it back in the envelope and throw it high into the air, turning away before it flutters to the ground. There are birds in the sky and it has started to rain.

'How'd it go?' asks David.
I take a deep breath and strain to keep my words clear and even.
'Fine,' I say. 'I just put it in a box around the back.'
'Did you read it at least?'
'Nah. Couldn't be bothered.'
'Liar.'

There could be no other conclusion: I was a liar, I could not be trusted. America had deceived me, and I, in turn, had betrayed America.

6.50 p.m. Brown Room

Dusk is falling on our last night in America. Tomorrow we catch a plane back to LAX and then another to Melbourne. For now though, we have to decide how to celebrate our having been here. But what befits our sixty-odd American Days?

'I dunno,' says David, rolling up a Robert Williams poster and tubing it into his pack. 'Go to a bar, get drunk. The usual.'

I suggest a big party. 'We'll invite Jennifer and Shaft the Bus Driver and Suzy and Cassis and Jane. Twitchy from Sanderson and our blackjack gang from the Casino Royale, Gracie and Walt and Herman Rothstein and I Am Barbara and everybody we met in LA, Brad Pitt, Gwyneth Paltrow, Beck and Jim Quillen, Blythe and Alanis and that talking dog from New Mexico. We'll get Chris and Ruth along, and Tito Puente. He could do some music for us and . . . and . . .'

'I think you'd better have a beer and a lie down,' suggests David. He rips open a Schlitz and hands it to me. I sink into the middle of the brown bed and try to think about America, but it defeats me and I just stare at the ceiling, eyes glazed, thoughts vagued. We've seen a great deal, but missed out on a lifetime more. There's so much here that I want to experience – but not as a tourist, as a regular guy. And although I miss Sally and home and reasonably priced coffee, I don't want to leave. I want to stay. I'll take the headaches, I want to be an American.

The Rockets' Red Glare

As soon as I'd calmed down we went out and got masterfully drunk. It wasn't a smart thing to do, and it wasn't cheap either. The only quality that it definitely possessed was inevitability.

It had plenty of that: I had to get drunk in order to try and forget about the poisoned paper ocean in which the not-blind man had set me adrift; David had to get drunk because he was with me.

We decided to take one last, long look at America so we went up to the bar at the top of Seattle's famous-ish Space Needle. It's been spinning around inducing nausea in drunks and wowsers alike since 1962, when it was built as part of Jack Kennedy's Interstellar Sewing Program. With our noses pressed to the glass, we spun and spun, catching a glimpse of Canada every fifteen minutes and drinking ourselves into 360° of stupidity. In honour of our hotel room we drank only brown liquors – beer, whisky, dark rum, brandy, bourbon and port. (This way, we figured, if we drank too much and threw up all over the room, nobody would notice.) We waved to New York, to Mississippi and Louisiana, to Texas, Arizona and New Mexico, and we smiled knowingly at California every time we faced south. We toasted the East Coast with Pabst Brown Ale, and raised Brown Cows to the West.

They threw us out at eleven and we slaked back to our hotel via a couple more bars where we threw down pints of cognac. Hideously dehumanised by the time we found Seneca Street, we had to climb its steep incline on all fours to reach our hotel. Back inside, I attempted to cross the cell to my bed, but along the way I tripped and fell. As soon as I remembered who I was, I picked up the thing that had caused my tumble – a plastic bag, now torn and spilling its contents. I smiled.
'Oh no,' said David.
'Oh yes indeed!' I said, standing with little help from gravity.

'We can't,' I heard him dribble, as I poked the fireworks back into the bag.

'We have to,' I told him. 'It's our duty.'

Up on the tar roof of the hotel we arranged the fireworks on a parapet – the Nutty Monkeys, the Catherine Wheels, the Emperor Balls, the Magic Heavens and Bursting Skyrockets. Our entire haul all the way from Tennessee. It was a beautiful sight and none of them had yet been touched by flame. I lit two cigarettes and handed one to David. 'Let's do it.'

In seconds the sky was afire: radioactive greens, glowing and humming like a beautiful infection; explosive, mezzotinted whites – a burst of shock inside your head; phosphorescent sea blue falling upward in undulating waves; a swarm of rich red, swelling like the heaving breath of a god; blazing arcs of orange, shot with a whistle and a scream; scintillating multitudes of colour and light and noise; red, white and blue, coruscating and dancing across the sky. Red, white and blue . . . red, white and blue . . . a message, a sign and a warning.

As the flashing faded and the thunder was silenced we saw that the night was still bright with a thousand northern stars. David was smoking the cigarette I'd given him, a glowing tip in the darkness down here on earth.

'Why are you smoking?'

'Well . . . I guess it calls for *some* sort of celebration.'

***The Long Goodbye.* A fond farewell to North America. Rated G (final).**

It was wonderful to find America, but it would have been more wonderful to miss it.
Mark Twain, *The Tragedy of Pudd'nhead Wilson*, 1894

7.15 a.m.

Woke up and vomited onto floor beside bed. As predicted, my insides blended well with carpet. Fell asleep again.

9.20 a.m.

Woke up and staggered to bathroom to get drink of water. Drank water. Regurgitated water. Came out brown.

When I emerged from the bathroom, David was sitting on the end of his bed, underpanted and clutching his head tenderly, as though feeling for bruises on ripe fruit. 'We have to get out of here and go back to Australia,' he said.

'I know,' I said. 'How?'

'Cab to airport. Plane to LA. Wait seven hours then catch plane home.'

'I don't know if I can. I might have to just live here,' I said, feeling a rolling brown in my stomach.

'Think of Sally.'

'Thank God she can't see me now. Am I naked?'

We both looked at me.

'Oh God,' moaned David. 'Where did that come from?'

'I don't know . . .' I said meekly. I was wearing a lemon yellow sundress, streaked with bilious brown.

303

2.30 p.m. On a Plane from Seattle to LA

Somehow we managed to pack and check out of Brownsville. I think we must smell like human cocktails, because we've been getting some pretty funny looks all day, especially from other alcoholics, who look as though they want to drink us.

David is a few rows ahead of me groaning quietly, his face hiding under a sleeping mask. I'm sitting next to two short-haired, fat English boys in their early teens. In the space of a minute the younger, fatter, Englisher one has called his bruvver a dick, a knob, a wally and a corpuscle. The older one has told Porky Jr to shut up, pipe down and get lost. Their parents must be very proud.

Connections

We made it to sprawling LAX. We caught a connecting flight from the United terminal to the Tom Bradley International terminal, then took a bus to the Qantas desk, checked in and hitch-hiked to the departure gate. David's taken a cab to the snack bar. I'd like to go outside for a final pre-flight cigarette, but it's a three-mile walk.

I'm thinking about the unpleasant hours ahead of us. If only it was possible to say, 'I'd like an aisle seat please, and no idiots nearby.' But on an Australian airline that's full of Australians going to Australia, it's not an easy request to fulfil. I bet the movies will suck too. Basically, I'm only in this for the food. And the touchdown.

QF 112. LA – Melbourne

It's late, some strange flight time just shy of midnight. They'll probably serve us lunch soon to acclimatise our stomachs to Melbourne time. We're just about to take off. The lights are dim and there's a quiet, amber glow throughout the plane. The final checks have been done and we're rumbling across the tarmac, climbing into the dark sky over the Pacific Ocean and leaving America behind. I miss it already.

And for now I might just pretend to be blind again so I don't have to talk to anybody about what I saw, tell them what it was like.

Acknowledgements

Apart from (nearly) every person or institution mentioned in the book, my most heartfelt thanks must go to the following people: first of all James Cunnack, whose parless punting skills immeasurably assisted in my going to America; Carolin Lenehan at Qantas for doing David and me a really, really big favour – quite apart from their enviable safety record, Qantas is the greatest airline in the world; the very charming Mr Richard Smith of the Soniat House in New Orleans (Sir, you are the living embodiment of Southern hospitality and grace); the gals at STA Travel in Prahran; Tamara Bues for tolerating me and David at our worst; Robyn McPeters in Santa Fe for being wonderfully hospitable and entertaining; Chris Potter for the backpack – again; Dr Chris Burns PhD for turning me on to the hip sounds of today; Heather Marmur for the computer & printer; Sue Negrau for her fantastic advice about everything; David Brown for providing certain jokes and my will – a big joke; my agent Fran Bryson for cutting her percentage; Michel Lawrence, Creative Director at J Walter Thompson, Melbourne, for kindly reneging on a deal and readjusting my future for the better; Pierre Archain, Kelly, Sonia and Francois in SF; Susan Ward Davies at British *Elle* for her enthusiasm and support; Anthony Kitchener for a well-timed letter of encouragement; Paul Giorgilli for wheeling and dealing; James Ursini at Rent-A-Mac for lending-a-mac; Tat and Tony up there in Stamford, Connecticut, for the sangria and sleeping bags; Lise LePage for showing us Montreal; the Windsor Court Hotel, New Orleans, for providing me with personalised stationery; Anne Stills at the Mansfield Hotel, NYC; the New York Hilton; the SoHo Grand Hotel; Nancy Friedman, the PR dynamo of NYC; the Fairmount Hotel in San Antonio; the Biltmore, the Nikko, the Regent Beverly Wilshire,

Loew's and the Ritz-Carlton, all in LA and all wonderful; Dawn Moreno-Freedman at Davidson Choy McWorter Publicity, for being neat; the Cadillac Cafe for a great dinner; the friendly staff at the San Francisco Marriott; the Westin St Francis, the Hilton, the Triton and the extremely beautiful Clift Hotel in SF; David Perry, at the Hotel Como in Melbourne – still a great place to stay; Susie Stenmark at the Regent Hotel, Sydney; Sally Morgan at the ANA, Sydney; everybody at Lonely Planet, Oakland Division, especially Carolyn Miller, Maria Mack and Eric Kettunen for letting me stay at his house; Sheryl Wilkinson and Fiona Le Brocq for all their help in the past and the future; and the Australian Customs Authority for a warm welcome home that I'll never forget.

And finally, to the eternally kind and patient Janet Austin, the rockin'-est editor on earth, and to Michelle de Kretser for being tough and smart and fun and for having faith in me twice. Without Michelle, none of this would have been possible. So blame her.

SEAN & DAVID'S LONG DRIVE

Sean Condon

Sean and David are young townies who have rarely strayed beyond city limits. One day, for no good reason, they set out to discover their homeland, and what follows is a wildly entertaining adventure that covers half of Australia. Highlights include the weekly Hair Wax Report and a Croc-Spotting with Stew adventure.

Sean Condon has written a hilarious, offbeat road book that mixes sharp insights with deadpan humour and outright lies.

After a couple of games of shuffleboard we drank some 'shooters', a very popular pastime here up north. And one which leads to another popular pastime – vomiting. Shooters are random, volatile and foolish 30-ml concoctions of spirits in a shot glass. You drink one, then a few moments later you poke your eyes back into their sockets and suddenly everybody looks like they just got off an interstate bus. After six of them, you have to be airlifted back home. David had one called a Snakebite, which consisted of tequila and chartreuse. He said it tasted like a chemical combination that would deform babies. I had a Buzz Bomb. It tasted just fine.

When I regained consciousness about an hour later I found myself doing something silly with a pair of maracas and a cigar in the middle of a large circle of people. The people were laughing at me.

LONELY PLANET JOURNEYS

JOURNEYS is a unique collection of travel writing – published by the company that understands travel better than anyone else.

It is a series for anyone who has ever experienced – or dreamed of – the magical moment when they encountered a strange culture or saw a place for the first time. They are tales to read while you're planning a trip, while you're on the road or while you're in an armchair, in front of a fire.

These outstanding titles explore our planet through the eyes of a diverse group of international writers. JOURNEYS books catch the spirit of a place, illuminate a culture, recount an adventure, or introduce a fascinating way of life. They always entertain, and always enrich the experience of travel.

'Lively, intelligent and varied . . . an important contribution to travel literature' – *Melbourne Age*

FULL CIRCLE
A South American Journey
Luis Sepúlveda (translated by Chris Andrews)

'A journey without a fixed itinerary' in the company of Chilean writer Luis Sepúlveda. Extravagant characters and extraordinary situations are memorably evoked: gauchos organising a tournament of lies, a scheming heiress on the lookout for a husband, a pilot with a corpse on board his plane . . . Part autobiography, part travel memoir, *Full Circle* brings us the distinctive voice of one of South America's most compelling writers.

WINNER 1996 Astrolabe – Etonnants Voyageurs award for the best work of travel literature published in France.

THE GATES OF DAMASCUS
Lieve Joris (translated by Sam Garrett)

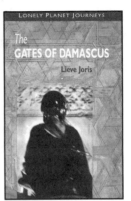

This best-selling book is a beautifully drawn portrait of day-to-day life in modern Syria. Through her intimate contact with local people, Lieve Joris draws us into the fascinating world that lies behind the gates of Damascus. Hala's husband is a political prisoner, jailed for his opposition to the Assad regime; through the author's friendship with Hala we see how Syrian politics impacts on the lives of ordinary people.

Written after the Gulf War, *The Gates of Damascus* offers a unique insight into the complexities of the Arab world.

IN RAJASTHAN
Royina Grewal

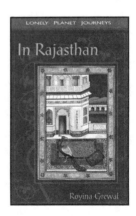

As she writes of her travels through Rajasthan, Indian writer Royina Grewal takes us behind the exotic facade of this fabled destination: here is an insider's perceptive account of India's most colourful state. *In Rajasthan* discusses folk music and architecture, feudal traditions and regional cuisine . . . Most of all, it focuses on people – from maharajas to camel trainers, from politicians to itinerant snake charmers – to convey the excitement and challenges of a region in transition.

ISLANDS IN THE CLOUDS
Travels in the Highlands of New Guinea
Isabella Tree

This is the fascinating account of a journey to the remote and beautiful Highlands of Papua New Guinea and Irian Jaya: one of the most extraordinary and dangerous regions on the planet. The author travels with a PNG Highlander who introduces her to his intriguing and complex world, which is changing rapidly as it collides with twentieth-century technology and the island's developing social and political systems. *Islands in the Clouds* is a thoughtful, moving book, full of insights into a region that is rarely noticed by the rest of the world.

KINGDOM OF THE FILM STARS
Journey into Jordan
Annie Caulfield

Kingdom of the Film Stars is a travel book and a love story. With honesty and humour, Annie Caulfield writes of travelling in Jordan and falling in love with a Bedouin with film-star looks.

The author offers fascinating insights into the country – from the tent life of traditional women to the hustle of downtown Amman. *Kingdom of the Film Stars* unpicks tight-woven Western myths about the Arab world, presenting cultural and political issues within the intimate framework of a compelling love story.

LOST JAPAN
Alex Kerr

Lost Japan draws on the author's personal experiences of Japan over thirty years. Alex Kerr takes his readers on a backstage tour, exploring different facets of his involvement with the country: friendships with Kabuki actors, buying and selling art, studying calligraphy, exploring rarely visited temples and shrines . . .

The Japanese edition of this book was awarded the 1994 Shincho Gakugei Literature Prize for the best work of non-fiction: the first time a foreigner has won this prestigious award.

THE OLIVE GROVE
Travels in Greece
Katherine Kizilos

Katherine Kizilos travels to fabled islands, troubled border zones and her family's village deep in the mountains. She vividly evokes breathtaking landscapes, generous people and passionate politics, capturing the complexities of a country she loves.

The Olive Grove tells of other journeys too: the life-changing journey made by the author's emigrant father; the migration of young Greeks to cities which is transforming rural life; and the tremendous impact of tourism on Greek society. A lyrical homage to Greece and its people.

THE RAINBIRD
A Central African Journey
Jan Brokken (translated by Sam Garrett)

The Rainbird is a classic travel story. Following in the footsteps of famous Europeans such as Albert Schweitzer and H.M. Stanley, Jan Brokken journeyed to Gabon in central Africa. A kaleidoscope of adventures and anecdotes, *The Rainbird* brilliantly chronicles the encounter between Africa and Europe as it was acted out on a side-street of history. It is also the compelling, immensely readable account of the author's own travels in one of the most remote and mysterious regions of Africa.

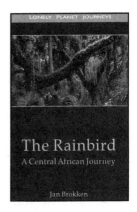

SHOPPING FOR BUDDHAS
Jeff Greenwald

Shopping for Buddhas is Jeff Greenwald's story of his obsessive search for the perfect Buddha statue. In the backstreets of Kathmandu, he discovers more than he bargained for . . . and his souvenir-hunting turns into an ironic metaphor for the clash between spiritual riches and material greed. Politics, religion and serious shopping collide in this witty account of an enlightening visit to Nepal.

WINNER of the Gold Medal for the Best Travel Book, Society of American Travel Writers' Lowell Thomas Journalism Awards.

SONGS TO AN AFRICAN SUNSET

A Zimbabwean Story

Sekai Nzenza-Shand

Songs to an African Sunset braids vividly personal stories into an intimate picture of contemporary Zimbabwe. Returning to her family's village after many years in the West, Sekai Nzenza-Shand discovers a world where ancestor worship, polygamy and witchcraft still govern the rhythms of daily life – and where drought, deforestation and AIDS have wrought devastating changes. With insight and affection, she explores a culture torn between respect for the old ways and the irresistible pull of the new.

LONELY PLANET GUIDES TO THE
USA AND CANADA

Follow in Sean and David's tyre tracks with these Lonely Planet travel guides – available in bookstores worldwide or online at www.lonelyplanet.com

Alaska

Baja California

California & Nevada

Canada

Deep South

Florida

Hawaii

Honolulu

Los Angeles

Miami

New England

New Orleans

New York City

New York, New Jersey & Pennsylvania

Pacific Northwest

Rocky Mountain States

San Francisco

Seattle

Southwest

Washington, DC & the Capital Region

Also available: Backpacking in Alaska and USA phrasebook

PLANET TALK

Lonely Planet's FREE quarterly newsletter

Every issue of PLANET TALK is packed with
up-to-date travel news and advice including:

- a letter from Lonely Planet founders Tony
  and Maureen Wheeler
- travel diary from a Lonely Planet author
  – find out what it's really like out on the road
- feature article on an important and topical
  travel issue
- a selection of recent letters from our readers
- the latest travel news from all over the world
- details on Lonely Planet's new and
  forthcoming releases

To join our mailing list contact any Lonely Planet office.

LONELY PLANET PUBLICATIONS

Australia: PO Box 617, Hawthorn 3122, Victoria
tel: (03) 9819 1877 fax: (03) 9819 6459
e-mail: talk2us@lonelyplanet.com.au

USA: Embarcadero West, 155 Filbert St, Suite 251,
Oakland, CA 94607
tel: (510) 893 8555 TOLL FREE: 800 275-8555
fax: (510) 893 8563   e-mail: info@lonelyplanet.com

UK: 10a Spring Place, London NW5 3BH
tel: (0171) 428 4800 fax: (0171) 428 4828
e-mail: go@lonelyplanet.co.uk

France: 71 bis rue du Cardinal Lemoine, 75005 Paris
tel: 1 44 32 06 20 fax: 1 46 34 72 55
e-mail: 100560.415@compuserve.com

World Wide Web: Lonely Planet is now accesible via the World
Wide Web. For travel information and an up-to-date catalogue, you
can find us at www.lonelyplanet.com

THE LONELY PLANET STORY

Lonely Planet published its first book in 1973 in response to the numerous 'How did you do it?' questions Maureen and Tony Wheeler were asked after driving, bussing, hitching, sailing and railing their way from England to Australia.

Written at a kitchen table and hand collated, trimmed and stapled, *Across Asia on the Cheap* became an instant local bestseller, inspiring thoughts of another book.

Eighteen months in South-East Asia resulted in their second guide, *South-East Asia on a shoestring*, which they put together in a backstreet Chinese hotel in Singapore in 1975. The 'yellow bible', as it quickly became known to backpackers around the world, soon became *the* guide to the region. It has sold well over half a million copies and is now in its 9th edition, still retaining its familiar yellow cover.

Today there are over 240 titles, including travel guides, walking guides, language kits & phrasebooks, travel atlases and travel literature. The company is the largest independent travel publisher in the world. Although Lonely Planet initially specialised in guides to Asia, today there are few corners of the globe that have not been covered.

The emphasis continues to be on travel for independent travellers. Tony and Maureen still travel for several months of each year and play an active part in the writing, updating and quality control of Lonely Planet's guides.

They have been joined by over 70 authors and 170 staff at our offices in Melbourne (Australia), Oakland (USA), London (UK) and Paris (France). Travellers themselves also make a valuable contribution to the guides through the feedback we receive in thousands of letters each year and on our web site.

The people at Lonely Planet strongly believe that travellers can make a positive contribution to the countries they visit, both through their appreciation of the countries' culture, wildlife and natural features, and through the money they spend. In addition, the company makes a direct contribution to the countries and regions it covers. Since 1986 a percentage of the income from each book has been donated to ventures such as famine relief in Africa; aid projects in India; agricultural projects in Central America; Greenpeace's efforts to halt French nuclear testing in the Pacific; and Amnesty International.

'I hope we send people out with the right attitude about travel. You realise when you travel that there are so many different perspectives about the world, so we hope these books will make people more interested in what they see.'

— Tony Wheeler